Close-up

TEACHER'S BOOK C1

Philip James

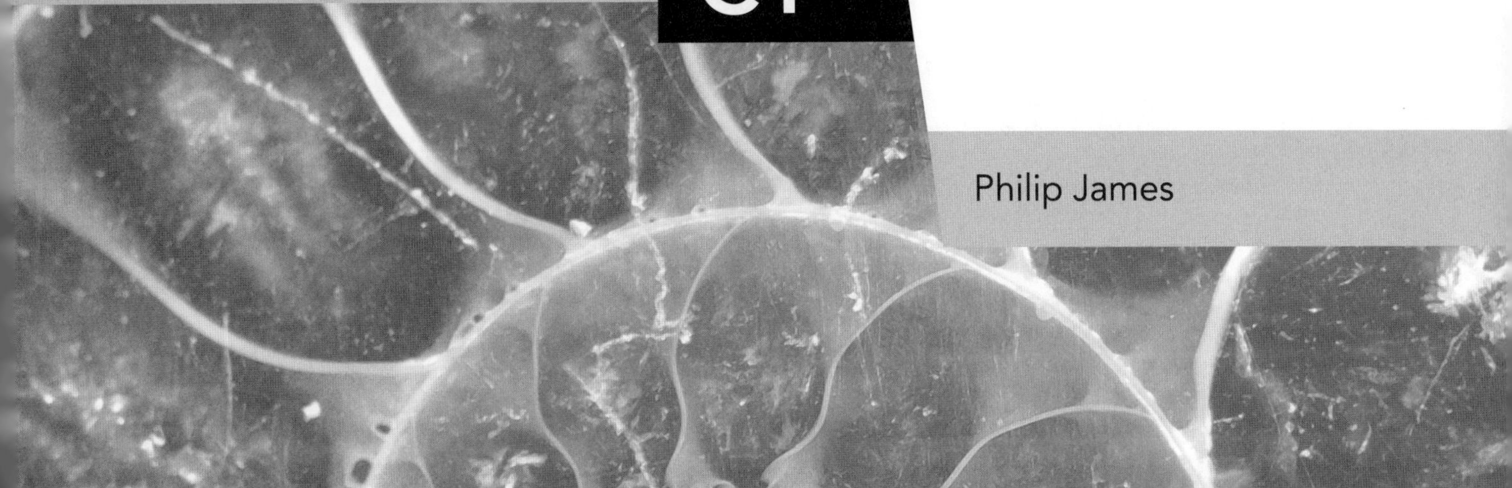

SECOND EDITION

NATIONAL GEOGRAPHIC LEARNING

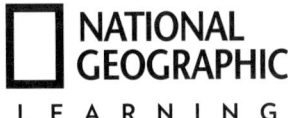

Australia • Brazil • Mexico • Singapore • United Kingdom • United States

Close-up C1 Teacher's Book Second Edition
Philip James

Publisher: Sharon Jervis
Commissioning Editor: Kayleigh Buller
Project Editor: Cathy Rogers
Editorial Assistant: Georgina McComb
Content Project Manager: Jon Ricketts
Compositor: Wild Apple Design Ltd

© 2017 National Geographic Learning, a Cengage Learning Company

ALL RIGHTS RESERVED. No part of this work covered by the copyright herein may be reproduced or distributed in any form or by any means, except as permitted by U.S. copyright law, without the prior written permission of the copyright owner.

"National Geographic", "National Geographic Society" and the Yellow Border Design are registered trademarks of the National Geographic Society ® Marcas Registradas

For product information and technology assistance, contact us at
Cengage Learning Customer & Sales Support, cengage.com/contact

For permission to use material from this text or product,
submit all requests online at **cengage.com/permissions**
Further permissions questions can be emailed to
permissionrequest@cengage.com

ISBN: 978-1-4080-9853-0

National Geographic Learning
Cheriton House, North Way, Andover, Hampshire, SP10 5BE
United Kingdom

National Geographic Learning, a Cengage Learning Company, has a mission to bring the world to the classroom and the classroom to life. With our English language programs, students learn about their world by experiencing it. Through our partnerships with National Geographic and TED Talks, they develop the language and skills they need to be successful global citizens and leaders.

Locate your local office at **international.cengage.com/region**

Visit National Geographic Learning online at **NGL.Cengage.com/ELT**
Visit our corporate website at **www.cengage.com**

Photo credits
Cover: (front cover) © Geanina Bechea/Shutterstock, (back cover) Sabena Jane Blackbird/Alamy

Printed in China by RR Donnelley
Print Number: 02   Print Year: 2018

Contents

Contents of Student's Book	4
Introduction to Close-up	6
Unit 1 – Scaling the Heights	8
Video 1 – Extreme Skydiving	18
Unit 2 – Like Comment Share	19
Video 2 – Orangutan Language	28
Review 1	29
Unit 3 – Just for the Health of it	31
Video 3 – Paraguay Shaman	41
Unit 4 – Lights, Camera, Action!	42
Video 4 – Skin Mask	51
Review 2	52
Unit 5 – Eat Up!	54
Video 5 – The Smelliest Fruit	65
Unit 6 – Living Planet	66
Video 6 – Holland Water	74
Review 3	75
Unit 7 – Eureka!	77
Video 7 – Lighting the Dark	87
Unit 8 – Money Mad	88
Video 8 – Art of the Deal	98
Review 4	99
Unit 9 – All That Jazz!	101
Video 9 – Eye Trick Town	110
Unit 10 – Modern Living	111
Video 10 – Zoo Dentists	120
Review 5	121
Unit 11 – Sports Crazy!	123
Video 11 – Flying Pumpkins	132
Unit 12 – Fast Forward	133
Video 12 – Space Walk	142
Review 6	143
Recording Script for Student's Book	145
C1 Workbook key	158

Contents

Unit	Reading	Vocabulary (topic vocab)	Grammar
1 Scaling the Heights p 5–16	multiple-matching, dealing with multiple matches	success, phrasal verbs, prepositions, collocations & expressions	review of present and past tenses, *used to* & *would*
2 Like Comment Share p 17–28	multiple-choice questions, choosing the correct option	social media, word formation, choosing the right part of speech, phrasal verbs, prepositions, idioms	future forms, future in the past, time expressions
REVIEW 1: Vocabulary & Grammar p 29–30			
3 Just for the Health of it p 31–42	missing paragraphs, looking for connections	health & medicine, word formation, phrasal verbs, collocations & expressions	demonstrative, reflexive, indefinite & reciprocal pronouns, adverbs & adverb phrases, adverb forms
4 Lights, Camera, Action! p 43–54	multiple-choice questions, identifying the purpose of a text	film & theatre, multiple-choice questions, choosing the correct word, word formation, compound nouns, prepositions	gerunds & infinitives, discourse markers
REVIEW 2: Vocabulary & Grammar p 55–56			
5 Eat Up! p 57–68	multiple texts, understanding the contexts in multiple texts	food, phrasal verbs, collocations & expressions, word formation	transitive & intransitive phrasal verbs, separable & Inseparable phrasal verbs, same-way question tags, question tags for polite requests, reinforcement tags
6 Living Planet p 69–80	missing paragraphs, understanding the text structure	environment & weather, word formation, phrasal verbs, prepositions, gapped text, dealing with gapped texts	modal verbs, perfect modal verbs
REVIEW 3: Vocabulary & Grammar p 81–82			
7 Eureka! p 83–94	multiple-matching, looking for specific information	technology & inventions, compound nouns, idioms	conditionals, other conditionals, unreal past, inversion
8 Money Mad p 95–106	multiple-choice questions, understanding opinion & attitude	money, phrasal verbs, collocation & expressions, word formation	relative clauses, participle clauses, cleft sentences
REVIEW 4: Vocabulary & Grammar p 107–108			
9 All That Jazz! p 109–120	multiple-matching, understanding the overall message	music & art, compound nouns, prepositions, collocations & expressions	comparison of adjectives & adverbs, other ways of comparing, qualifiers, *too* & *enough*, *so*, *such*
10 Modern Living p 121–132	multiple-choice questions, finding your own method	work & lifestyle, word formation, phrasal verbs, collocation & expressions	passive voice, reporting with passive verbs, *seem* & *appear*, passive causative
REVIEW 5: Vocabulary & Grammar p 133–134			
11 Sports Crazy! p 135–146	multiple-choice questions, dealing with different text types	sport, phrasal verbs, prepositions, collocations & expressions	reported speech, reporting verbs, reported questions
12 Fast Forward p 147–158	missing paragraphs, checking for coherence & cohesion	space, science, technological advances & the future, word formations, prepositions, sentence transformation	clauses of reason, clauses of purpose & result, clauses of contrast, *neither ... nor either ... or*
REVIEW 6: Vocabulary & Grammar p 159–160			

Grammar Reference: p 161–172
Irregular Verbs: p 173–174
Writing Reference: p 175–184
Speaking References: p 185–186

Listening	Speaking	Writing	Video
multiple-choice questions, listening to short extracts	talking about achievements, comparing photographs, understanding instructions, dealing with all parts of the question, challenges & overcoming obstacles	reference, understanding the purpose of a reference, writing a formal letter, opening, introduction, supporting your opinion, discussing attributes, recommending, ending	Extreme skydiving
sentence completion, preparing to listen	decision-making, talking about social networking sites, preparing to speak, presenting opinions & reaching a decision	essay (1), planning & structuring an essay, preparing an essay, introducing & countering an argument	Orangutan Language
multiple-choice questions, dealing with scientific information	talking about health, comparing photographs, using relevant words & expressions, topic vocabulary	information sheet, writing a good information sheet, giving information clearly	Paraguay Shaman
multiple-matching, dealing with two tasks simultaneously	talking about film genres & cinema, decision-making, presenting an argument, presenting your options & handing over to your partner	review, understanding the purpose of a review, structuring a review, liking, disliking & recommending	Skin mask
multiple-choice questions, identifying distractors	talking about food & eating, follow-up questions, answering follow-up questions, adding ideas, contrasting, involving your partner	proposal, understanding the purpose of a proposal, creating a proposal, stating purpose, introducing talking about positives & negatives, recommending	The Smelliest Fruit
multiple-choice questions, identifying opinion & attitude	natural disasters, comparing photographs, starting and finishing, selecting photos	contribution, using the appropriate register, planning a contribution, engaging the reader, describing a problem, explaining effects, recommending a course of action	Holland Water
sentence completion, making notes	decision-making, giving opinions with reasons & examples, justifying choices	nomination, nominating someone for achievement, writing an effective nomination, talking about reputations, influence & achievements	Lighting the Dark
multiple-choice questions, dealing with specific questions	money, shopping & poverty, comparing photos, answering follow-up questions, linking ideas	article (1), making an article interesting, using appropriate language, engaging the reader, expressing positives & negatives, giving your opinion	Art of the Deal
multiple-choice questions, listening again	talking about art & artists, decision-making, speculating, evaluating & negotiating, evaluating	report, recognising the purpose of a report, structuring a report, introducing positives & negatives, making recommendations	Eye Trick Town
multiple-matching, focusing on attitude & opinion	talking about skills, qualities & qualifications, decision-making, assessing strengths & weaknesses, comparing options	article (2), understanding the aim of an article, composing an article, comparing & contrasting, providing information, offering advice, describing places	Zoo Dentists
multiple-choice questions, focusing on adverbs & time expressions	talking about sport, discussing questions, opening questions, developing answers to personal questions	informal letter, following letter writing conventions, responding appropriately, acknowledging a letter, using suitable openings & endings, giving opinions & advice, recommending	Flying Pumpkins
sentence completion, spelling & numbers	talking about life in the future, follow-up questions, interacting with your partner, supporting opinions with examples, talking about the future	essay (2), using formal expressions in moderation, writing an effective essay, introducing talking about the future, predicting	Space Walk

Collocations & Expressions: p 187   Phrasal Verbs: p 189
Prepositions: p 188

Introduction to Close-up

Introduction to Close-up

Welcome to *Close-up Second Edition*, an exciting advanced course which brings English to life through spectacular National Geographic photography and facts carefully selected to appeal to the inquisitive minds of students.

Course Components

Close-up C1 Student's Book with online student zone

The Student's Book is divided into twelve topic-based units. Each unit starts with a stunning photograph linked to the theme of the unit and a summary of the contents of the unit. There are five two-page lessons in each unit covering reading, vocabulary, grammar, listening & speaking and writing. The unit ends with a video page to accompany the National Geographic video clips found on the online student zone. The video clips are designed to expand students' knowledge of the world they live in, and the tasks in the Student's Book aid comprehension and further discussion of the topic.

Each unit also contains:

- tasks that actively develop students' reading, listening, speaking and writing skills.
- *Exam close-up* boxes and *Exam Tasks* that provide step-by-step advice and strategies for how to best to approach exam tasks and have the opportunity to put the advice into practice.
- *Useful Expressions* boxes in the speaking & writing sections that provide students with appropriate language when doing communicative tasks.
- plenty of opportunity for discussion of the topics in the *Ideas Focus* sections.

Close-up C1 Student's Book also contains six reviews, one after every two units, which consolidate the vocabulary and grammar taught within those units.

At the back of the Student's Book, there is a wealth of reference material. The Grammar Reference and Irregular Verbs List support the Grammar Focus within each unit. The Writing Reference provides a summary of the important points to remember for each genre of writing as well as a check list. There is also a Speaking Reference, bringing the *Useful Expressions* presented throughout the course together in one place. In addition, the collocations, expressions, prepositions and phrasal verbs actively taught in the Student's Book are also listed for easy reference.

The online student zone includes the Student's Book audio and video, and the Workbook audio available to download.

Close-up C1 Workbook

The Workbook accompanies *Close-up C1 Student's Book*. Like the Student's Book, it is divided into twelve units and six reviews. Each unit consists of reading, vocabulary, grammar, listening and writing. The reviews include multiple-choice grammar and vocabulary items. The audio on the online student zone contains the recordings for use with the listening tasks.

The Workbook's clear and simple format means that it can be used at home as well as in class. The Workbook is available with or without the *Online Workbook*.

Close-up C1 Teacher's Book

Close-up C1 Teacher's Book provides clear lesson plans with detailed instructions and tips for teachers on how to make the best of the material in the Student's Book. The key to all tasks in the Student's Book and Workbook are included, along with the Student's Book transcripts with justification for the answers to the listening tasks underlined.

Close-up C1 online teacher zone

The online teacher zone contains a comprehensive testing package in printable PDF format. The multiple choice quizzes, one for each unit of *Close-up C1 Student's Book*, focus on the key vocabulary and grammar items presented in the unit. Progress Tests, one for use after every two units of *Close-up C1 Student's Book*, include a reading comprehension task, a writing task as well as vocabulary and grammar tasks. There is also a Mid-Year Test *(Units 1-6)* and an End-of-Year Test *(7-12)* that provide a written test covering reading comprehension and writing, as well as a listening test. There is a section of photocopiable vocabulary and grammar tasks which can be used with students who finish early in class, as a way of revising prior to a test, or as extra practice of the vocabulary and grammar. All keys to these tests are included.

The *Close-up C1 online teacher zone* also includes the Student's Book audio and video along with the Workbook audio and transcripts, plus the Workbook transcripts with justification for the answers to the listening tasks underlined. In addition, there is a Student's Record document, which can be printed for each student, where test results can be recorded.

Close-up C1 Interactive Whiteboard Software is downloadable from the online teacher zone.
Close-up C1 Interactive Whiteboard Software includes content from the Student's Book, plus the audio and video. The Interactive Whiteboard has easy to navigate, interactive tasks, word definition functions, grammar animation and a series of games for further practice.

Justification for reading comprehension and listening tasks is available at the touch of a button, as is the key to all tasks. *Close-up C1 Interactive Whiteboard Software* also contains the Content Creation Tool, which allows teachers to create their own interactive tasks to use in class, and is compatible with any interactive whiteboard hardware.

1 Scaling the Heights

Reading:	multiple-matching, dealing with multiple-matchings
Vocabulary:	success-related vocabulary, phrasal verbs, prepositions, collocations & expressions
Grammar:	review of present & past tenses, *used to* & *would*
Listening:	multiple-choice questions, listening to short extracts
Speaking:	talking about achievements, challenges & overcoming obstacles, comparing photographs, understanding instructions, dealing with all parts of the question
Writing:	reference, understanding the purpose of a reference, writing a formal letter, opening, introduction, supporting your opinion, discussing attributes, recommending, ending

Unit opener

- Ask students to look at the title of the unit and to guess what it might mean *(being successful at something)*.
- Ask them which other words they know that can mean *scaling the heights* in this context *(excel, prevail, triumph)*.
- Ask students to tell the rest of the class one positive and one negative thing about being successful.
- Ask students to look at the picture and to read the caption. Then ask them how the man might be feeling and why he might be feeling that way.
- Ask them how the picture corresponds to the theme of the unit *(success)* and whether they feel that this type of success is worth achieving.

Reading

A

- Ask students to look at the picture in the top right-hand corner of page 6 and to say what the people are trying to accomplish. Ask them if they would ever take on such an extreme challenge.
- Ask students to read the instructions and the list of achievements in A. Answer any questions they might have about them. Ask students to think about what they personally think of as success and to rank the achievements in the order that they consider to be impressive. Then ask students to work in groups of four to compare and discuss their answers.
- Write numbers 1–8 as headings on the board and ask students which achievement they chose as the most impressive. Call out each of the achievements in turn and ask students from each group to report on how each one was ranked. Write their answers on the board under the headings with the number of students who chose this as the most impressive. Encourage students to discuss the results.

Teaching Tip

Stress that there are no right or wrong answers in task A, but ask students to justify their choices.

Answers

Students' own answers

Background Information

Every year *National Geographic*, one of the world's leading magazines, holds a competition to choose the Adventurers of the Year. After the nominees have been selected, people then have the opportunity to visit the *National Geographic* website to view photos, listen to interviews and watch videos before voting for their personal favourite adventurer. Adventurers of the Year are selected for their extraordinary achievement in fields ranging from exploration to conservation to innovators of adventure.

B

- Ask students to look at the pictures relating to the article and ask them what the people in the pictures all have in common *(they are all doing something adventurous and challenging)*.
- Ask students to read the title of the article and elicit how it relates to the pictures *(the people in the pictures may have been in the running for 'People's Choice Adventurers of the Year')*.
- Ask students to read the instructions for B and check that they understand what they have to do. Tell them to skim read the text to find the answer to the question. Remind them that they don't have to read the text in detail at this point as they will have an opportunity to do that later. Ask students to do the task individually, but check answers as a class.
- Ask students at random round the class whether they feel the person/people deserved to win and why or why not. Encourage students to justify their answers.

Answers

Sano Babu Sunuwar and Lakpa Tsheri Sherpa
Students' own answers

Word Focus

- Ask students to look at the words and phrases in red in the text and to re-read the sentences they are found in. Ask students to work in pairs to decide what each of the words/phrases means in the *Word Focus* box and to then find synonyms, if any, for each word.
- Ask students to compare their answers with another pair.

C

- Draw students' attention to the *Close-up* box and tell them that these boxes are used throughout the book to give them tips about how to do specific tasks.
- Ask students to read the information in the box and then ask a student to explain what it says in their own words.
- Explain that they should select their answers based on all four sections *(not only one)* and that they should pay attention to any small details to see which section fits best. Encourage students to underline any information in the texts that relates to the ideas in the questions, but point out that the ideas will be paraphrased in some way.
- Ask students to read the questions in the *Exam Task* before reading the text again so that they know what information to pay attention to.
- Encourage students to guess the meaning of unfamiliar words from the context they are in before using their dictionaries. Explain any problem words and correct their pronunciation where necessary.
- Ask students to read the text again and to underline any information related to the questions.
- Ask students to do the task individually, but check as a class.

Answers

1b (She showed fellow competitors and surfing fans … picked up first prize in two events.)
2a (… and a bare-bones budget, …)
3a (With borrowed gear …)
4c (MacAskill makes us reimagine our daily environments as he and his bike become one.)
5d ('You have to see opportunity when it knocks on your door.')
6b (Moore has pocketed a staggering $225,000 and has attracted top-notch sponsors.)
7d (Snowboarder Travis Rice, whose father was a ski patroller, was raised to take risks in snowy mountains.)
8c (In 2011, a short film … became an instant sensation on YouTube.)
9a (Wasting no time, they then launched a tandem paraglider … being only the third team to do so.)
10c (… as he rides through abandoned Scottish factories, …)

D

- Explain to students that this exercise allows them to practise new vocabulary that they have met in the reading passage.
- Ask students to look at the words in the yellow box and to scan the text to find and underline them.
Ask them to say each of the words after you and elicit that they are all verbs. Correct their pronunciation where necessary. Stress that the verbs may be in a different form in the text and might need to be changed for the task.

- Remind them that they should always try to work out the meaning of the word from its context and ask them to read the sentences in the text in which each word is contained.
- Ask students to read the instructions and check that they understand what they have to do. Encourage them to read all the sentences in D once before writing any answers.
- Ask students to do the task individually, but check as a class.

Answers

1 pocketed
2 snatch
3 crush
4 executed
5 leap
6 hailed

Ideas Focus

- Explain to students that they are going to answer some questions about success. Ask them to read the questions and explain anything they don't understand.
- Ask students to answer the questions in pairs and encourage them to draw on personal experience.
- Go round the class monitoring students to ensure they are carrying out the task properly. Don't correct any mistakes at this point, but make a note of any problems in structure or pronunciation.
- Ask students at random to answer each of the questions and encourage the other students to give their opinions.
- Write any structural mistakes made by students on the board without saying who made them, and ask them to correct them. Deal with any problems in pronunciation that came up.

Answers

Students' own answers

Teaching Tip

Allowing students time to discuss their own personal experiences helps to improve their fluency and gives them a reason to communicate in English. Try to be aware of any sensitivities students may have in talking about themselves, however, and don't insist when they seem reluctant to talk about particular subjects.

Vocabulary

Teaching Tip

Encourage students to record new vocabulary in a vocabulary notebook. Explain that at this level, it is essential to record the meanings of words in English rather than translating them into their own language.

A

- Ask students to look at the picture to the right of the text in A and ask them to describe it. Ask them what it shows *(the different features on modern technology)*.
- Ask students to look at the title of the text and elicit what a *millennial* is *(the name of the generation born between 1980 and 2000)*. Ask them if they know the

1 Scaling the Heights

names of any other generations (e.g. Baby Boomers – born between 1946 and 1964; Generation X – born between 1965 and 1980; Boomlets – born after 2001) and if they know anyone from these generations.
- Ask students to read the text all the way through without filling in any answers at this stage.
- Say each of the words in red in the text and ask students to repeat them after you. Correct their pronunciation where necessary.
- Ask students to read the instructions and check that they understand what they have to do. Encourage them to think about the general meaning of the sentences that the options are contained in to help them decide which is appropriate in the context of the text.
- Ask students to do the task individually, but check as a class.

Answers
1 generation   5 aim
2 distinguishes   6 realise
3 digital   7 riches
4 revolution   8 industrious

B
- Ask students to read the instructions and check that they understand what they have to do.
- Read the words in the yellow boxes and ask students to repeat them after you. Correct their pronunciation where necessary.
- Encourage students to read both sentences in each pair before filling in any answers.
- Ask students to do the task individually, but check as a class.

Answers
1 accomplishes   5 resolve
2 achieve   6 solve
3 insisted   7 defeat
4 persist   8 failure

Teaching Tip

Ask students to write a sentence of their own for each of the words in the yellow boxes. This will help them to consolidate any new vocabulary.

C
- Ask students to read the instructions and check that they understand what they have to do.
- Read the sets of words 1–8 to the students and ask them to repeat them after you. Correct their pronunciation where necessary.
- Ask students to work in pairs to encourage discussion, but check the answers as a class. Ask students to explain why one of the words is the odd one out in each item.

Answers
1 mediocre (The others are ways of describing someone who is 'brave', but 'mediocre' means of average quality.)
2 vain (The others are positive virtues, but 'vain' is a negative virtue meaning to be overly proud of one's appearance.)
3 selfless (The others describe someone who cares very little for others, but 'selfless' means to put other people first.)
4 touchy (The others describe someone who is not sincere, but 'touchy' means to be easily upset or irritated.)
5 sentimental (The others are positive ways of describing someone's mood, but 'sentimental' means to often be over emotional.)
6 timid (The others are ways of describing neutrality, but 'timid' means to be very shy.)
7 cautious (The others mean to make decisions quickly and without thinking about the consequences, but 'cautious' means to think carefully before doing something.)
8 candid (The others are ways to describe someone who does what they want, but 'candid' means to be honest and open.)

D
- Ask students to read the instructions and check that they understand what they have to do.
- Read the words and the opposites to the students and ask them to repeat them after you. Correct their pronunciation where necessary.
- Ask students to do the task individually, but check as a class.

Answers
1d 2e 3a 4b 5f 6c

E
- Read the phrasal verbs in the yellow box to the students and ask them to repeat them. Correct their pronunciation where necessary.
- Tell students that they have to consider the meaning of the verb and the particle together and not just focus on the verb.
- Ask students to read the instructions and check that they understand what they have to do.
- Ask them to read the sentences on their own to work out the meaning of the missing phrasal verb. Also encourage them to underline the subject of each sentence so that they write the verbs in the correct form.
- Ask students to do the task individually, but check as a class.

Answers
1 knuckle down   5 get ahead
2 come up against   6 falls through
3 pull ... off   7 blow ... away
4 break through   8 hang on

Teaching Tip

Encourage students to copy the phrasal verbs, their meanings and an example sentence into their notebooks.

F
- Ask students to read the instructions and check that they understand what they have to do. Point out that they have to use the phrasal verbs from E in the correct form to fill the gaps.
- Ask students to first read the sentences for gist to work out which phrasal verb might be missing from each one. Remind them to pay attention to the subject and also other tenses used in the sentences to help them write the verbs in the correct form.
- Ask students to do the task individually, but check as a class.

Answers

1 get ahead
2 pull ... off
3 blown away
4 knuckle down
5 fell through
6 hung on
7 came up against
8 break through

G
- Read the prepositions in the yellow box to the students and explain that they will use these to complete the sentences. Point out that they should use each preposition only once.
- Ask students to read the sentences carefully and to pay attention to the words before or after the gap and try to think of a preposition which follows or precedes the words without filling in any answers.
- Ask students to do the task individually, but check as a class.

Answers

1 for
2 on
3 around
4 by
5 under
6 without

H
- Write the verbs *do*, *get* and *go* on the board and ask students to come up with at least two collocations for each verb. Explain that learners of English often confuse these verbs in common collocations as similar expressions in their own language may use only one verb.
- Ask students to read the instructions. Make sure they realise they should fill in the correct form of each verb.
- Ask students to read the sentences, without filling in the answers, and to underline the words that appear immediately after the gaps. Explain to students that they should decide which of the three verbs each word can collocate with.
- Ask students to do the task individually, but check as a class.

Answers

1 get
2 do
3 went
4 did
5 get
6 going

I
- Ask students to read the instructions and check that they understand what they have to do.
- Read the phrases to the students and ask them to repeat them. Correct their pronunciation where necessary. Ask the students to work in pairs to discuss what the phrases mean.
- If students are totally unfamiliar with these phrases, write the sentences below on the board to help them to understand their meaning.
   – Johnny, I've asked you three times to be quiet, now *wise up* and get on with your assignment.
   – Why do some newspapers *dumb down* the words they use? Do they think their readers are not clever enough to understand challenging vocabulary?
   – Maria is *box clever*; she always comes up with innovative ideas before anyone else.
   – Tim asked me if we should be doing anything to help the environment. I told him that was *a no-brainer* and that his question didn't even require an answer.
   – My brother is travelling round Europe, but I'm not worried about him because he's very *streetwise* and knows how to take care of himself.
- As a class, ask each pair to give their definition of one of the phrases.

Answers

wise up – *to become aware of or informed about something*
dumb down – *to simplify or reduce the intellectual content of something so as to make it accessible to a larger audience*
box clever – *to use your intelligence to get ahead*
a no-brainer - *something that requires little mental effort*
streetwise – *to have the necessary knowledge to deal with modern urban life*
a bright spark – *an intelligent person who is full of energy*

Grammar

- Write the sentences below on the board and ask students what the verbs are. Then ask them what tenses have been used and what they express.
   – Water boils at 100 degrees Celsius. *(boils; Present Simple; This sentence talks about a scientific fact.)*
   – The water is getting hotter and hotter. *(is getting; Present Continuous; This sentence talks about a changing situation with a comparative.)*
   – The water has boiled. *(has boiled; Present Perfect Simple; This sentence talks about an event that happened at an unspecified time in the past.)*
   – The water has been boiling for five minutes. *(has been boiling; Present Perfect Continuous; This sentence talks about an event happening repeatedly up until now.)*
- Revise the affirmative, negative, question forms and short answers of these four tenses. Then elicit the time expressions used with each one.

1 Scaling the Heights

A

- Ask students to read the instructions and check that they understand what they have to do.
- Ask students to focus on the words in bold in each sentence as well as any time expressions.
- Ask students to do the task individually, but check as a class.

Answers

1 Present Perfect Simple
2 Present Continuous
3 Present Simple
4 Present Perfect Continuous

B

- Ask students to read the instructions and check that they understand what they have to do.
- Ask them to read a–d and explain anything they don't understand. Then encourage them to read the sentences in A again.
- Ask students to do the task individually, but check as a class.

Answers

a3 b4 c2 d1

C

- Write the sentences below on the board and, in pairs, ask students to find the verbs, identify the tenses and discuss what each expresses.
- Ask students to work in pairs to encourage discussion, but check as a class.
  - They have just won the gold medal! *(have (just) won; Present Perfect Simple; an action that has just finished.)*
  - Tony always goes skiing at the weekend. *(goes; Present Simple; a routine or habit.)*
  - We've been talking about life's great challenges. *('ve been talking; Present Perfect Continuous; a recent or unfinished action.)*
  - Joanne is an adventurous person. *(is; Present Simple; a permanent state.)*
  - I'm reading an article about success. *('m reading; Present Continuous; an action that is in progress around the time of speaking.)*
  - Why are you always wearing my clothes? *(are (always) wearing; Present Continuous; an annoying habit.)*
  - She's been living in Madrid for ten years. *('s been living; Present Perfect Continuous; emphasises how long an action has been in progress.)*
  - She has had the same hairstyle for five years. *(has had; Present Perfect Simple; something that started in the past and has continued up until now.)*
- Ask students to read the instructions and check that they understand what they have to do.
- Ask students to read 1–4 and explain anything they don't understand.
- Ask students to do the task individually, but check as a class.

Suggested answers

1 To express routines or habits, permanent states, and timetabled events in the future.
2 To express situations and actions happening around the time of speaking, temporary situations and future plans.
3 To express something that happened in the past but has a present result, or an action that has just finished.
4 To express a recent or unfinished action, or an action that started in the past and is still in progress.

Now read the Grammar Reference on pages 161 & 162 (1.1 to 1.4) with your students.

D

- Ask students to read the instructions and check that they understand what they have to do.
- Encourage students to read the whole sentence to look for any clues before circling the correct answer. Tell them they should pay particular attention to time expressions, adverbs of frequency and the tenses of other verbs in the sentences.
- Remind students to re-read the sentences once they have finished to check their answers.
- Ask students to do the task individually, but check as a class.

Answers

1 We've been waiting
2 seem
3 have been training
4 is working
5 Has she managed
6 I'm trying
7 haven't received
8 departs

E

- Ask students to read the instructions and check that they understand what they have to do. Point out that they have to use the verbs in brackets after each sentence in the correct form (Present Simple, Present Continuous, Present Perfect Simple or Present Perfect Continuous).
- Ask students to read the first sentence and to decide what it expresses (a scientific fact). Then ask them which tense is used to express a scientific fact (Present Simple).
- Remind students to look back at the Grammar box as they do the task and to pay attention to time expressions, adverbs of frequency and the tenses of other verbs in the sentences.
- Ask students to do the task individually, but check as a class.

Answers

1 sets
2 've/have been looking
3 are ... complaining
4 've/have completed
5 don't/do not watch
6 haven't/have not been working
7 'm/am writing
8 hasn't/has not been

- Ask the questions below at random around the class.
  - When did you last do something you were really proud of?
  - How long did you study for the last test you did really well on?
  - Which famous person interested you the most when you were younger? Why?
  - How old were you the first time you had to face a big challenge? What was the challenge?
- Ask students which tense the questions and their answers were in *(Past Simple)* and elicit how this tense is formed. Revise the affirmative, negative, question forms and short answers of this tense.
- Write the following sentences on the board and ask students what tense has been used this time *(Past Continuous)*.
  - The hikers were carrying a lot of equipment.
  - The cyclist was practising this time yesterday.
  - They weren't trying their hardest.
  - We were resting after the long walk.
- Elicit that the first and third person singular *(I, he, she, it)* form the Past Continuous with *was* followed by the main verb with *-ing*, and that the second person singular/plural, and first and third person plural *(you, we, they)*, form it with *were* followed by the main verb with *-ing*. Revise the affirmative, negative, question forms and short answers.
- Write the following sentences on the board and ask students what the difference in meaning between them is.
  - They had practised their shooting skills many times, so they were ready for the basketball match. *(The act of practising was a completed action in the past which took place before they played in the match.)*
  - They had been practising their shooting skills for hours when they decided to take a break. *(The act of practising was in progress for some time before it was interrupted by them taking a rest.)*
- Ask a student to come up to the board and underline the verbs in both sentences. Elicit that the tenses are Past Perfect Simple *(had practised)*, Past Simple *(were)*, and Past Perfect Continuous *(had been practising)* and Past Simple *(decided)*.
- Revise the affirmative, negative, question forms and short answers of Past Perfect Simple and Past Perfect Continuous.

F

- Ask students to read the instructions and check that they understand what they have to do.
- Ask students to focus on the words in bold in each sentence as well as any time expressions.
- Ask students to do the task individually, but check as a class.

Answers

1 Past Perfect Simple
2 Past Continuous
3 Past Simple
4 Past Perfect Continuous

G

- Ask students to read the instructions and check that they understand what they have to do. Explain that they should complete the gaps with the tense that describes each use.

- Ask students to read uses 1–4 and explain anything they don't understand.
- Ask students to do the task individually, but check as a class.

Answers

1 Past Simple
2 Past Continuous
3 Past Perfect Simple
4 Past Perfect Continuous

H

- Read the information to the students and elicit that we can't use *would* with stative verbs to talk about habits, but that we can use it with active verbs.
- Ask students to read the three sentences and to decide whether to use *used to* or *would* to fill the gaps. Ask them to justify their answers.

Answers

1 used to
2 used to
3 used to, would

Now read the Grammar Reference on page 162 (1.5 to 1.9) with your students.

I

- Ask students to read the title and look at the picture to the right of the text. Then ask them to skim read the text to find out how the title relates to it *(it is about various types of dog intelligence)*.
- Explain to students that they should think about which use of each tense is being used in each item, which verbs are stative, and the time expressions that are used with these tenses.
- Ask students to do the task individually, but check as a class.

Answers

1 had bred
2 used to
3 attacked
4 banned
5 had been wondering
6 was researching
7 published
8 had consulted

Listening

A

- Ask students to read the instructions and make sure they understand what they have to do.
- Ask students to do the task on their own and to then compare their answers with a partner. Don't check answers as a class yet.

Teaching Tip

You could expand this task further by asking the students to tell a partner about a situation or an experience that wasn't up to scratch for them, or, where they had achieved something great. Also, ask students to discuss a book they couldn't put down.

1 Scaling the Heights

B
- Ask students to read the instructions and make sure they understand what they have to do.
- Explain that students will hear a conversation between two people. Tell them to look back at the statements in A and ask students at random to guess what the conversation might be about *(a book that they have read)* and what the statements in A mean.
- Play the recording once all the way through and ask students to check their answers from A. Ask students to compare their answers with a partner and to justify any answers they have that are different.
- Play the recording again to check their answers or to fill in any missing answers.
- Check answers as a class.

Answers
1 N
2 P
3 P
4 N
5 P

C
- Ask students to read the instructions and make sure they understand what they have to do.
- Ask students to read the questions and the options and to underline any key words. Ask them to work with a partner to discuss other ways of saying the main ideas in the options.
- Remind students that in listening tasks, ideas are often paraphrased and that it's a good idea to get into the habit of reading the questions before listening and to think of other words and phrases that they might hear on the recording. Explain that students will hear the same conversation again.
- Play the recording all the way through and ask students to circle their answers. Then ask students to discuss their answers with a partner and to justify any answers they have that are different.
- Play the recording again and ask students to check their answers and to fill in any missing answers.
- Check the answers as a class and ask students to justify their answers using the words and expressions they heard on the recording.

Answers
1b 2c

D
- Ask students to read the *Exam Close-up*.
- Remind students of any differences in any answers they might have had in C and explain that this task shows how important it is to read and understand the questions properly in this type of listening task.
- Point out that as all the options will be related in some way to information on the recording, it is essential that they underline negative verb forms in expressions and try and work out how else they could be expressed to understand what they actually mean. This will help them decide which one answers the focus of the question.

- Stress that students should use the time between the first and second listening wisely. They should check their answers and see which information they need to focus on during the second listening.

E
- Ask students to read the instructions and check they understand what they have to do.
- Explain that they will hear two different extracts and that there are two questions for each extract.
- Explain that in this type of listening task, the situation is always given and that they should read it carefully so they will be able to predict, to a degree, what might be said in each extract.
- Give students time to read questions 1–4 and to underline any key words in the situations, the questions and the options. Answer any questions they might have about them.
- Play the recording once all the way through and ask students to mark their answers. Ask students to discuss their answers with a partner and to justify any they have that are different.
- Play the recording again and ask students to check their answers and to complete any missing answers.
- Check the answers as a class and ask students to justify their answers.

Answers
1b 2c 3c 4a

Extra Class Activity
If time allows, you could ask students to write a different conversation between the man and woman in the picture on page 12. Then ask them to write down a question and three possible options on a separate piece of paper. Go round the class giving students any help they may need. Then, ask students to swap questions and options with a partner. Each student should take it in turns to read their conversation while the other student answers the question.

Speaking

A
- Ask students to read the three questions and answer any queries they may have.
- Ask students to work in pairs and to take it in turns to ask and answer the questions about themselves.
- Go round the class monitoring students to make sure they are carrying out the task properly. Don't correct any mistakes at this point, but make a note of any problems in structure or pronunciation.
- Ask each pair to ask and answer one question and repeat until each student has had a turn.
- Write any structural mistakes made by students on the board without saying who made them, and ask them to correct them. Deal with any problems in pronunciation that came up.

Answers
Students' own answers

B
- Ask students to read the instructions and check that they understand what they have to do. Make sure that each pair has a watch.
- Ask students to read the four topics and answer any queries they may have.
- Go round the class monitoring students to make sure they are carrying out the task properly. Don't correct any mistakes at this point, but make a note of any problems in structure or pronunciation.
- As a class, ask one student from each pair to tell the rest of the class what he or she said about a topic, making sure all four topics are covered. Ask the others if they agree or if they have anything else to add.
- Write any structural mistakes made by students on the board without saying who made them, and ask them to correct them. Deal with any problems in pronunciation that came up.

Answers
Students' own answers

C
- Ask students to read the *Exam Close-up*.
- Ask students to quickly read the instructions for the *Exam Task* and elicit that they will have one long and one short turn.
- Stress that they should spend a minute or two brainstorming ideas to answer each of the questions about the photos.

Useful Expressions
- Read the *Useful Expressions* to the students and ask them to repeat them. Correct their pronunciation and intonation where necessary.
- Ask students for examples of which expressions they can use to deal with all the parts of the question: to compare the photos (*Photo ... shows ..., whereas the third photo shows ...*), to talk about similarities (*The photos are similar as / in that they both ...*), to talk about differences (*While there are some similarities between the photos, they are different because ...*), to talk about what aspects of achievement are shown (*Achievement is depicted / shown in photo ... by ..., but in photo ... it is shown by ...*) and to say how success is measured in the photos (*The main measure of success in photo ... is ..., while/whereas in photo ..., success is measured in terms of ...*).
- Point out that they should use some of these expressions when they do D.

D
- Ask students to read the instructions again and check that they understand what they have to do.
- Ask them to work in pairs and to decide who will be Student A and who will be Student B. Ask them to read the instructions for their role and to spend a few minutes looking at their own set of photos.
- Remind students that this kind of task isn't a discussion and that each student is expected to speak for one minute on his or her photos (*two*) answering the questions provided or to respond briefly (*30 seconds*) to the follow-up question about his or her partner's photos.
- Ask Student A to begin answering the questions about the two photos they have chosen from the three and for Student B to answer the follow-up question once Student A has finished. Then ask Student B to answer their questions about the two photos they have chosen from the three and Student A to answer the follow-up question.
- Go round the class monitoring students to make sure they are carrying out the task properly. Don't correct any mistakes at this point, but make a note of any problems in structure or pronunciation.
- Ask one pair of students to carry out the task in front of the class and ask the other students afterwards if they have anything to add.
- Write any structural mistakes made by students on the board without saying who made them, and ask them to correct them. Deal with any problems in pronunciation that came up.

Answers
Students' own answers

Writing: a reference

- Ask students what a reference is and why they are written (*a letter or statement recommending someone be considered for a new job*). Ask if they or anyone they know has had a reference written for them. If so, ask them if they or the person for whom the reference was written got the job they had applied for.
- Explain to students that in this lesson they are going to deal with writing references.
- Read the *Learning Focus* on understanding the purpose of a reference to the students and explain anything they don't understand. Ask students why they must explain who they are and what their relationship is to the person (*so that the reader will know that the reference is valid*) and why they should present the person in a positive light (*to improve their chances of getting the job*).

A
- Ask students to read the instructions and check that they understand what they have to do.
- Read out 1–7 and deal with any queries students might have about unfamiliar words.
- Ask students what they think a job as a receptionist might entail.
- Ask students to do the task individually, but check as a class.

Suggested answers
2, 3, 5, 6, 7

- Ask students to read the instructions and check that they understand what they have to do.
- In pairs, ask them to look at their answers from A and encourage them to make lists in their notebooks.
- As a class, discuss the points raised by each pair and make a list on the board of suitable ideas.

1 Scaling the Heights

Suggested answers

efficient, helpful, neat, patient, polite, presentable, respectful, responsible, tidy, trustworthy

B
- Ask students to read the instructions and check that they understand what they have to do.
- Read the words and phrases in the yellow box and ask students to repeat them after you. Correct their pronunciation where necessary. Deal with any queries students might have about unfamiliar words.
- Ask students to work in pairs to encourage discussion, but check as a class.

Answers
communication, computer, customer service, multi-tasking, organisational, people, secretarial

C
- Ask students to read the instructions and check that they understand what they have to do.
- Ask students to read the writing task and explain anything they don't understand.
- Ask students to do the task individually, but check as a class.

Answers
1. reference, friend, receptionist, good at dealing with people, excellent organisational skills, character, skills, previous relevant experience, reasons why they should be considered
2. people skills and organisational skills
3. four main paragraphs: (1) character, (2) skills, (3) previous experience, (4) reasons your friend should be considered
4. formal / neutral

D
- Ask students to read the instructions and check that they understand what they have to do.
- Ask students to read the example reference and to underline any information that relates to the main points in the writing task. Then ask them to compare the parts they underlined with a partner.
- As a class, ask students if every point has been dealt with and developed to its fullest and to quote the parts in the reference that deal with each part. Then discuss whether Sarah Crocker is a good candidate for the job. Ask students to justify their answers.

Answers
The writer has dealt with every point fully. Her friend Sarah appears to be a good candidate for the job.

E
- Ask students how many things the task asks them to do (two – to say how the writer has made a case for their friend and supported his/her opinion, to write the answers).
- Ask students to work in pairs to encourage discussion, but check as a class.

Answers
1. example of her good character: gives up all her free time to help with under-privileged youth; shows she is dependable and hard-working
2. example of her skills set in use: maintains youth club's web site, multi-tasks
3. work experience: the positions she has held make her ideal for the available post
4. summary of reasons that make her an ideal candidate

F
- Ask students to read the instructions and check that they understand what they have to do.
- Read out the two set phrases (To whom it may concern, Yours faithfully) and elicit why each is used (because the name of the recipient of the letter is unknown, because Yours faithfully is used when the name of the recipient is unknown).
- Ask students to do the task individually, but check as a class.

Answers
To whom it may concern: because the writer doesn't know the name of the recipient
Yours faithfully: used when the recipient is not addressed by name; optional for a reference

G
- Ask the students to read the Exam Close-up box and point out that the writer of the example reference did all the things on the list.
- Remind students that they can use the information here as a checklist when writing their own references.
- Ask students to read the Exam Task and ask them to underline any key words and phrases. Explain anything they don't understand.
- Ask students to answer the questions in C about this writing task so that they know what they have to do.
- As a class, ask students the following questions.
  - What job has your friend applied for? (student services assistant in an English-language college)
  - What qualities and skills should a suitable candidate have? (personable, a good multi-tasker, excellent computer and organisational skills).
- Ask students to read the paragraph plan and to make notes for each paragraph, if time allows. Then ask them how they will begin and end their references (To whom it may concern, Yours faithfully).
- Set the writing task for homework.
- Encourage students to use the Writing Reference and checklist for references on page 175.

Suggested answer

To whom it may concern,

I am writing to recommend Jane Barrie for the position of Student Services Assistant at your English-Language College. I first met Jane in 2005 when she attended my summer camp programme in the New Forest. She later went on to work as a camp host for five years.

Jane is a very friendly person and is well-liked by everyone she meets. She is also incredibly helpful and while at summer camp would always take care of the younger children.

Jane is highly capable of multi-tasking in demanding situations. She was always able to keep a cool head and deal with several jobs at once. For this reason, she always becomes a very important part of any team she is in. Jane also has excellent computer skills and a talent for organising events. She was able to arrange a summer party for the camp attendees with only a couple of days' notice.

Jane's experience co-ordinating summer camp programmes and various part-time positions doing office work have enabled her to become a proficient communicator as well as attaining a high level of organisational skills.

For these reasons, Jane would be an ideal candidate for any position where a personable manner combined with good multi-tasking and organisational skills are valued.

In summary, I have no hesitation in recommending Jane for the position and believe she would be a great asset to any company.

Yours faithfully,

Olivia Morton

Useful Expressions

- Read the *Useful Expressions* to the students and ask them to repeat them. Correct their pronunciation and intonation if necessary.
- Ask students to circle words and phrases from the list that are used in the example reference (*To whom it may concern, ..., I am writing to recommend ..., I have known ... since..., Her ... is such that..., For this reason..., Yours faithfully,...*)
- Elicit in which part of their reference they can use each category of expressions and tell them that they can use them when writing their reference for the Exam Task.

Video 1 Extreme Skydiving

General Note

The National Geographic videos can be used as an interesting way to introduce your students to other cultures. They are authentic National Geographic videos, and it is not necessary for students to understand everything they hear to benefit from them. The videos have the option to play English subtitles so that students can read on screen exactly what is said in the documentary. This feature may help students with some of the tasks in the worksheets. The videos are also a good way to encourage your students to watch TV programmes and films in English so that they can get used to the sound of the language. The more students are exposed to English, the easier it will be for them to pick up the language.

Background Information

Skydiving has an interesting history that goes back much further than the 20th century. The Chinese began parachuting without aeroplanes way back in the 10th century. Like today's base diving, they jumped from a height so they could then float to the ground. In the 18th century, Andre Jacques Garnerin of France was one of the first to use a parachute after he jumped out of a hot air balloon, Nowadays, skydiving is done both as a recreational pastime and as a highly-competitive sport.

Before you watch

A

- Explain to students that in this lesson they are going to watch a video about a special kind of sport. Ask them to look at the globe in the top-right corner of the page and tell you in which part of the world the sport is done (North England). Elicit what they know about North England and the sports that people do there.
- Read the words and phrases 1–4 to the students and ask them to repeat them. Then ask students to read meanings a-d and explain anything they don't understand.
- Ask students to do the task individually, but check as a class.

Answers

1c 2b 3d 4a

While you watch

B

- Tell students that they are going to watch the video and do a task based on the information they hear.
- Ask students to read statements 1–6 and ask them what the documentary will be about (extreme skydiving). Ask students to think about which statements may be true and which ones may be false before they watch.
- Explain anything in the statements that the students don't understand. Then play the video all the way through without stopping and ask students to mark their answers. Ask students to compare their answers with a partner's and to justify any answers they have that are different.
- Play the video again so that they can check their answers. Ask students to do the task individually, but check as a class.

Answers

1 T (00:07)   4 F (02:57)
2 F (01:03)   5 T (04:43)
3 T (02:24)   6 F (06:03)

After you watch

C

- Explain to students that this is a summary of the information they heard on the video.
- Read the words in the yellow box to the students and ask them to repeat them. Ask them to write N, V or Adj beside each of the words depending on whether it is a noun, verb or adjective.
- Explain to students that they should read the whole summary before writing any answers first to work out what part of speech is missing.
- Tell students to read the text again once they have finished to check their answers.
- Ask students to do the task individually, but check as a class.

Answers

1 exceed   6 holds
2 resistance   7 challenger
3 competitive 8 harnesses
4 lure   9 inflate
5 recorded   10 place

Ideas Focus

- Ask students to read the three questions and answer any queries they might have.
- Ask students to work in pairs and explain that they should both give their opinions on all three questions.
- Go round the class monitoring students to make sure they are carrying out the task properly.
- Ask each pair to answer one of the questions and repeat until each pair has had a turn.
- Write what the advantages and disadvantages of extreme sports are on the board as they give their answers.
- Deal with any problems in structure or pronunciation that came up.

Answers

Students' own answers

2 Like Comment Share

Reading:	multiple-choice questions, choosing the correct option
Vocabulary:	social media-related vocabulary, word formation, choosing the right part of speech, phrasal verbs, prepositions, idioms
Grammar:	future forms, future in the past, time expressions
Listening:	sentence completion, preparing to listen
Speaking:	talking about mobile phone use, social networking sites, decision making, preparing to speak, presenting opinions & reaching a decision
Writing:	essay (1), planning & structuring an essay, writing an essay, introducing & countering an argument

Unit opener

- Ask students to look at the title of the unit and to guess what it might mean (*'like', 'comment' and 'share' are three of the most common functions on social media sites such as Facebook*).
- Ask them to look at the picture and to read the caption, and then say how it might relate to the unit (*the picture is of a drawing of a social network structure*).
- Ask students to come up with as many adjectives related to social media as they can. Then, ask them to say if each word describes a positive, negative or neutral aspect of social media

Reading

A

- Ask students if they feel that social media brings people closer together and makes the world a smaller place.
- Ask students to say each of the words in the yellow box after you and elicit their meanings. Correct their pronunciation where necessary.
- Ask students to read the instructions in A and the questions above the yellow box. Check that they understand what they have to do.
- Ask them to work in pairs to encourage discussion, but check as a class.

Answers

Students' own answers

Extra Class Activity

Do a class survey to see if students feel social media is generally a 'good' or a 'bad' thing. Ask students to justify their answers.

B

- Ask students to look at the title of the first text and the picture that accompanies it. Elicit what they know about *Twitter*. Then ask them to do the same for the second text on cyborg anthropology.
- Ask students to read the instructions for B and check that they understand what they have to do.
- Ask them to skim read the texts to find relevant information regarding the question. Explain that they don't have to read in detail at the moment as they will have another opportunity to do that later.
- Ask students to do the task individually, but check answer as a class.

Answers

Joe Simpson is a user of modern technology and has a Twitter account.
Amber Case is a cyborg anthropologist who studies the relationship between people and technology and how technology is affecting and changing people's lives and the world they live in.

Word Focus

- Ask students to look at the words in red in the text and to re-read the sentences they are found in. Ask students to work in pairs to decide what each of the words means in the *Word Focus* box and to then find synonyms, if any, for each word.
- Ask students to compare their answers with another pair.

C

- Ask students to read the *Exam Close-up* and then ask one to explain what it says in his or her own words.
- Explain that before they attempt the multiple-choice task they should always underline the key words in the questions and then scan (*not re-read*) the texts to find and underline information that deals with the focus of the questions.
- Remind students that options are usually paraphrased so it is a good idea to try to answer the question in their own words before choosing the option closest to their own answer.
- Ask students to read the instructions in the *Exam Task* and items 1–4 with their options. Explain anything they don't understand.
- Ask students to do the task individually, but check as a class.

19

2 Like Comment Share

Answers

1 c (*While Simpson's mountaineering and survival skills are second to none, …*)
2 b (*Simpson sees the funny side of it all. He said that it was quite comical …*)
3 c (*'These are the kinds of questions my work tries to help answer,' says Case.*)
4 a (*She claims that mobile phones have become like miniature children. 'If they cry … when they're lost, we panic.*)

Teaching Tip

Always give students plenty of time to discuss their opinions on the theme of the reading texts. This will not only help their fluency, but will also help them to better understand the key ideas of the text. The images that accompany the texts often provide a good starting point for discussion.

D

- Ask students to read the instructions and check that they understand what they have to do.
- Ask students to look at the words in the yellow box and to scan the texts again to find and underline them. Ask them to say each of the words after you and elicit that they are all nouns. Correct their pronunciation where necessary.
- Remind them that they should always try to work out the meaning of the word from its context and ask them to read the sentences in the text in which each word is contained.
- Ask students to do the task individually, but check as a class.

Answers

1 views
2 reaction
3 scratch
4 criticism
5 choice
6 contact

Ideas Focus

- Explain to students that they are going to answer some questions about social media. Ask students to read the questions and explain anything they don't understand.
- Ask students to answer the questions in pairs and encourage them to draw on personal experience.
- Go round the class monitoring students to ensure they are carrying out the task properly. Don't correct any mistakes at this point, but make a note of any problems in structure or pronunciation.
- Ask students at random to answer each of the questions. Then ask the other students if they agree or if they have anything else to add.
- Write any structural mistakes made by students on the board without saying who made them, and ask them to correct them. Deal with any problems in pronunciation that came up.

Answers

Students' own answers

Vocabulary

A

- Ask students to read the instructions and check that they understand what they have to do.
- Read the sets of words 1–6 to the students and ask students to repeat them after you. Correct their pronunciation where necessary.
- Ask students to work in pairs to encourage discussion, but check the answers as a class. Ask students to explain why one of the words is the odd one out in each item.

Answers

1 purpose (*The others relate to ways of talking or observing something, but 'purpose' refers to the reason why something is done.*)
2 defend (*The others are ways of showing disapproval, but 'defend' is when you show support in the face of criticism.*)
3 avoid (*The others refer to human interaction, but 'avoid' means to keep out of the way of or to stop doing something.*)
4 burdens (*The others refer to positive aspects of human behaviour, but 'burdens' means when something is difficult to put up with.*)
5 resist (*The others refer to ways you could force someone into a bad reaction, but 'resist' means to oppose something you don't agree with.*)
6 shock (*The others refer to positive feelings, but 'shock' means to experience a nasty surprise.*)

B

- Ask students to read the title of the text and ask them what they think *phishing* is. Then ask them to skim read the text, without filling in any answers, to find out (*the criminal activity of sending emails or having a website that is intended to fool someone into divulging information, such as their bank account number. This information is then used to illegally obtain money or goods*). Ask students if they know of any other ways that the Internet can be used illegally and encourage a short class discussion on the topic.
- Ask students to read the *Exam Close-up* and then to complete the *Exam Task* individually, but check as a class.

Answers

1 personal
2 users
3 scammers
4 validate
5 username
6 included
7 access
8 identity
9 directed

C

- Read phrasal verbs 1–8 to the students and ask them to repeat them. Correct their pronunciation where necessary.
- Ask students to read definitions a–h without filling in any answers at this stage.

- Ask students to do the task individually, but check as a class.
- Encourage students to copy the phrasal verbs and their meanings into their notebooks.

Answers

1 d 2 h 3 e 4 c 5 g 6 b 7 a 8 f

D

- Ask students to read the instructions and check that they understand what they have to do. Point out that they have to use the phrasal verbs from C in the correct form.
- Ask students to first read the sentences for gist to work out which phrasal verb might be missing. Remind them to pay attention to the subject and also the other tenses used in the sentences to help them write the verbs in the correct form.
- Ask students to do the task individually, but check as a class.

Answers

1 come in for
2 got back at
3 stir up
4 bringing down
5 set out
6 taken aback
7 cut in
8 took to

E

- Ask students to read the instructions and check that they understand what they have to do. Encourage students to read the sentences carefully and to pay attention to the words before and after the options before circling their answers.
- Remind students to re-read the sentences once they have finished to check their answers.
- Ask students to do the task individually, but check as a class.

Answers

1 under
2 Without
3 in
4 out of
5 on
6 at
7 to

F

- Ask students to read the instructions and check that they understand what they have to do.
- Read the words in the yellow box to students and ask them to repeat them. Correct their pronunciation where necessary.
- Ask students to look at the phrases in italics quickly. Explain that in English there are lots of colourful expressions and that some of these expressions are called idioms. Tell them that in this task they will be dealing with idioms related to animals.
- Ask students to work in pairs to encourage discussion, but check as a class.
- Point out that they will be better able to remember idioms if they record them in their notebooks and include their definitions as well as a sentence demonstrating their use.

Answers

1 horse
2 canary
3 goose
4 bird
5 frog
6 Cat

Teaching Tip

You could extend this task by asking students if they have animal idioms in their language. If they do, tell students to say the idiom in English and ask the other students to try and guess its meaning.

Ideas Focus

- Explain to students that they are going to answer two questions about which social media they use and what they use them for. Ask students to read the questions and explain anything they don't understand.
- Ask students to answer the questions in pairs and encourage them to draw on personal experience.
- Go round the class monitoring students to ensure they are carrying out the task properly. Don't correct any mistakes at this point, but make a note of any problems in structure or pronunciation.
- Ask students at random to answer each of the questions. Then ask the other students if they agree or if they have anything else to add.
- Write any structural mistakes made by students on the board without saying who made them, and ask them to correct them. Deal with any problems in pronunciation that came up.

Answers

Students' own answers

Grammar

- Ask students to work in pairs to discuss what they think social media will be like in 50 years time. Ask them which aspects of social media they think will stay the same and which will change. You could also ask them whether or not they think sites like *Facebook* will still be popular.
- Ask students to look back at the Reading texts about modern technology on pages 18 and 19 to find as many examples of the future tense as they can: *Text 1, 'my entire year will fail'; Text 2, 'What will the next life-shaping breakthrough in technology be?', 'Which new products will fail or succeed,' 'technology will make us'.* Ask students which of the future tenses is demonstrated in the examples they found (Future Simple).
- Revise the affirmative, negative, question forms and short answers of this tense with the class. Then elicit the adverbs of frequency and time expressions that are used with it. Explain to students that in this lesson they will concentrate on this tense as well as other future forms.

A

- Ask students to read the instructions and check that they understand what they have to do.
- Ask them to read sentences 1–8 quickly and to underline all the future forms.
- Ask students to do the task individually, but check as a class.

2 Like Comment Share

Answers

1 Shall ... help
2 will be talking
3 're opening
4 'm going to return
5 visit
6 will have updated
7 'll find
8 will have been using

- Explain to students that they should pay attention to the context of each missing verb to help them to decide which tense is appropriate each time. Encourage them to look back at A, B and C if they need help while doing the task.
- Ask students to do the task individually, but check as a class.

Answers

1 will continue
2 will enter
3 will have replaced
4 will happen/are going to happen
5 will be looking

B

- Ask students to look at what they have underlined in A and ask them which future tenses and forms are used (Future Simple, Future Continuous, Future Perfect Simple, Future Perfect Continuous, Present Simple, Present Continuous, be going to, shall).
- Ask students to read uses a–h and point out that some tenses and forms have more than one function.
- Ask students to do the task in pairs to encourage discussion, but check as a class.

Answers

a6 b8 c4 d2 e5 f7 g1 h3

E

- Ask students to read the instructions and check that they understand what they have to do. Explain that they mustn't change the word in bold in any way in the second sentence.
- Ask students to read the two sentences in item 1. Then ask them to underline the part in the first sentence that is missing from the second sentence. Explain that in order to complete the second sentence they will have to make a structural change.
- Ask students to complete the first item and correct it before they move on to do the rest of the task.
- Ask students to do the task individually, but check as a class.

C

- Ask students to read the instructions and check that they understand what they have to do.
- Encourage them to re-read the uses in B before they do the task.
- Ask students to do the task in pairs to encourage discussion, but check as a class.

Answers

Future Simple **f**
Future Continuous **d**
Future Perfect Simple **a**
Future Perfect Continuous **b**
Present Simple **e**
Present Continuous **h**
be going to **c**
shall **g**

Answers

1 will have been building
2 am going (to go)
3 will get into trouble
4 will not have finished
5 are you doing

- Write the sentences below on the board:
  - Jake said he **would text** us from America. (Future in the past; Jake went to America).
  - We knew that our newly-designed social networking site **was going to be** a great success. (Future in the past; we designed our social networking site).
  - I had to call a taxi because I **was meeting** my BFF in an hour. (Future in the past; I called a taxi).
- In pairs, ask students to look at the verbs in bold and ask them if the sentences refer to the past, present or future. Elicit which event or situation occurred first in each sentence.
- Ask students to work in pairs to encourage discussion, but check the answers as a class.

Extra Class Activity

You could extend this task by asking students to write a sentence of their own for each of the future tenses and forms covering all the uses mentioned in B.

Now read the Grammar Reference on pages 162 & 163 (2.1 to 2.6) with your students.

F

- Ask students to read the instructions and check that they understand what they have to do.
- Ask students to read sentences a, b and c carefully and to focus on the verbs in bold before answering the questions.
- Ask students to do the task in pairs to encourage discussion, but check as a class.

D

- Ask students to look at the title and the picture to the right of the text and ask them the questions below. Accept any logical answers.
  - How is the title related to the picture?
  - What does the title mean?
  - What will the woman probably do later?
  - How will the English language have changed by 2050?
- Explain to students that they are going to read a text that talks about future language developments similar to those illustrated in the title of the text. Ask them to read the text without filling in any answers, and to guess what the terms contained in the third to last line of the text might mean (LOL = laugh out loud, FYI = for your information, IMHO = in my humble opinion, BFF = best friend(s) forever, OMG = oh my goodness).

Answers

1 the past
2 Janet promised, I had a feeling, We had to hurry

G

- Ask students to read the rules carefully and to refer back to sentences *a*, *b* and *c* before filling in the gaps.
- Ask students to do the task individually, but check as a class.

Answers

1 would
2 was/were going to
3 Past Continuous

- Write the following sentences on the board.
  - Maria said that <u>when</u> she got to Athens she would call us.
  - <u>As soon as</u> I saw the new social networking site I knew it was going to be a great success.
- Elicit what the list of words and phrases are called (*time expressions*).
- Ask students if the sentences refer to the past, present or future (*Future in the past*). Then elicit what tense is used with the underlined time expressions (*Past Simple*).
- Ask students to read the information and explain anything they don't understand.
- If necessary, give students extra practice by asking them to write their own sentences using time expressions.

Now read the Grammar Reference on page 163 (2.7 & 2.8) with your students.

H

- Ask students to read the instructions and check that they understand what they have to do.
- Encourage students to read the whole sentence before underlining the time expressions. Remind them that Future in the past cannot be used with time expressions, instead the Past Simple is used.
- Explain to students that they should pay attention to the context of each missing verb to help them decide which tense is appropriate. Encourage them to look back at the grammar point if they need help while doing the task.
- Ask students to do the task individually, but check as a class.

Answers

1 while – 'll/will wait, shop
2 As soon as – get, 'll/will send; got, sent
3 before – was going to withdraw, went; withdrew, went
4 until – wouldn't/would not fix, showed; won't fix, shows
5 After – have had, 'll/will be able

I

- Ask students to read the instructions and check that they understand what they have to do. Point out that they have to use *was/were going to* or *would* to complete the sentences.
- Ask students to read the first sentence and to decide what it expresses (*a prediction in the past based on evidence*).
- Ask them which tense or form is used to express a prediction in the past based on evidence (*was/were going to*).
- Ask students to do the rest of the task individually, but check as a class.

Answers

1 were going to
2 was going to/would
3 would
4 were going to
5 would
6 was going to

J

- Ask students to read the instructions and check that they understand what they have to do. Explain that they mustn't change the word in bold in any way in the second sentence.
- Ask students to read the two sentences in item 1. Then ask them to underline the part in the first sentence that is missing from the second sentence. Explain to students that in order to complete the second sentence they will have to make a structural change.
- Ask students to complete the first item and correct it before they move on to the rest of the task.
- Ask students to do the task individually, but check as a class.

Answers

1 once you have packed
2 was going to buy
3 he wouldn't/would not reply
4 wasn't/was not planning
5 as soon as we get

Listening

- Ask students to work in pairs to describe the bottom picture on page 24. Ask them to describe the people and the situation. Ask them what the people are doing (*a mobile phone is being used*).
- In pairs, ask students to talk about mobile phones and what they can be used for (*talking to people, using apps, listening to music, taking photos/videos*). Finish off by discussing the topic of mobile phones and apps as a class and explain that in this part of the lesson they will learn more about this subject.

A

- Explain that in this lesson they will be improving their technique in note-taking listening tasks.
- Ask students to read the instructions and make sure they understand what they have to do.
- Ask students to read the sentences and decide what kind of information or part of speech (*name, number, noun, etc.*) is needed to complete the sentences.
- Elicit that they are not expected to complete the sentences at this stage, but only to guess what kind of information is needed.
- Give students time to think about their answers and then ask them to compare them with a partner.
- Check answers as a class.

Answers

1 a noun referring to an object/device
2 number of years
3 adverb/adjective
4 a verb
5 a noun referring to a person
6 a date/year

2 Like Comment Share

B

- Ask students to read the instructions and make sure they understand what they have to do.
- Explain to students that they are now going to hear someone talking about mobile phones and apps. Ask them to look back at the statements in A again and to underline any key words that will help them focus on the information in the recording. Explain that what they hear on the recording will probably be paraphrased in the sentences, so it is a good idea to listen out for synonyms and synonymous phrases.
- Play the recording once all the way through and ask students to write their answers in the gaps in A. Ask students to compare their answers with a partner and to justify any answers they have that are different.
- Play the recording again and ask students to check their answers and to fill in any missing answers.
- Check answers as a class and ask students to justify their answers.

Answers

1 iPad
2 two months
3 completely cut-off
4 chat with
5 (team) leader
6 1999

C

- Ask students to read the instructions and make sure they understand what they have to do.
- Explain to the students that questions 1–3 in C refer to the sentences in the Exam Task.
- Explain that in question 3 students are not expected to guess the specific words needed to complete the sentences. At this stage they only need to guess what kind of information is needed.
- Ask the students to work with a partner to discuss how they decided on their answers.
- Check answers as a class.

Answers

1 use of mobile phones
2 negative because phrases like *are to blame for/have affected our privacy/is worried* are used
3 Information missing in each question:
  1 a date
  2 a noun referring to a company
  3 a noun referring to an aspect of technology
  4 a phrase
  5 a noun
  6 an adjective
  7 a verb

D

- Ask students to read the Exam Close-up box.
- Refer them back to A and elicit that reading the sentences and predicting what kind of information was needed to complete the sentences made it more likely that they would complete this type of listening task successfully.
- Also point out that their answers were the exact words heard on the recording while the sentences themselves may have been paraphrased or contained synonyms or synonymous phrases.
- Encourage students to spend a minute thinking about the information needed to complete the sentences in the Exam Task and underlining any key words that will help them to focus on the information in the recording.
- Stress that students should use the time between the first and second listening wisely. They should check their answers and see which information they need to specifically focus on during the second listening.
- Ask students to read the instructions and check they understand what they have to do.
- Play the recording once all the way through and ask students to write their answers. Then ask students to discuss their answers with a partner and to justify any answers they have that are different.

E

- Play the recording again and ask students to check their answers and to fill in any missing answers.
- Check the answers as a class and ask students to justify their answers.

Answers

1 1997
2 service providers
3 tracking systems
4 stalking people
5 an alert
6 intrusive
7 can access

Teaching Tip

If students have problems with listening, suggest that they make time to listen to English more outside the classroom. Suggest that they watch films and TV programmes in English, preferably without subtitles. Point out that it is not necessary to understand every word as long as they understand the general idea of what is being said. Explain that they must listen as often as possible to the language being spoken naturally for their ears to become accustomed to it.

Speaking

A

- Ask students to read the three questions and answer any queries they may have about them.
- Ask students to work in pairs and to take it in turns to ask and answer the questions about themselves.
- Go round the class monitoring students to make sure they are carrying out the task properly. Don't correct any mistakes at this point, but make a note of any problems in structure or pronunciation.
- Ask each pair to ask and answer one question and repeat until every student has had a turn.
- Write any structural mistakes made by students on the board without saying who made them, and ask them to correct them. Deal with any problems in pronunciation that came up.

Answers

Students' own answers

B

- Ask students to read the information in the *Exam Close-up*. Ask students to then look at the *Exam Task* and decide the types of ideas they will discuss.
- Stress the importance of discussing all the options as fully as possible. Point out that this will help them prepare logical reasons for their decisions. You should also point out that in an exam situation, the examiner won't be able to assess their language level properly if they don't discuss each option in detail.
- Elicit from students that in decision-making tasks, they should be having a two-way conversation, so they should encourage each other to give opinions and ask for reasons to justify them.
- Ask students to quickly read the instructions in the *Exam Task* and ask them what kind of decision they will have to make *(what part might technology play in the people in the pictures lives and in whose life technology plays the most important part)*.
- Explain to students that they will learn various structures for presenting opinions and reaching a decision in the *Useful Expressions* box.

Useful Expressions

- Read the *Useful Expressions* and ask students to repeat them. Correct their pronunciation and intonation where necessary.
- Explain that they can use these structures when presenting their opinions and reaching a decision.
- Point out that they should practise using some of these structures when they are trying to reach a decision when they do the *Exam Task*.

C

- Ask students to read the instructions again and ask them how many things they have to do *(two)* and what they are *(talk about the role of technology in different people's lives; decide which person finds technology most important in their life.)*.
- Explain to students that in decision-making tasks like this, they should base their decision on the pictures in the task and not on a personal situation.
- As a class, elicit what type of technology might each person use in each situation.
- Ask students to do the task in pairs and to use the structures in *Useful Expressions* to present their opinions and reach a decision.
- Go round the class monitoring students to make sure they are carrying out the task properly. Don't correct any mistakes at this point, but make a note of any problems in structure or pronunciation.
- Ask each pair to tell the rest of the class which option(s) they chose and to say why.
- Write any structural mistakes made by students on the board without saying who made them, and ask them to correct them. Deal with any problems in pronunciation that came up.

Answers
Students' own answers

Ideas Focus

- Ask students to read the questions quickly and deal with any queries they may have.
- Ask students to work in pairs and to take it in turns to answer the questions.
- Go round the class monitoring students to make sure they are carrying out the task properly. Don't correct any mistakes at this point, but make a note of any problems in structure or pronunciation.
- Ask a student from each pair to answer one of the questions until each pair has had a turn. Ask the other students if they agree or if they have anything else to add.
- Write any structural mistakes made by students on the board without saying who made them, and ask them to correct them. Deal with any problems in pronunciation that came up.

Answers
Students' own answers

Writing: an essay (1)

- Explain to students that in this lesson they are going to deal with writing essays.
- Ask students to read the *Learning Focus* on planning and structuring an essay and explain anything they don't understand. Ask them what the main purpose of an essay is *(to present an argument and give reasons for it)*. Explain that they need to look carefully at the essay task and topic area before considering what register, functions, grammatical structures and vocabulary they will need to use.
- Remind students that a well-developed essay should include an introduction, two or three main paragraphs and a conclusion and that the paragraphs should follow on logically from one another. Also remind students that that each paragraph should have one main idea which is introduced by a topic sentence and supported by details and reasons.
- When proofreading their essays, students should not only look out for spelling, grammatical and lexical errors, but also check that they have written in the appropriate register.

A

- Ask students to read the instructions and check that they understand what they have to do.
- In pairs, give students time to write down five ways in which people can interact via the Internet and then ask them to work together in order to answer the question based on their ideas.
- Ask one student from each pair for one way in which people can interact via the Internet and ask the other student in the pair to talk about a negative aspect that is associated with it. Repeat until each pair has had a turn.

2 Like Comment Share

Suggested answers

email – phishing and other Internet scams
instant messaging – no inflection, one can be misunderstood
Internet forums – as above
blogs and microblogs (*e.g. Twitter*) – posts can get you into trouble
social networking sites (*e.g. Facebook*) – you can say too much about yourself; some of your 'friends' are really strangers
content communities (*e.g. YouTube*) – anyone can post almost anything/inappropriate content
virtual game worlds (*e.g. World of Warcraft*) – time-wasting, addictive, violent
virtual social worlds (*e.g. Second Life*) – time-wasting, addictive
collaborative projects (*e.g. Wikipedia*) – misinformation

B
- Ask students to read the instructions and check that they understand what they have to do.
- Ask students to look at their answers from A and encourage them to write a paragraph about one of their answers in their notebooks.
- Elicit that students must explain what the way of interacting is *(e.g. email)* and what its benefits are. Also elicit how many words they have to write *(60)*.
- When they have finished, ask some students to read out their paragraphs to the rest of the class. You could hang all the paragraphs on the wall and ask students to read each other's work.

Answers
Students' own answers

C
- Ask students to read the instructions and check that they understand what they have to do.
- Then ask students to read the writing task and explain anything they don't understand.
- Point out that in question three students must tick the correct box to indicate how essays can be made more formal.
- Ask students to do the task individually, but check as a class.

Answers
1 a teacher
2 two: 1) agree or disagree with the statement, 2) discuss disadvantages of Internet interaction
3 d

D
- Ask students to read the instructions and check that they understand what they have to do.
- Ask them to read the example essay and to pay particular attention to the writer's view.
- As a class, ask students what the writer's view on the topic is and if they agree with it.

Answers
The Internet has revolutionised the way we communicate, but there are serious risks attached to it. Students' own answers

E
- Tell students that they are going to look back at the example essay to analyse and comment on how it is organised, the language used and its content.
- Ask students to read the questions and explain anything they don't understand.
- Ask students to work in pairs to encourage discussion, but check as a class.

Answers
1 The Internet has changed how we communicate and who we communicate with.
It is a good response to the prompt because it addresses the magnitude of the Internet's effect and alludes to making the world a smaller place.
2 At the end of the introduction, 'has brought the world into our homes and work' is echoed by 'nobody and nothing is out of reach' in the main paragraph.
3 With the Internet, nobody and nothing is out of reach. Supporting points: helps us to stay in touch with family and friends; certain gadgets make the presence of the other person more real; we can meet people we might never have met otherwise; information is gathered with ease; exposes us to international points of view and broadens our horizons.
There is, nonetheless, cause for much concern in a number of areas. Supporting points: privacy is threatened; misinformation; no peace and quiet
4 Yes, it does summarise the writer's view. No, it doesn't introduce any new ideas. No, it is not repetitive.
5 allows information *to be gathered*, is threatened, being connected, must be set off
6 Suggested answers (*alternatives in brackets*)
Main paragraph 1: What is more (*In addition*); Aside from (*Apart from*); Beyond (*Further to*); thus (*thereby*)
Main paragraph 2: nonetheless (*however*); To begin with (*Firstly*); Furthermore (*Moreover*); Finally (*Last but not least*)
Conclusion: All in all (*In summary*)

F

- Ask students to read the instructions and check that they understand what they have to do.
- Remind students to use two of their answers from A to write their paragraph.
- Allow no more than ten minutes for them to write their paragraph and go round the class offering help where necessary.
- When students have finished, remind them that when they have finished a piece of writing they should always proofread it to check for spelling, grammatical and punctuation errors.
- Ask students to swap paragraphs with a partner and give them a few minutes to read and underline any mistakes they find in their partner's work. Explain that they don't have to correct them.
- Ask students to hand the notebooks back to their partners and to correct any mistakes that have been noted.
- As a class, ask several students to read out their paragraph.

Answers

Students' own answers

Teaching Tip

Some students might be embarrassed about another student looking at their work. It's important to build up an atmosphere of trust in the classroom and for students to see that they all have a common goal. Explain to students that reading each other's work is an important part of the learning process and it allows them to see how other people deal with tasks as well as giving them an opportunity to read English.

G

- Ask the students to read the *Exam Close-up* and ask students to underline the topic sentences in the two main paragraphs of the example essay *(With the Internet ... out of reach.; There is ... in a number of other areas.)* and remind them to use topic sentences like these in their essay.
- Remind students that they can use the information here as a checklist when writing their own essays.
- Ask students to read the instructions and the *Exam Task* and ask them to underline any key words and phrases in the task. Explain anything they don't understand.
- Ask students to answer the questions in C about this *Exam Task* so they know what they have to do.
- As a class, ask students to answer the two questions *(Do you agree that our relationships have suffered as a consequence of social media?; How do you think social media will affect human relationships in the future?)*.
- Ask students to read the paragraph plan and to make notes on each paragraph, if time allows. Ask students what kind of language they will need to use for their essay *(formal)*.
- Set the *Exam Task* for homework.
- Encourage students to use the Writing Reference and checklist for essays on page 176.

Suggested answer

It is a well-known fact that social media sites have changed the nature of human relationships today. A large section of society believe that they have had a negative effect whereas others may disagree.

There is no doubt that relationships have changed since the introduction of social media sites like Facebook and Twitter, but I don't agree that this has caused them to suffer. For one thing, it is now easier to keep in touch with people. No matter where you are you can send emails, text messages or tweets from your mobile phone, tablet or laptop. This has led to enhanced relationships as you can stay in contact with people you're not able to see regularly. What is more, social media sites enable us to find friends that we have lost contact with for one reason or another. This would be far more difficult if we tried to do it via traditional means.

Far from being detrimental I think that social media sites will continue to enrich our relationships in the future. It is widely thought that people sometimes endanger themselves by coming into contact with people they don't know and counting them as 'friends'. On the contrary, I believe this can be a good thing and that in future, people will have as many virtual friends as they do actual friends.

All in all, I feel that, if used with caution, social media sites can only improve our relationships with existing friends and help us to make new relationships with people that we have things in common with.

Useful Expressions

- Read the *Useful Expressions* to the students and ask them to repeat them. Correct their pronunciation and intonation if necessary.
- Elicit in which part of their essay they can use each category of expressions and tell them to use them when writing their essay for the *Exam Task*.

2 Orangutan Language

General Note

Please see the information about the National Geographic videos on page 18 of this Teacher's Book.

Background Information

Orangutans are truly amazing creatures. In Malay, the word *orangutan* means 'person of the forest'. They are large animals with arms that are about twice as long as their bodies. Wild orangutans live in Sumatra and Borneo and are the only great apes found today outside of Africa. Orangutans are famous for their dexterity and use both their hands and feet when gathering food. They can live for 45 to 60 years in the wild. Sadly, the Sumatran orangutan is now classified as critically endangered. The Bornean orangutan has a larger habitat range than its cousin and therefore is at less risk of immediate extinction and is classified as endangered.

Before you watch

A

- Explain to students that in this lesson they are going to watch a video about orangutans in a zoo in Washington DC. Ask them to look at the globe to see where Washington DC is *(USA)*. Elicit what they know about Washington DC and ask them if they know anything about the zoo there.
- Ask students to answer the questions in pairs. Encourage them to draw on their own knowledge of orangutans and how they communicate.
- Go round the class monitoring students to make sure they are carrying out the task properly. Don't correct any mistakes at this stage, but make a note of any problems in structure and pronunciation.
- Ask each pair to answer one of the questions and repeat until each pair has had a turn.
- Deal with any problems in pronunciation that came up.

Answers

1	Indonesia and Malaysia
2 & 3	Students' own answers

While you watch

B

- Explain to students that they are now going to watch the video and do a task based on the information they hear.
- Ask students to read sentences 1–6 and explain anything they don't understand.
- Ask them to think about which words may be correct before watching.
- Play the video all the way through without stopping and ask students to circle their answers. Ask students to compare their answers with a partner's.
- Play the video again so that they can check their answers.
- Ask students to do the task individually, but check as a class.

Answers

1 coordinator (00:28)	4 social (02:18)
2 voluntary (00:55)	5 extinct (03:04)
3 identify (01:46)	6 personally (03:21)

After you watch

C

- Explain to students that this is a summary of the information they heard on the video.
- Read the words in the yellow box to the students and ask them to repeat them. Ask them to write N, V or Adj beside each of the words depending on whether it is a noun, a verb or an adjective.
- Explain to students that they should read the whole summary first before writing any answers to work out what part of speech is missing.
- Tell students to re-read the text once they have finished to check their answers.
- Ask students to do the task individually, but check as a class.

Answers

1 primates	6 simple
2 captivity	7 communicating
3 choices	8 research
4 connects	9 efforts
5 performs	10 regard

Ideas Focus

- Ask students to read the three questions and answer any queries they might have.
- Ask students to work in pairs and explain that they should both give their opinions on all three questions.
- Go round the class monitoring students to make sure they are carrying out the task properly. Don't correct any mistakes at this stage, but make a note of any problems in structure and pronunciation.
- Ask each pair to answer one of the questions and repeat until each pair has had a turn.
- Write about how technology may or may not be able to help us communicate with animals in the future on the board.
- Deal with any problems in structure or pronunciation that came up.

Answers

Students' own answers

Review 1

Units 1 & 2

Objective
- To revise vocabulary and grammar from Units 1 and 2
- To practise exam-type tasks

Revision
- Explain to students that there will be a review after every two units in *Close-up C1*. Tell them that Review 1 revises the material from Units 1 and 2.
- Explain that students can ask for help with the exercises or look back at the units if they're not sure about an answer. Stress that the review is not a test.
- Decide how you will carry out the review. You could ask students to do one task at a time and then correct it immediately, or ask students to do all the tasks and correct them together at the end. If you do all the tasks together, let students know every now and again how much time they have got left to finish.
- Ask students not to leave any answers blank and to find any answers they aren't sure about in the units.
- When checking students' answers to the review tasks, make a note of any problem areas in vocabulary and grammar that they still have. Try to do extra work on these areas so that your students will progress well.

Vocabulary Revision
- Ask students to write down as many character adjectives as they can think of. Then ask them to write down synonyms or antonyms of these adjectives.
- Elicit from students the phrasal verbs they learnt in Unit 1 which are related to success (*blow away, break through, come up against, fall through, get ahead, hang on, knuckle down, pull off*) and ask them to write sentences of their own using these phrasal verbs.
- Ask students to explain the difference between the following pairs of words: *accomplish/achieve, insist/persist, resolve/solve, defeat/failure*.
- Say the words *construction, warning, confidence, context, occasion, a guess* and *my face* one by one to students and ask them which prepositions come before them.
- Ask students to work in pairs to tell each other about a situation in which:
  - they got something straight from the horse's mouth
  - they sang like a canary
  - they had a frog in their throat
  - the cat got their tongue
  - a little bird told them something

Grammar Revision
- Write these sentences on the board and ask students to say which tenses have been used and whether they are in the affirmative, negative or question form. Then revise all forms of the tenses students learnt in Unit 1 as well as the time expressions used with them.
  - They had never used Facebook until now. *(Past Perfect Simple; negative)*
  - Had they been waiting in the Internet café for long? *(Past Perfect Continuous; question)*
  - She soon grew bored of her new video game. *(Past Simple; affirmative)*
  - We go mountain climbing every year. *(Present Simple; affirmative)*
  - Are they interviewing you this morning? *(Present Continuous; question)*
  - I haven't finished my assignment yet. *(Present Perfect Simple; negative)*
  - He has been travelling around Europe this month. *(Present Perfect Continuous; affirmative)*
  - Was Petra getting on the train when she fell? *(Past Simple and Past Continuous; question)*
- Write the sentences below on the board and ask students to complete them with *used to* or *would*, or their negative forms. Explain that if both structures can be used, then they should write both options in. Then, as a class, revise the rules for *used to* and *would* to talk about repeated actions in the past.
  - Barry _____ hate extreme sports. *(used to)*
  - Kate _____ be addicted to her mobile phone. *(used to)*
  - When he was young, he _____ dream about being a famous actor. *(used to / would)*
  - My father _____ drive in the city because he was frightened of the traffic. *(didn't use to / wouldn't)*
- Revise the future tenses and forms students learnt in Unit 2 by asking the questions below at random round the class. Make sure each student answers at least one question and revise any forms they have problems with.
  - What are you going to do this evening?
  - Where will you spend your holidays this year?
  - How many texts will you have sent by this time next week?
  - Did your parents promise they would get you something new if you passed your exams?
  - What job do you think you will be doing in the year 2030?
  - Did you have the feeling that Facebook was going to be a success?
- Write the beginnings of the sentences below on the board and ask students to complete them in their own words. Make sure that they remember that future tenses cannot be used with time expressions in the sentences.
  - Let's go to a desert island when _____.
  - We should wait here in case _____.
  - Tell your teacher about missing your deadline as soon as _____.
  - Make sure you buy your ticket before _____.
  - Why don't we go to the park after _____.

A

- Ask students to read the instructions and check that they understand what they have to do.
- Ask students to read the title of the text and ask them what they think the text will be about. Then ask them to skim read the text, without circling any answers, to find out what *dumbing down* means in the context of the text *(making people less intelligent)*.
- Point out to students that they should read all four options for each item before deciding which word best fits each gap. Remind them to pay attention to the whole sentence as the context will help them understand what word is missing.
- Remind students to re-read the text once they have finished to check their answers.

Answers

1 B 2 D 3 A 4 D 5 C 6 A 7 D 8 B 9 A 10 C

B

- Ask students to read the instructions and check that they understand what they have to do.
- Ask students to read the title of the text and ask them what it might mean. Ask them to skim read the text, without filling in any answers, to find out what *progressive ideas* are mentioned in the text *(the Internet, writing)*. Ask students which of the two inventions was probably more important and to say why.
- Read the words in capital letters to the right of the text to students and ask them to repeat them. Correct their pronunciation where necessary.
- Ask students to re-read the text and to decide which part of speech is missing from each gap. Then ask them to complete the gaps using the correct form of the words given.
- Remind students to re-read the text once they have finished to check their answers.

Answers

11 ignorant
12 achievement
13 revolutionary
14 developments
15 Industrial
16 significance
17 objectively
18 interaction
19 dramatic
20 unwise

C

- Ask students to read the instructions and check that they understand what they have to do.
- Encourage students to read all three sentences before filling in any answers.
- Explain to students that the missing word in each set of sentences will be a fairly common one and that students should not spend time trying to find overly-difficult words.
- Tell students that the missing word in each set of sentences will be the same part of speech and that the word will have a different meaning each time.
- Remind students to re-read the sentences once they have finished to check their answers.

Answers

21 aim
22 places
23 all
24 post
25 clock

D

- Ask students to read the instructions and check that they understand what they have to do.
- Ask students to read both sentences in each item and to underline the information in the first sentence that is missing from the second sentence. Then ask them to look at the word given to decide how the missing information could be inserted into the second sentence using this word. Remind students that they will have to use a different structure in order to keep the meaning the same.
- Remind students that they mustn't change the word given in bold in any way.
- Encourage students to re-read the sentences once they have finished to check their answers.

Answers

26 used to be (very/really) lazy
27 were all taken aback by
28 had no choice
29 reported my words/took it out of context
30 distinguish between the websites/them
31 too much on my plate
32 came up against some problems

3 Just for the Health of it

Reading:	missing paragraphs, looking for connections
Vocabulary:	health- and medicine-related vocabulary, word formation, phrasal verbs, collocations & expressions
Grammar:	demonstrative, reflexive, indefinite and reciprocal pronouns, adverbs and adverb phrases, adverb forms, intensifying adverbs
Listening:	multiple-choice questions, dealing with scientific information
Speaking:	talking about health, comparing photographs, using relevant words and expressions, topic vocabulary
Writing:	information sheet, writing a good information sheet, giving information clearly, introducing, giving advice / suggesting

Unit opener

- Ask students to look at the title of the unit and ask if they know of another phrase that sounds similar to it *(just for the heck of it)* and elicit what it means *(for no particular reason)*. Ask students what the title must mean in this context *(simply for health reasons)*.
- Ask students to look at the picture and to read the caption. Then ask them to describe the person in the picture and guess why he might have what he has on his head *(to improve his memory)*.
- Ask them how the picture corresponds to the theme of the unit *(it shows a kind of medical treatment or a way to improve the 'health' of the brain)* and whether they feel that this type of treatment would actually be effective or not.

Reading

Teaching Tip

Stress that A is meant to be a fun activity and that some people have better memories than others, so it is unimportant if they can't remember all the items.

A

- Ask students to look at the picture in the top right-hand corner of page 32 and ask what it has to do with memory *(photos help people to remember the past)*. Ask them if they have ever looked at an old photo and suddenly remembered something about the past. If they would like to share these experiences with the class, allow a little time for them to do so.
- Ask students to read the instructions for A and answer any questions they might have about them.
- Ask students to work in pairs. Explain that one student will look at the first item while their partner counts to five, then they must try and write down what they remember about the item. The students then swap roles and the student who did the counting before, now looks at the item while their partner counts to five. Then they must try and write down what they remember about the item. Repeat for the other four items.
- When students have completed the task, ask students at random around the class to answer each of the questions. Encourage students to discuss the results for the first two questions and to add their thoughts and opinions when the third question is answered.

Answers

Students' own answers

B

- Ask students to read the instructions for B and check that they understand what they have to do.
- Tell them to skim read the text to find the answers to the question. Explain that they should concentrate on information that deals with the question and that they don't have to read in detail as they will have an opportunity to do that later.
- Ask students to do the task individually, but check answers as a class.

Answers

They both have unusual memories. AJ remembers her past with precise detail. EP suffers from two types of amnesia which cause him to forget everything and to be unable to make new memories.

Word Focus

- Ask students to look at the words in red in the text and to re-read the sentences they are found in. Ask students to work in pairs to decide what each of the words means in the *Word Focus* box and to then find synonyms, if any, for each word.
- Ask students to compare their answers with another pair

C

- Ask students to read the *Exam Close-up* and ask one to explain what it says in his or her own words.
- Explain that in missing paragraph tasks it is important that each missing paragraph links with the sentences immediately before and after each gap. Ask students why they should pay attention to pronouns *(pronouns are used to refer back to something that has already been mentioned, so if the first paragraph after the gap contains a pronoun, the missing paragraph should contain the noun it refers to and vice versa)*.

3 Just for the Health of it

- Ask students for examples of phrases that express time (*first, next, then, after that, etc.*) and explain that these words and phrases as well as synonyms and verb tenses offer valuable clues for finding the correct missing paragraph.
- Explain to students that it's a good idea to get into the habit of underlining these clues in the text and in the missing paragraphs when they read them through for the first time.
- Ask students to read the instructions and check that they understand what they have to do.
- Elicit that this is a missing paragraph task and that five paragraphs have been removed from the text and that students must choose from seven paragraphs the one which fits each of the five gaps in the text (*there are two extra paragraphs they don't need to use*).
- Ask students to read paragraphs A–G and to underline the clues which might help them understand what information they can follow on from (*A: These, his, he, gets up, then, etc., B: Every sensation, we, our, etc., C: the other end, following, his, he, etc., D: In this sense, has allowed him, etc., E: My, says AJ, her, she, etc., F: they, us, etc., G: she, her, etc.*).
- Ask students to read the text again and to decide where each paragraph should go. Tell them to pay attention to the sentences before and after each gap.
- When they have finished tell them to re-read the text to make sure the paragraphs they have chosen make sense in the gaps and to check that the paragraphs they haven't used don't fit anywhere else.
- Ask students to do the task individually, but check as a class.
- Once the answers have been checked, ask students to explain the title of the text and to say how it relates to the pictures that accompany the text (*the two pictures depict the brain generally and memory [which allows us to remember things] specifically*).
- If students seem interested, give them further information using the Background Information box below.

Answers

1 E 2 C 3 D 4 A 5 F

Background Information

Point out to students that they can watch a very interesting National Geographic video on mapping memory by going to the site below: http://ngm.nationalgeographic.com/2007/11/memory/brain-interactive. Alternatively, if time allows and the equipment is available, you could watch the video with the students during class.

D

- Ask students to look at the words in the yellow box and to scan the text again to find and underline them. Ask them to say each of the words after you and elicit that they are all adjectives. Correct their pronunciation where necessary.
- Remind them that they should always try to work out the meaning of the word from its context and ask them to read the sentences in the text in which each word is contained.
- Ask students to read the instructions and check that they understand what they have to do. Encourage them to read all the sentences in D before writing any answers. Ask students to do the task individually, but check as a class.

Answers

1 precise 4 vast
2 oblivious 5 photographic
3 mixed 6 vivid

Ideas Focus

- Explain to students that they are going to answer some questions on memory. Ask students to read the questions and explain anything they don't understand.
- Ask students to answer the questions in pairs and encourage them to draw on personal experience.
- Go round the class monitoring students to ensure they are carrying out the task properly. Don't correct any mistakes at this point, but make a note of any problems in structure or pronunciation.
- Ask students at random to answer the questions. Then ask the other students if they agree or if they have anything else to add.
- Write any structural mistakes made by students on the board without saying who made them, and ask them to correct them. Deal with any problems in pronunciation that came up.

Answers

Students' own answers

Extra Class Activity

You could extend this activity by asking students to make up their own quiz questions and options about memory. Students could then work in pairs and exchange their questions to see if their partner can guess the correct answers.

Vocabulary

A

- Ask students to read the instructions and check that they understand what they have to do.
- Point out that they will have to change the form of the verb in some sentences.
- Read the words in the yellow box to students and ask them to say them after you. Correct their pronunciation where necessary.
- Ask students to read all the sentences first to work out the meaning of the missing verb and which form it should be in.
- Remind students to re-read the sentences once they have finished to check their answers.
- Ask students to do the task individually, but check as a class.

Answers

1 prescribed
2 nursed
3 responding
4 consult
5 monitor
6 sprained
7 relieve
8 practising

B

- Ask students to read the instructions and check that they understand what they have to do.
- Read the sets of words 1–6 to the students and ask students to repeat them after you. Correct their pronunciation where necessary.
- Ask students to work in pairs to encourage discussion, but check answers as a class. Ask students to explain why one of the words is the odd one out in each item.

Answers

1 physical (The others are all states of mind, but 'physical' refers to the body.)
2 muscular (The others describe the state of being deprived of moisture, but 'muscular' means to have well-developed muscles.)
3 sane (The others are all positive adjectives related to a healthy diet, but 'sane' means to have a sound and rational mind.)
4 disorder (The others all describe a state whereby someone is prone to very emotional outbursts, but 'disorder' is another word for an illness or health complaint.)
5 delicate (The others describe the state of being very thin, but 'delicate' means to be fragile or weak.)
6 contented (The others describe someone who has difficulty remembering things, but 'contented' means when someone is happy and satisfied.)

Teaching Tip

If time allows, ask students to work in pairs to think of one more word that could go with the three words in each item 1–6.

C

- Ask students to look at the picture to the right of the text in C and ask them to describe it. Elicit that the picture is blood cells and that they relate to the subject of the text.
- Read the words in the yellow box to students and ask them to repeat them. Correct their pronunciation where necessary.
- Ask students to read the text all the way through without filling in any answers.
- Ask students to do the task individually, but check as a class.

Answers

1 intravenous
2 vessel
3 donors
4 pressure
5 type
6 bank

D

- Ask students to read the instructions and check that they understand what they have to do. Explain that they have to decide which order each of the verbs comes in, in each sentence.
- Point out that they will have to change the form of the verb in some sentences.
- Read the words in the yellow boxes and ask students to repeat them after you. Correct their pronunciation where necessary.
- Encourage students to read the whole sentence each time before filling in any answers.
- Ask students to do the task individually, but check as a class.

Answers

1 recover, heal
2 injured, wounded
3 damage, harm

E

- Ask students to read the title of the text and to look at the accompanying picture. Ask them how the insect – do not reveal what it is at this stage – in the picture might relate to the title (it can transmit malaria).
- Read the words in capitals to the students and ask them to repeat them. Correct their pronunciation where necessary.
- Ask students which part of speech each word is (verbs: discover, treat, poison; nouns: thirst, poison, miracle, medicine, effect).
- Ask students to read the instructions and check that they understand what they have to do. Ask them to work out what part of speech is missing from each gap before they write their answers.
- Remind students to re-read the text once they have finished to check their answers.
- Ask students to do the task individually, but check as a class.

Answers

1 discovery
2 treatment
3 accidentally
4 thirsty
5 poisonous
6 miraculously
7 medicinal
8 effective

Teaching Tip

Encourage students to keep a special section in their vocabulary notebook for *word families*. Tell them that they could have a table containing headings for the various parts of speech and that every time they come across a word formation task in their student's book they could record the words in the table.

F

- Read the phrasal verbs 1–6 to the students and ask them to repeat them. Correct their pronunciation where necessary.
- Ask students to also read definitions a–f without filling in any answers at this stage.
- Ask students to do the task individually, but check as a class.

3 Just for the Health of it

- Encourage students to copy the phrasal verbs and their meanings into their notebooks.

Answers

1 d 2 f 3 b 4 a 5 e 6 c

G

- Ask students to read the instructions and check that they understand what they have to do. Point out that they have to use the phrasal verbs from F in the correct form.
- Ask students to first read the sentences for gist to work out which phrasal verb might be missing from each one. Remind them to pay attention to the subject and also other tenses used in the sentences to help them write the verbs in the correct form.
- Ask students to do the task individually, but check as a class.

Answers

1 threw up   4 took out
2 fight off   5 passed out
3 came down with   6 picked up

H

- Ask students to read the instructions and check that they understand what they have to do.
- Ask students to read the sentences without filling in any answers at this stage.
- Read the words in red to students and ask them to repeat them. Correct their pronunciation where necessary. Point out that the task tests collocations so the correct answers will depend on how naturally each option goes with the following word or phrase.
- Ask students to do the task individually, but check as a class.

Answers

1 bodily   5 sores
2 failing   6 fit
3 internal   7 imbalance
4 terminal   8 splitting

I

- Ask students to read the instructions and check that they understand what they have to do.
- Read the idioms to the students and ask them to repeat them. Correct their pronunciation where necessary.
- Ask the students to work in pairs to discuss what the idioms mean.
- If students are totally unfamiliar with these idioms, write the sentences below on the board to help them.
  - I've had a change of heart. I'll run the marathon with you after all.
  - OK! OK! I only asked you a simple question. You don't have to bite my head off!
  - Make sure my fiancé makes it to the church. A lot of grooms get cold feet and decide not to get married at all!
  - Those two don't get along at all. They're at each other's throats the whole time.
  - I think dad's really angry. I can hear him shouting at the top of his lungs at my brother.
  - I know you're frustrated about your new job, but keep your chin up and everything will turn out fine.
  - Jason was a good student, so the teacher turned a blind eye to the fact that he was late for class.
  - What *is* that girl's name? It's on the tip of my tongue but I simply can't remember it.
- As a class, ask each pair to give their definition of one of the idioms.

Answers

- If you change the way you think or feel about something, you have a change of heart.
- If you bite someone's head off, you criticise them angrily.
- If you get cold feet about something, you lose the courage to do it.
- If people are at each other's throats, they are fighting, arguing or competing ruthlessly.
- If you shout at the top of your lungs, you shout as loudly as you possibly can in an angry way.
- If you keep your chin up you go on having confidence and hope at a difficult time.
- When people turn a blind eye, they deliberately ignore something, especially if people are doing something wrong.
- If a word is on the tip of your tongue, you know you know the word, but you just can't quite remember it at that moment.

Extra Class Activity

Ask students to choose one of the idioms from I and to draw a picture that represents it. Then ask students at random round the class to come to the front and show their pictures. Ask their classmates to guess which idioms they have tried to depict.

Grammar

- Write the sentences below on the board and elicit what kind of word the underlined words and phrases in the sentences are (*pronouns*).
  1 <u>This</u> substance here is quinine, and <u>that</u> substance over there is called arsenic.
  2 We decided to start dieting <u>ourselves</u>; a doctor didn't tell us to do it.
  3 <u>Some</u> of the patients may have malaria. In Africa, <u>anything</u> is possible.
  4 My mother and I email <u>each other</u> at least once a week.
- Ask students more specifically what type of pronoun is underlined in each sentence and elicit what other pronouns they know for each type.
  1 *demonstrative; these, those*
  2 *reflexive; myself, yourself, herself, himself, etc.*
  3 *indefinite pronouns; any, all, nothing, something, etc.*
  4 *reciprocal; one another, each other's, one another's*

- Ask students to look back at the Reading text about memory on pages 32 and 33 to find as many examples of pronouns as they can and to say what type of pronoun each is: *Paragraph 2: herself (reflexive); Paragraph 3: This (demonstrative), everything (indefinite), Paragraph F: each other (reciprocal).*
- Explain that in this lesson they are going to revise these four types of pronouns.

A

- Ask students to read the instructions and check that they understand what they have to do.
- Ask students to read the sentences and underline the demonstrative pronouns.
- Ask students to do the task individually, but check as a class.

Answers

1 this, That
2 These, those

B

- Ask students to read the rule from start to finish and to then look back at the example sentences in A to focus on the demonstrative pronouns that they underlined before choosing any answers.
- Ask students to do the task individually, but check as a class.

Answers

1 near
2 far

C

- Read the information on reflexive pronouns to the students and explain anything they don't understand.
- Read the instructions and check that they understand what they have to do.
- Ask students to read sentences 1–3 before trying to match them to their uses. Explain anything they don't understand.
- Ask students to do the task individually, but check as a class.

Answers

1 c 2 a 3 b

D

- Write the sentences below on the board. In pairs, ask students to find the indefinite pronouns and identify which ones refer to specific nouns and which refer to non-specific nouns. Ask students to work in pairs to encourage discussion, but check answers as a class.
  - Why are you shouting? I didn't do anything. *(anything; non-specific noun).*
  - I'm ill; I need some medicine. *(some; specific noun – medicine).*
- Ask students to read the instructions and check that they understand what they have to do.
- Ask students to read a and b and then 1 and 2 and explain anything they don't understand about the indefinite pronouns.
- Ask students to do the task individually, but check as a class.

Answers

1 Some, all 2 anything, nothing

E

- Read the instructions and check that they understand what they have to do.
- Ask students to read the sentences and items 1–3 before marking their answers. Explain anything they don't understand about reciprocal pronouns.
- Ask students to do the task individually, but check as a class.

Answers

1 true
2 true
3 false

Now read the Grammar Reference on pages 163 & 164 (3.1 to 3.4) with your students.

F

- Ask students to read the title and then skim read the text to find out how the title relates to the picture. *(The text is about how music therapy can have a positive effect on a person's physical and mental health. This relates to the picture because the woman is listening to music and she appears to be both physically and mentally healthy.)*
- Explain to students that they should think about the type and use of each pronoun in each item and to refer back to the Grammar box if they need help when choosing their answers.
- Remind students to re-read the text once they have finished to check their answers.
- Ask students to do the task individually, but check as a class.

Answers

1 one's   5 themselves
2 Those   6 Much
3 ones   7 Another
4 others   8 Anything

- Write the sentences below on the board and elicit what is underlined in each one *(adverbs and adverb phrases).*
  a   She will be operated on now.
  b   She will be operated on to improve her mobility.
  c   She will be operated on in an hour.
  d   She will be operated on when she is ready.
Ask students at random the following questions:
  – Which sentence uses a prepositional phrase as an adverb phrase? *(c)*
  – Which sentence uses an adverb clause? *(d)*
  – Which sentence uses an infinitive phrase as an adverb phrase? *(b)*
  – Which sentence uses a single adverb? *(a)*
  – Ask students to look back at Paragraph A in the Reading text on page 33 and underline and identify an adverb or adverb phrase *(Later; a single adverb).*

G

- Ask students to read the instructions and check that they understand what they have to do.
- Ask students to read sentences 1–4 and to say how the adverbs and adverb phrases in bold are used in each sentence.

3 Just for the Health of it

- Afterwards, read a–d with the students and explain anything they don't understand. Ask students to do the task individually, but check as a class.

Answers

a 2, in an hour
b 3, when you are ready
c 4, to take your temperature
d 1, now

- Write the sentences below on the board and ask a student to come up and underline an adverb in each sentence. Ask students what the adverbs mean.
  - The nurses were working hard. *(hard, busily)*
  - The nurses were hardly working. *(hardly, almost not at all)*
- Elicit that adverbs can have more than one form. Explain that sometimes adverbs end with *-ly* and sometimes they don't
- Ask students if they can think of any other adverbs like this *(late/lately; high/highly)*.

H

- Ask students to read the instructions and check that they understand what they have to do.
- Ask students to read the sentences and to say what the words in bold have in common before moving on to *Be careful!*.

Answers

They are both adverbs.

I

- Ask students to read the instructions and check that they understand what they have to do.
- Allow students time to write their sentences in their notebooks.
- Ask students to do the task individually, but check as a class.

Answers

Students' own answers

Be careful!

- Read the information in *Be careful!* to the students and explain anything they don't understand.
- Ask students to write sentences of their own with the adverbs *hard* and *hardly* based on the theme of health.

Answers

Students' own answers

- Write the sentence below on the board.
  - You took four of the tablets? What a totally ridiculous thing to do!
- Ask a student to read the sentence aloud and elicit from the class what adverb is used in the sentence *(totally)*. Ask students what word follows *totally (ridiculous)* and elicit what part of speech it is *(an adjective)*. Explain to students that *totally* is an intensifying adverb and that adverbs of this type modify adjectives and adverbs *(e.g., enough)*.
- Ask students to look back at the third paragraph in the Reading text on page 32 and underline the intensifying adverbs *(entirely, perfectly, completely)*. Elicit or explain that intensifying adverbs, and the words they modify, can come at the beginning, in the middle or at the end of a sentence, but that if they come at the beginning of a sentence, the adverb, and the word it modifies, must be followed by a comma.

J

- Ask students to read the instructions and check that they understand what they have to do.
- Read the sentences and items 1–3 to the students and explain anything they don't understand.
- Ask students to do the task in pairs to encourage discussion, but check as a class.

Answers

1 adjectives and other adverbs
2 at the beginning, middle or end
3 a comma

Now read the Grammar Reference on page 164 (3.5 to 3.7) with your students.

K

- Ask students to look at the title of the text and the picture to the right of the text and ask them what the text might be about. Ask them what the relationship is likely to be between the women in the picture.
- Ask students to read the instructions and check that they understand what they have to do. Then ask them to read the words in the yellow box.
- Ask students to read the text all the way through without filling in any answers. Ask students to think about which word might fill each gap and to look for clues in the surrounding sentences as to which form of the word they should use.
- Remind students to re-read the text once they have finished to check their answers.
- Ask students to do the task individually, but check as a class.

Answers

1 absolutely   4 Ideally
2 barely   5 wide
3 Firstly   6 uncomfortable

Teaching Tip

You could extend this task by asking students to come up with intensifying adverbs and the adjectives or adverbs they modify to describe how the woman in the chair is feeling both mentally and physically.

Listening

A
- Ask students to read the instructions and check that they understand what they have to do.
- Ask students to work in pairs and give them enough time to discuss the medical conditions, their symptoms and how they think they can be cured.
- As a class, ask each pair to talk about one of the medical conditions, its symptoms and how they think it can be cured and ask the others if they agree or have anything to add.

Answers
Students' own answers

Extra Class Activity
If the students have access to computers in the classroom, ask them to use them to add to the knowledge they already have about the medical conditions discussed in A.

B
- Ask students to read the instructions and make sure they understand what they have to do.
- Explain that students will hear a conversation between two people about common illnesses.
- Ask students to read sentences 1–4 and to discuss the difference in meaning between the three options in each question with a partner.
- Play the recording once all the way through and ask students to circle their answers. Then ask students to compare their answers with a partner and to justify any answers they have that are different.
- Play the recording again and ask students to check their answers and to fill in any missing answers.
- Check answers as a class and ask students to justify their answers.

Answers
1 can lead to death
2 can bring on tooth decay
3 can be cured with medication
4 suffer from a lack of sleep

C
- Ask students to read the *Exam Close-up* and then ask one of them to explain what it says in his or her own words. Remind students that in multiple-choice question tasks they will often be required to listen to long talks and interviews which deal with difficult topics like medicine, science or technology.
- Point out that it is very important to read the questions and the options carefully before listening and to underline any key words so as to avoid making mistakes.

D
- Ask students to read the instructions and check that they understand what they have to do.
- Elicit that the topic of the interview is the Black Death. Ask students to look at the picture in the bottom-right corner of the page and ask them how it is related to the Black Death (*the picture is of the Grim Reaper who signifies death*).
- Give students time to read through questions 1–6 and their options carefully. Remind them to underline the key words and phrases in both the questions and the options. Explain anything they don't understand.
- Play the recording once all the way through and ask students to circle their answers. Then ask students to discuss their answers with a partner and to justify any answers they have that are different.

E
- Play the recording again and ask students to check their answers and to fill in any missing answers.
- Check the answers as a class and ask students to justify their answers.

Answers
1 a 2 c 3 b 4 b 5 b 6 d

Speaking

A
- Ask students to read the three questions and answer any queries they may have about them.
- Ask students to work in pairs and to take it in turns to ask and answer the questions about themselves.
- Go round the class monitoring students to make sure they are carrying out the task properly. Don't correct any mistakes at this point, but make a note of any problems in structure or pronunciation.
- Ask each pair to ask and answer one question and repeat until each student has had a turn.
- Write any structural mistakes made by students on the board without saying who made them, and ask them to correct them. Deal with any problems in pronunciation that came up.

Answers
Students' own answers

B
- Ask students to read the instructions and the list of ideas for keeping in good health in B. Answer any questions they might have about them. Ask students to work in pairs and to think about what they believe is important for keeping in good health and to rank the ideas in the order that they consider to be important.
- Go round the class monitoring students to make sure they are carrying out the task properly. Don't correct any mistakes at this point, but make a note of any problems in structure or pronunciation.
- Write numbers 1–8 as headings on the board and ask students which idea they chose as the most important. Call out each of the ideas in turn and ask each pair to report how each one was ranked. Write their answers on the board under the headings with the number of students who chose this to be most important. Encourage students to discuss the final results.
- Write any structural mistakes made by students on the board without saying who made them, and ask them to correct them. Deal with any problems in pronunciation that came up.

3 Just for the Health of it

Answers

Students' own answers

D

- Ask students to read the *Exam Close-up* and then ask a student to explain what it says in his or her own words.
- Ask students to quickly read the instructions in the *Exam Task* and elicit that during their long turn they will have to discuss two of the three photos shown.
- Ask students to decide on which two photos to talk about. They should also think about the vocabulary required to talk successfully about each one. Point out that it is only logical to avoid a photo that they don't understand or that they don't have the vocabulary needed to talk about it.
- Stress that before they answer the questions they should make a mental list of the vocabulary they will need to answer them appropriately.

Useful Expressions

- Read the *Useful Expressions* to the students and ask them to repeat them. Correct their pronunciation and intonation where necessary.
- Explain that these words and expressions are topic vocabulary and that they should use some of these words and expressions when answering the *Exam Task*.

E

- Ask students to read the instructions again and check that they understand what they have to do.
- Ask students to work in pairs and to decide who will be Student A and who will be Student B. Ask them to read the instructions for their role and to spend a few minutes looking at their own set of photos and deciding which two they will talk about.
- Remind students that this kind of task isn't a discussion and that each student is expected to speak for one minute on his or her photos answering the questions provided or to respond briefly *(30 seconds)* to the follow-up questions about his or her partner's photos.
- Ask Student A to begin answering the questions about the two photos they have chosen from the three and for Student B to answer the follow-up question once Student A has finished. Then ask Student B to answer their questions about the two photos they have chosen from the three and Student A answers the follow-up question.
- Go round the class monitoring students to make sure they are carrying out the task properly. Don't correct any mistakes at this point, but make a note of any problems in structure or pronunciation.
- Ask one pair of students to carry out the task in front of the class and once they have finished ask the other students if they have anything to add.
- Write any structural mistakes made by students on the board without saying who made them, and ask them to correct them. Deal with any problems in pronunciation that came up.

Answers

Students' own answers

Ideas Focus

- Ask students to read the questions quickly and deal with any queries they may have. Then ask students to work in pairs and to take it in turns to answer the questions.
- Go round the class monitoring students to make sure they are carrying out the task properly. Don't correct any mistakes at this point, but make a note of any problems in structure or pronunciation.
- Ask a student from each pair to answer one of the questions until each pair has had a turn. Ask other students if they agree or if they have anything else to add.
- Write any structural mistakes made by students on the board without saying who made them, and ask them to correct them. Deal with any problems in pronunciation that came up.

Answers

Students' own answers

Writing: an information sheet

- Ask students what an information sheet is and why they are written (*a sheet giving clear, factual, succinct information about a certain subject*). Ask if they have ever written an information sheet for anyone. If so, ask them who they wrote it for and what the topic was.
- Explain to students that in this lesson they are going to deal with writing information sheets.
- Read the *Learning Focus* on writing a good information sheet out to the students and explain anything they don't understand.
- Point out that normally information sheets are written for a specific target reader so they should be careful with register when they are writing their own information sheet.

A

- Ask students to look at the photo on page 40 and ask them if anyone has ever visited Barcelona.
- Ask students to read the instructions and check that they understand what they have to do.
- Read out the two texts and deal with any queries students might have about unfamiliar words.
- In pairs, ask students to discuss the similarities and differences between the two texts. Then discuss as a class before moving on to the final question.
- Ask students, again in pairs, to discuss the final question bearing in mind what they have learnt about information sheets from reading the *Learning Focus* at the top of the page.
- Do a class survey to see which text students thought was better. Make sure students justify their answers.

Answers

Both texts give information and advice, but text 2 is more informative (*it says what the daily high temperature can be*), clearer and easier to understand (*due to bullets being used*).

B

- Ask students to read the instructions and check that they understand what they have to do.
- Ask students to read the writing task and explain anything they don't understand.
- Give students time to answer the questions and make notes about the four areas that they must cover.
- Ask students to do the task individually, but check as a class.

Answers

1 students; friendly and informal / semi-formal
2 Students' own answers, but some suggested answers are: hot weather: wear loose clothes, don't go out in the middle of the day, drink lots of water; transport: scooters are fun to ride but dangerous, take public transport instead or ride a bicycle; insects: mosquitoes can be a problem, use an insect repellent; food: lots of cheap, healthy options

C

- Ask students to read the instructions and check that they understand what they have to do.
- Read the question to the students and explain anything they don't understand.
- Ask students to read the example information sheet and to underline information that relates to ways of dealing with hot weather. Then ask them to discuss the question with a partner.
- Ask a student from each pair to talk about a way to deal with hot weather until each pair has had a turn. Ask the others if they agree or if they have anything else to add.

Answers

Students' own answers

D

- Ask students to read the instructions and check that they understand what they have to do.
- Read questions 1–3 to students and explain anything they don't understand.
- Ask students to read the example information sheet again and to underline any information that relates to the main points in the questions. Then ask them to discuss the three questions with a partner.
- Ask a student from each pair to answer one of the questions until each pair has had a turn. Ask the others if they agree or if they have anything to add.

Answers

1 There is a title, a brief introduction and a conclusion, four distinct sections with headings some of which include bullets.
2 friendly, chatty tone; contractions; idiomatic language
3 imperative; it's short and succinct

E

- Ask students how many things the task asks them to do (*two – write a section for the information sheet and supply a proper heading*).
- Ask students to look at the example information sheet in C again and to write a section with a heading in their notebooks.
- Give students no more than ten minutes to write their sections. Go round the class offering help where necessary.
- Ask some students to read out their headings and sections to the rest of the class. You could hang all the sections on the wall and ask students to read each other's work when they have time.

Answers

Students' own answers

F

- Ask the students to read the *Exam Close-up* and remind students that they can use the information here as a checklist when writing their own information sheet.
- Ask students to look at the final point and elicit why this is important (*because information sheets are written for a target reader who needs specific information, advice or help*).
- Ask students to read the *Exam Task* and ask them to underline the key words and phrases in the task. Explain anything that they don't understand.
- Ask students to answer the questions in B about this writing task so that they will know what they have to do. Elicit from students how many areas they have to cover (*four*).
- Ask students to read the paragraph plan and ask them to make notes for each point, if time allows.
- Ask students how many words they must write (*220-260 words*).
- Set the *Exam Task* for homework.
- Encourage students to use the Writing Reference and checklist for information sheets on page 177.

3 Just for the Health of it

Suggested answers

The Smart Guide for Students

Welcome to our college! We hope you will have a wonderful year. Here are a few tips to make your time at college even better.

Calling all sports fans!

If you love to keep fit, Greenham College is the perfect place for you. We offer a wide range of team sports including football, basketball and rugby. We also have a huge timetable full of the latest fitness classes like zumba, pilates and tai chi. So you can give your body a workout as well as your mind!

999–Emergency!

There are several hospitals within a few miles of the college, so you are never far away from the very best medical care. But do remember, if you feel unwell but don't think it's anything serious please call the campus nurse instead and she can give you all the help and advice you need.

Smile!

If you have toothache, need a check-up or just want to brighten up your smile, get yourself down to our campus dentist. The surgery is open from 9-5, Monday to Friday. He is also available for emergency appointments, just ring 023 92 823445.

Headaches be gone!

Need shampoo, headache pills or even suntan lotion in a hurry? Visit our 24-hour pharmacy on campus. Our friendly staff are on hand to help out whether it's night or day!

So now, you have all the information you need to stay healthy, wealthy and wise while studying at Greenham College!

Useful Expressions

- Read the *Useful Expressions* to the students and ask them to repeat them. Correct their pronunciation and intonation if necessary.
- Elicit in which part of their information sheet they can use each category of expressions *(Introducing: in the introduction; Giving advice / Suggesting: in the middle sections when giving information or advice)* and tell them to use them when writing their information sheet for the *Exam Task*.

3 Paraguay Shaman

General Note

Please see the information about the National Geographic videos on page 18 of this Teacher's Book.

Background Information

The word *shaman*, which comes from the Tungusic language of North Asia, was introduced to the western world after Russian warriors captured the state of Khanate of Kazan in 1552. Shaman is defined as 'a priest or priestess who uses magic for the purpose of curing the sick, divining the hidden, and controlling events'.

Before you watch

A

- Explain to students that in this lesson they are going to watch a video about a special kind of 'doctor'. Ask them to look at the globe and tell you in which part of the world the person lives (Paraguay). Elicit what they know about Paraguay and the plants that grow there.
- Read words 1–4 to the students and ask them to repeat them. Then ask students to read meanings a–d and explain anything they don't understand.
- Ask students to do the task individually, but check as a class.

Answers

1 d 2 c 3 a 4 b

While you watch

B

- Explain to students that they are now going to watch the video and do a task based on the information they hear.
- Ask students to read statements 1–6 and ask them what the documentary will be about (a shaman and how he heals people).
- Explain anything in the statements that the students don't understand and encourage them to think about which statements may be true and which may be false before they watch.
- Play the video all the way through without stopping and ask students to mark their answers. Ask students to compare their answers with a partner's and to justify any answers they have that are different. Play the video again so that they can check their answers.
- Ask students to do the task individually, but check as a class.

Answers

1 T (00:26)   4 F (01:35)
2 T (00:52)   5 F (01:58)
3 F (01:10)   6 F (02:17)

After you watch

C

- Explain to students that this is a summary of the information they heard on the video.
- Read the words in the yellow box to the students and ask them to repeat them. Ask them to write N, V or Adj beside each of the words depending on whether it is a noun, a verb or an adjective.
- Explain to students that they should first read the whole summary before writing any answers to work out what part of speech is missing.
- Tell students to re-read the text once they have finished to check their answers.
- Ask students to do the task individually, but check as a class.

Answers

1 rainforests   6 chants
2 illnesses   7 root
3 deforestation   8 cancer
4 healers   9 analysing
5 extensive   10 cures

Ideas Focus

- Ask students to read the three questions and answer any queries they might have.
- Ask students to work in pairs and explain that they should both give their opinions on all three questions.
- Go round the class monitoring students to make sure they are carrying out the task properly. Don't correct any mistakes at this stage, but make a note of any problems in structure and pronunciation.
- Ask each pair to answer one of the questions and repeat until each pair has had a turn.
- Write students' views on whether serious illnesses will be cured in the future on the board.
- Write any structural mistakes made by students on the board, without saying who made them, and ask them to correct them. Deal with any problems in pronunciation that came up.

Answers

Students' own answers

41

4 Lights, Camera, Action!

Reading:	multiple-choice questions, identifying the purpose of the text
Vocabulary:	film- and theatre-related vocabulary, multiple-choice questions, choosing the correct word, word formation, compound nouns, prepositions
Grammar:	gerunds, infinitives, discourse markers
Listening:	multiple-matching, dealing with two tasks simultaneously
Speaking:	talking about film genres and cinema, decision-making, presenting an argument, presenting your options, handing over to your partner
Writing:	review, understanding the purpose of a review, writing a review, liking, disliking, recommending

Unit opener

- Write *Lights, Camera, Action!* on the board and ask students what comes to mind when they read it *(films, film-making)*. Explain to students that *Lights, Camera, Action!* is the title of Unit 4.
- Direct students' attention to the picture and the caption and ask them how the picture corresponds to the theme of the unit *(it depicts the act of making a film, but in extreme circumstances)*.
- Ask students who usually instructs a cameraman or woman on the kind of footage required *(a director)*. Ask students to tell the rest of the class what they think one positive and one negative thing about being a director might be.
- Ask students to look at the picture and ask them how the people might be feeling and why they might be feeling that way.

Reading

A

- Ask students to cover up the instructions and to look at the pictures in A. Ask them what pictures 1–5 have in common *(they could all be stills from films)*.
- Ask students to read the instructions and explain anything they don't understand.
- In pairs, get students to talk about what kind of film they think the stills are from and what the film might be about and to discuss the questions that follow.
- Ask students to think about what three criteria from the list they personally think is important for deciding how good a film is and why. Then ask students to work in groups of four to compare and discuss their answers.
- Write numbers 1–7 as headings on the board then call out each of the criteria in turn and ask students from each group to report if each one was chosen. Write their answers on the board under the headings with the number of students who chose the criteria as the most important. Encourage students to discuss the results and why the criteria that were least chosen were considered less important than the ones that were most chosen.

Answers
Students' own answers

Teaching Tip
You could extend this activity further by asking a student what genre of film they like best and why. Encourage a discussion on the topic and ask the others whether they agree or whether they have anything to add.

Background Information
In 2007, National Geographic brought together its magazine, book publishing, television, film, and other diverse units to create a new Global Media group called National Geographic Ventures. The film part of this venture, called National Geographic Films, has produced many popular films featuring some of the world's biggest stars. The themes of these films range from a Russian submarine commander *(played by Harrison Ford)* to a bunch of very persistent penguins *(narrated by Morgan Freeman)*.

B

- Ask students to read the instructions in B and check that they understand what they have to do.
- Ask students to discuss the questions in pairs.
- Discuss the answers as a class. Ask the students if they enjoy reading film reviews.

Answers
You might find the article in a magazine or on a website. Its purpose is to inform people about the films that National Geographic Entertainment have to offer. People reading this will either be film buffs or people that enjoy other National Geographic content and want to explore the movies they have to offer.

C

- Ask students to read the instructions in C and check that they understand what they need to do.
- Tell them to skim read the text to find the answers to the first question. Remind them that they don't have to read in detail as they will have another opportunity to do that later. Ask students to do the task individually, but check answer as a class.
- Ask students at random round the class which film appeals to them most and why. Encourage students to justify their answers.

Answers

1 Life in a Day
2 Flying Monsters 3D
3 The First Grader
4 Desert Flower
5 U23D

Students' own answers

Word Focus

- Ask students to look at the words in red in the text and to re-read the sentences they are found in.
- Ask students to work in pairs to decide what each of the words means in the *Word Focus* box and to then find synonyms, if any, for each word.
- Ask students to compare their answers with another pair. Explain anything they don't understand.

D

- Ask students to read the *Exam Close-up* box and then ask a student to explain what it says in his or her own words.
- Encourage students to look carefully for words and expressions in the text that refer to the options in the *Exam Task*.
- Ask students to read the instructions and items 1–6 with their options. Explain anything they don't understand.
- Encourage students to guess the meaning of any unfamiliar words from the context before looking them up in their dictionaries. Explain any problem words and correct their pronunciation where necessary.
- Ask students to underline any key words in the items and options and to underline the parts of the text that refer to each of the items and options. Remind students that the information in the items follows the same order as the text.
- Ask students to read the text again and to underline any information related to the questions while reading.
- Ask students to do the task individually, but check as a class.

Answers

1d (Whatever your taste in films, National Geographic Entertainment has something for everyone.)
2c (… YouTube contributors were asked to submit film footage of their lives …)
3a (Maruge's application, while receiving the support of head teacher Jane Obinchu … faces fierce opposition from parents who don't want to see a place wasted on such an old man.)
4b (The First Grader is … true story of one man's battle to gain the education …; Desert Flower is the heart-rending tale of Waris Dirie … at the tender age of 13, fled her family's nomadic camp in the Somalian desert.)
5c (… a groundbreaking film that uses cutting-edge 3D filming technology to bring the story of giant flying monsters and their pre-historic world to life.)
6b (… it all sounds like a too-good-to-be-true Cinderella story ,…)

E

- Ask students to look at the phrases in the yellow box in D and to scan the text again to find and underline them. Ask them to say each of the phrases after you and elicit that they are all adjectives. Correct their pronunciation where necessary.
- Remind them that they should always try to work out the meaning of the phrase from its context and ask them to read the sentences in the text in which each word is contained.
- Ask students to read the instructions and check that they understand what they have to do. Encourage them to read all the definitions in D once before writing any answers. Ask students to do the task individually, but check as a class.

Answers

1 heart-warming
2 groundbreaking
3 sugary-sweet
4 heart-rending
5 state-of-the-art
6 cutting-edge

Ideas Focus

- Explain to students that they are going to answer some questions about film reviews. Ask students to read the question and explain anything they don't understand.
- Ask students to answer the question in pairs. Then go round the class monitoring students to ensure they are carrying out the task properly. Don't correct any mistakes at this point, but make a note of any problems in structure or pronunciation.
- Write any structural mistakes made by students on the board without saying who made them, and ask them to correct them. Deal with any problems in pronunciation that came up.

Answers

Students' own answers

Vocabulary

A

- Ask students to read the instructions and check that they understand what they have to do.
- Read the words in the yellow box to students and ask them to say them after you. Correct their pronunciation where necessary.
- Ask students to read all the sentences first to work out the meaning of the missing word.
- Remind students to re-read the sentences once they have finished to check their answers.
- Ask students to do the task individually, but check as a class.

Answers

1 set
2 foyer
3 row
4 backstage
5 wings
6 aisles
7 interval
8 usher

4 Lights, Camera, Action!

B

- Ask students to look at the picture and elicit what kind of building is being shown *(a cinema)*. Ask them to imagine they are inside the building. Ask them what they would probably be doing and how they might be feeling *(watching a film, feeling happy and excited)*.
- Ask students to read the *Exam Close-up* and then ask one to explain what it says in his or her own words.
- Ask students to read the instructions in the *Exam Task* and check that they understand what they have to do.
- Ask them to skim read the text, without circling any answers, and elicit what the text is about *(film preferences)*.
- Read the words in options 1–6 and ask students to repeat them after you. Correct their pronunciation where necessary. Explain anything they don't understand.
- Remind students that they should consider all four options before circling their answers.
- Remind students to re-read the text once they have finished to check their answers.
- Ask students to do the task individually, but check as a class.

Answers
1 b 2 b 3 c 4 a 5 c 6 a

C

- Ask students to read the title of the text and to look at the accompanying picture. Ask them how the picture might relate to the title *(the title of the text might be the title of a film)* – don't check their answer yet.
- Read the words in capital letters to the students and ask them to repeat them. Correct their pronunciation where necessary.
- Ask students which part of speech each word is *(verbs: perform, animate, narrate, race, portray; nouns: race)* and which other parts of speech of these words they know.
- Ask students to read the text, without filling in any answers, to find out how the title relates to the picture *(as above)*.
- Ask students to read the instructions and check that they understand what they have to do. Ask students to work out what part of speech is missing from each gap before they write their answers.
- Remind students to re-read the text once they have finished to check their answers.
- Ask students to do the task individually, but check as a class.

Answers
1 performances   4 racially
2 animation   5 portrayal
3 narrative

D

- Read the nouns in the yellow box to the students and ask them to repeat them. Correct their pronunciation where necessary.
- Ask students to read the instructions and check that they understand what they have to do.
- Ask them to read all the sentences for meaning and underline the words that come before the gaps. Explain that the missing word in each case can form a compound noun with these words.
- Remind students to re-read the sentences once they have finished to check their answers.
- Ask students to do the task individually, but check as a class.
- Encourage students to copy the compound nouns and their meanings into their notebooks.

Answers
1 room   5 rehearsal
2 lead   6 festival
3 role   7 night
4 fright   8 ovation

E

- Read the prepositions in the yellow box to the students and explain that they will use these to complete the sentences. Point out that they should use each preposition only once except for *in* (which they will use three times).
- Ask students to read the sentences carefully and to pay attention to the words before or after the gap and think of a preposition which follows or precedes the words without filling in any answers at this stage.
- Ask students to do the task individually, but check as a class.

Answers
1 in   5 on
2 without 6 in
3 in   7 to
4 by   8 At

F

- Ask students to close their books. Elicit different film genres from students and write them on the board. If necessary give the following clues:
  - scary films *(horror)*
  - films about the future and worlds other than our own *(science fiction and fantasy)*
  - films about love *(romance)*
  - funny films *(comedies)*
  - films about cowboys *(westerns)*
  - films with singing and dancing *(musicals)*
  - films about fighting and battles *(war)*
  - films that are like cartoons *(animation)*
  - films with heroes or super heroes *(action or adventure)*
  - films about the past *(historical drama)*
- Ask students to open their books and read the instructions. Check that they understand what they have to do.
- Ask students to think about what their favourite films are for each genre and to write them in their notebooks. Then ask students to work in groups of four to compare and discuss their answers. Do a class survey by calling out each of the genres in turn and asking students from each group to report what the favourite film for each

genre was. Write their answers on the board under the correct headings and ask students from the other groups to report whether anyone in their group had chosen the same film to see which films were the most popular. Encourage students to discuss the results.

Answers

Students' own answers

Teaching Tip

If you are short of time in class, don't be tempted to skip this type of task. Although at first glance they may not seem as important as other types of vocabulary tasks, they are actually extremely useful to language learners. Tasks like this are an excellent opportunity to practise spoken English with others while discussing something they are sure to be interested in and knowledgeable about.

Grammar

- Write the caption below on the board and ask students to rewrite the information in the caption in two different ways: one beginning *Wearing* and the other beginning *Walking*.
  - American actress Anne Hathaway wears a beautiful designer dress as she walks along the red carpet at an awards show in Hollywood, California.
  - *Wearing a beautiful designer dress, American actress Anne Hathaway walks along the red carpet at an awards show in Hollywood, California.* and *Walking along the red carpet at an awards show in Hollywood, California, American actress Anne Hathaway wears a beautiful designer dress.*)
- Ask students to underline the words *Wearing* and *Walking* in their sentences and elicit that they are gerunds and act as the subject of these sentences. Ask students what the bare and full infinitive forms would be (*wear/to wear, walk/to walk*).
- Explain to students that in this lesson they will concentrate on gerunds and forms of the infinitive.

A

- Ask students to read the instructions and check that they understand what they have to do.
- Read uses a–d to the class and explain anything they don't understand.
- Ask students to then read sentences 1–4 and to focus on the words in bold in each sentence. Elicit that each sentence contains a gerund, but each gerund has got a different use.
- Ask students to do the task individually, but check as a class.

Answers

a4 b1 c3 d2

B

- Ask students to read the instructions and check that they understand what they have to do.
- Ask students to read the sentences and to focus on the words in bold.
- In pairs, ask students to discuss whether the words in bold contain bare infinitives or full infinitives and why each is used.
- Check answers as a class (hate <u>to say</u> (full infinitive; after certain verbs), can't <u>act</u> (bare infinitive; after modal verbs), confident enough <u>to be</u>, too scared <u>to admit</u> (full infinitive; with too and enough), don't know how <u>to apply</u> (full infinitive; after certain verbs), why not <u>have</u> (bare infinitive; after verbs with interrogatives), <u>to become</u> (full infinitive; to express purpose), determination <u>to succeed</u> (full infinitive; after certain nouns), <u>to take</u> (full infinitive; to express purpose), difficult <u>to improve</u> (full infinitive; after certain adjectives) before students move on to complete the rules.
- Ask students to read the rules carefully and to refer back to the sentences before filling in the gaps.
- Ask students to do the task individually, but check as a class.

Answers

1 full infinitive
2 bare infinitive

C

- Ask students to read the instructions and check that they understand what they have to do.
- Elicit that they have to do two things here: circle the infinitives and the gerunds in the sentences and then answer the question.
- Ask students to do the first part of the task and check their answers before moving on to the second part. As you check the verbs underlined, ask students to say what form they are.
- Ask students to do the task in pairs to encourage discussion, but check as a class.

Answers

1 expected her to win
2 recall Mark saying
3 made them speak
Form: verb + object + infinitive/gerund

D

- Ask students to look at the title and the picture to the left of the text and ask them the questions below. Accept any logical answers.
  - How is the title related to the picture? (*Rupert Grint first appeared in the Harry Potter films as a child, so he was a child star who grew up in the limelight.*)
  - What does the title mean?
- Explain to students that they are going to read a text which talks about the effect of fame on the lives of child stars. Ask them to read the text without filling in any answers at this stage and to find out if the effect of fame on child stars is negative or positive.
- Explain to students that they should pay attention to the context of each missing verb to help them decide which form is appropriate each time. Encourage them to look back at A, B and C if they need help while doing the task.
- Remind students to re-read the text once they have finished to check their answers.
- Ask students to do the task individually, but check as a class.

4 Lights, Camera, Action!

Answers

1 entering
2 watching
3 to play
4 to strive
5 becoming
6 grow up
7 follow
8 to be

Answers

1 I mean
2 Mind you
3 that is
4 Obviously
5 As a matter of fact
6 Apparently

Extra Class Activity

You could extend this task by reading out some of the verbs from Grammar Reference 4.3 to 4.5 on page 164 of the Student's Book and asking students to say whether they are followed by the full infinitive, bare infinitive or both.

Now read the Grammar Reference on page 164 (4.1 to 4.5) with your students.

E

- Read the information about discourse markers to the students and elicit what the two main purposes of discourse markers are *(to connect a sentence to what comes before or after it and to show one's attitude to what they are writing or saying)*.
- Ask students to look back at the last sentence of the Reading text about National Geographic Entertainment on page 45 to find as many examples of discourse markers as they can *(Admittedly, but)* and elicit what the main purpose of each is *(Admittedly: to show one's attitude to what they are writing or saying; but: to connect a sentence to what comes before or after it)*. Ask students which of the discourse markers is used to show contrast *(but)* and which one is used to express unwillingly that something is true *(Admittedly)*.
- Ask students to read the instructions and check that they understand what they have to do.
- Ask students to read sentences a–j before trying to match them to their uses and explain anything they don't understand.
- Ask students to do the task individually, but check as a class.

Answers

1j 2f 3d 4a 5i 6b 7c 8g 9e 10h

Now read the Grammar Reference on page 165 (4.6) with your students.

F

- Ask students to read the instructions and check that they understand what they have to do.
- Encourage students to read the whole sentence before circling any answers to look for any clues. Tell them they should pay particular attention to how the discourse marker connects a sentence, to what comes before or after it or what attitude it expresses.
- Encourage them to look back at E if they need help while doing the task.
- Remind students to re-read the sentences once they have finished to check their answers.
- Ask students to do the task individually, but check as a class.

G

- Ask students to read the instructions and check that they understand what they have to do.
- Encourage students to read the whole sentence before writing any answers to look for any clues. Tell them they should pay particular attention to how the discourse marker connects a sentence, to what comes before or after it or what attitude it expresses.
- Encourage them to look back at E if they need help while doing the task.
- Remind students to re-read the sentences once they have finished to check their answers.
- Ask students to do the task in pairs to encourage discussion, but check as a class.

Answers

1 Admittedly
2 by the way
3 After all
4 Quite honestly
5 No doubt
6 Still

Listening

A

- Ask students to read the instructions and make sure they understand what they have to do.
- Read the words in the yellow box to students and ask them to repeat them. Correct their pronunciation where necessary. Elicit what part of speech the words are *(adjectives)* and whether they express something positive or negative *(positive: delighted, proud, relieved, satisfied, surprised; negative: annoyed, ashamed, bitter, frustrated, regretful)*.
- Explain that they will hear four people talking in four different situations and that they must choose adjectives from the yellow box to describe how they sound. Remind students that in all cases more than one answer is correct and that they should be prepared to justify their choices.
- Play the recording once all the way through and ask students to write their answers. Ask students to compare their answers with a partner and to justify any answers they have that are different.
- Play the recording again to check their answers or complete any missing answers.
- Check answers as a class and ask students to justify their answers.

Answers

1 relieved / satisfied / proud
2 annoyed / bitter / frustrated
3 regretful / frustrated / ashamed / annoyed
4 proud / satisfied / delighted / surprised

Teaching Tip

You could expand this task further by asking the students to tell a partner about a situation where they have felt the emotions expressed by the adjectives in the yellow box. Alternatively, they could use their imaginations and make up a situation.

B

- Ask students to read the instructions and make sure they understand what they have to do.
- In pairs, ask students to discuss why the speakers feel the way they do.
- Ask a student from each pair to answer about one of the speakers. Repeat until each student has had a turn. Ask the others if they agree or if they have anything to add.

Answers

1 at being given a good part
2 that a bad actor got a part just because she was related to director
3 at not having done a good job
4 that a show went well against all odds

C

- Ask students to read the instructions and make sure they understand what they have to do.
- Explain that students will hear the same four speakers again. Elicit that they have to do two things here: to decide who the people are and to match the speakers to what they are expressing.
- Ask students to read 1–4 and a–g and to underline any key words. Ask the students to work with a partner to discuss how the speakers in 1–4 might feel.
- Remind students that they won't need to use three of items a–g.
- Play the recording all the way through and ask students to mark their answers. Then ask students to discuss their answers with a partner and to justify any answers they have that are different.
- Play the recording again and ask students to check their answers and to fill in any missing answers.
- Check the answers as a class and ask students to justify their answers using the words and expressions they heard on the recording.

Answers

Speaker 1: a successful actor, b
Speaker 2: an unsuccessful actor, e
Speaker 3: a film editor, g
Speaker 4: a director, f

Teaching Tip

Remind your students that they must do both tasks and that they will only hear the series of monologues twice. Explain that there are various strategies for attempting this type of task. Point out that they can either attempt one task on each listening, or perhaps approach both tasks simultaneously, answering the most accessible questions on the first listening and the more challenging questions when the recording is repeated. Allow students time to identify the best method of approaching this task for themselves. Don't force them to do it either one way or the other.

D

- Ask students to read the *Exam Close-up*.
- Remind students of any difficulties they might have had completing both tasks simultaneously in C and explain that this task shows how important it is to read both parts of the task in multiple matching before listening for the first time.
- Remind students that in this type of listening task there will be three items in each of the tasks that they won't need to use.
- Stress that these might be difficult to spot as they will often contain information that is similar to what a speaker on the recording is saying (*this is called a red-herring*) but is not exactly correct, so as they listen they must try to work out why these items are wrong while trying to work out why the other answers are correct.
- Ask students to read the instructions and check they understand what they have to do.
- Explain that they will hear five people talking in five different situations, but that they will all be talking about their roles in film and cinema.
- Explain that in this type of listening task, the topic is always given and that they should read it carefully so they will be able to predict, to a degree, what might be said by each speaker.
- Elicit that they have to do two things here (*decide who the people are and match the speakers to what they are expressing*).
- Ask students to read A–H in both tasks and to underline any key words. Answer any questions they might have about them.
- Ask students to work with a partner to discuss how speakers A–H might feel. Encourage them to look back at the adjectives in A for ideas if they need to.
- Remind students that they won't need to use three of items A–H in each of the tasks.
- Play the recording all the way through.
- Ask students to mark their answers. Then ask students to discuss their answers with a partner and to justify any answers they have that are different.

E

- Play the recording again and ask students to check their answers and to complete any answers they haven't already marked.
- Check the answers as a class and ask students to justify their answers and say why the red herrings were wrong.

Answers

Task 1
1D 2F 3A 4C 5G
Task 2
6D 7A 8B 9H 10C

Speaking

A

- Ask students to read the two questions and answer any queries they may have about them.
- Ask students to work in pairs and to take it in turns to ask and answer the questions about themselves.
- Go round the class monitoring students to make sure they are carrying out the task properly. Don't correct any mistakes at this point, but make a note of any problems in structure or pronunciation.

4 Lights, Camera, Action!

- Ask each pair to ask and answer one question and repeat until each student has had a turn.
- Write any structural mistakes made by students on the board without saying who made them, and ask them to correct them. Deal with any problems in pronunciation that came up.

Answers
Students' own answers

B

- Ask students to read the instructions and check that they understand what they have to do. Read the genres to students and elicit what they mean.
- In pairs, ask students to discuss the characteristics of each genre.
- Go round the class monitoring students to make sure they are carrying out the task properly. Don't correct any mistakes at this point, but make a note of any problems in structure or pronunciation.
- Ask each pair to talk about the characteristics of one of the genres until each pair has had a turn. Ask the others if they agree or have anything else to add.
- Write any structural mistakes made by students on the board without saying who made them, and ask them to correct them. Deal with any problems in pronunciation that came up.
- Ask students to think about how they personally feel about each of the genres and to rank them in the order that they like them best and why. Then ask students to work in groups of four to compare and discuss their answers.
- Write numbers 1–8 as headings on the board and ask students which genre they chose as their favourite. Call out each of the genres in turn and ask students from each group to report how each one was ranked. Write their answers on the board under the headings with the number of students who chose the genre as their favourite. Encourage students to discuss why they ranked the genres in the order that they did.

Answers
Students' own answers

C

- Ask students to read the *Exam Close-up*.
- Then ask them to quickly read the instructions in the *Exam Task* and elicit that they will be working in pairs with prompt cards and that they have to do two things here: tell each other about the films (*present options to a partner*) and decide together which film the club will show next week (*weigh up the pros and cons of each film bearing in mind the tastes of the members of the film club*).
- Stress that when they are presenting their options, they should do so in a clear and coherent way by deciding on which points are positive and which are negative, then go on to talk about the positive points before moving on to the negative points.
- Explain that when it is their partner's turn to discuss their options, they should listen carefully so they will be able to come to a decision together.
- Ask students to read the instructions again and check that they understand what they have to do.
- Ask students to work in pairs and to decide who will be Student A and who will be Student B. Ask them to spend a few minutes looking at their prompt cards and explain anything that they don't understand.
- Remind students that this is a decision-making task and that each student is expected to speak about and discuss their options with a partner before coming to a mutual decision about which film the club will show.
- Ask Student A to begin presenting their options (*A and B*) and for Student B to listen very carefully and to agree or disagree with what their partner is saying and to justify why they agree or disagree in a polite, logical manner.
- Then ask them to reverse the process so that Student B talks about their options (*C and D*) and Student A listens very carefully and agrees or disagrees with what their partner is saying and justifies why they agree or disagree in a polite logical manner. Once both presentations have been made, encourage students to reach a decision on which film should be shown.
- Go round the class monitoring students to make sure they are carrying out the task properly. Don't correct any mistakes at this point, but make a note of any problems in structure or pronunciation.
- Ask one pair of students to carry out the task in front of the class and ask the other students if they agree or if they have anything to add.
- Write any structural mistakes made by students on the board without saying who made them, and ask them to correct them. Deal with any problems in pronunciation that came up.

Answers
Students' own answers

Useful Expressions

- Read the *Useful Expressions* to the students and ask them to repeat them. Correct their pronunciation and intonation where necessary.
- Ask students for examples of expressions they can use to deal with all the parts of the question: to begin their presentation (*Let me begin by telling you about ...*), to compare their options (*On the one hand, this film ..., but on the other ...*), to add points about one of their options (*Not only is / does this film ..., but it also, ...*), summing up opinions about one of their options (*For me / To my mind / In my opinion, the biggest advantage / drawback is...*), to move on to the second option (*The next film is ...*) and to hand over to their partner (*What films do you have to suggest?*).
- Point out to students that they should use some of these expressions when they do *Exam Task*.

Teaching Tip
Remind students that in this type of task they have to do two things and that the instructions make these two parts of the task clear by saying 'First, talk to each other about ...'. and 'Finally decide ...'. Point out that in the second part of the task the decision should only be made after the students have explored each of the issues as illustrated by the pictures. Stress that students do not lose marks if they cannot reach a negotiated decision.

Ideas Focus
- Ask students to read the questions quickly and deal with any queries they may have.
- Ask students to work in pairs and to take it in turns to answer the questions.
- Go round the class monitoring students to make sure they are carrying out the task properly. Don't correct any mistakes at this point, but make a note of any problems in structure or pronunciation.
- Ask a student from each pair to answer one of the questions until each pair has had a turn. Ask the other students if they agree or have anything else to add.
- Write any structural mistakes made by students on the board without saying who made them, and ask them to correct them. Deal with any problems in pronunciation that came up.

Answers
Students' own answers

Writing: a review

- Ask students what a review is and why they are written. Ask if they have ever written a review about anything before. If so, ask them what the review was about and if it was a positive or a negative review.
- Explain to students that in this lesson they are going to deal with writing reviews.
- Read the *Learning Focus* on understanding the purpose of a review to the students and explain anything they don't understand.
- Ask students to look at the picture to the right of the information and elicit what is being shown (*Broadway, a street in New York famous for its theatre productions*). Ask students what readership would be most interested in a review about this kind of entertainment (*theatre-lovers*). Elicit what style they should use for a review with a readership of this kind (*formal, informative*).
- Ask them what the main functions of reviews are (*to describe, to express an opinion, and often to recommend*).

A
- Ask students to read the instructions and check that they understand what they have to do.
- Point out to students that they should bear in mind the tone and style of the sentences when making their decisions.
- Ask students to read the sentences and explain anything they don't understand.
- Ask students to work in pairs to encourage discussion, but check as a class before asking them to rewrite the sentences in their notebook.
- Once students have finished rewriting the sentences, ask students at random round the class to read out one of their sentences until everyone has had a turn. Ask the other students for their opinion on the sentences.

Suggested answers
2 Contrary to popular opinion, I found this book exceedingly dull.
5 I was not impressed with the actors at all.
6 I would have preferred it if they'd played some of their old classics instead of just the new songs.

B
- Ask students to read the instructions and check that they understand what they have to do.
- Ask students to read the writing task and explain anything they don't understand.
- Ask students to do the task individually, but check as a class.

Answers
1 young people, informal
2 a theatre performance
3 play, musical, comedy show, etc.
4 Suggested answers
play: acting, costumes, plot; musical: music, dancing, costumes, lighting; comedy show: acts, rapport with audience

C
- Ask students to read the instructions and check that they understand what they have to do.
- Ask students to look at the example review in C and to then write an introduction for the theatre performance they chose in B in their notebooks.
- Give students no more than five minutes to write their introductions and go round the class offering help where necessary.
- Ask some students to read out their introductions to the rest of the class.

Answers
Students' own answers

D
- Ask students how many things the task asks them to do (*two – say where the discourse markers are placed in the review and to replace them with other suitable ones*).
- Ask students to work in pairs to encourage discussion, but check as a class.

Answers
The discourse markers are placed immediately before a point is made.
Suggested answers for different markers:
For starters – To begin with
In addition to – Aside from
Well – So
namely – that is
As for – Regarding
despite (there being) – although (there is)
Add to that – Throw in

4 Lights, Camera, Action!

E

- Ask students to read the instructions and check that they understand what they have to do.
- Give students time to find the three adverb + adjective pairs and to create new phrases.
- Ask students to do the task individually, but check as a class.

Answers

1 absolutely spectacular –> absolutely breathtaking, absolutely stunning
2 technically complex –> incredibly complex, technically challenging
3 fairly mediocre –> pretty mediocre, fairly ordinary

F

- Ask the students to read the *Exam Close-up* and point out that the writer of the example review did all the things on the list.
- Remind students that they can use the information here as a checklist when writing their own reviews.
- Ask students to read the *Exam Task* to underline the main points their review should focus on. Explain anything they don't understand.
- Ask students to answer the questions in B about this writing task so that they know what they have to do.
- Point out to students that the number of paragraphs may vary, but elicit that they must write at least four. Ask students what these paragraphs should be about (*say which film you are reviewing and a little about it, describe and give your opinion on one aspect of the film, describe and give your opinion on another aspect of the film, summarise your points and give your recommendation*).
- As a class, discuss some of the positive and negative things a reviewer could write about a film. Create a list on the board of related adjectives and ask students to collocate them with suitable adverbs. Ask them if each adverb + adjective pair is positive or negative.
- Ask students to think about the film they will review and to decide whether their review will be positive, negative or a mixture of positive and negative points.
- Ask students to read the paragraph plan and to make notes for each paragraph, if time allows.
- Set the *Exam Task* for homework.
- Encourage students to use the *Writing Reference* and checklist for reviews on page 178.

Suggested answers

The Great Gatsby
On a recent trip to London, I saw the new Baz Lurhmann film, *The Great Gatsby* at the Apollo cinema in Piccadilly Circus. This fantastic spectacle of a film, which is an adaptation of the F. Scott Fitzgerald novel of the same name, is set in the 'Roaring Twenties' and stars Leonardo DiCaprio, Tobey Maguire and Carey Mulligan.
One of the highlights of the film for me was the stunning cinematography. Everything was so colourful, from the scenery to the beautiful costumes that perfectly reflected the 1920s. The film had a really lavish and vibrant feel. What I liked the most though was the soundtrack. The film score was directed by rapper, Jay-Z and it perfectly mixed songs from the 20s with tracks by Beyonce and Lana Del Ray which gave it a really contemporary feel.
I was a bit disappointed with how some of the characters were portrayed in the film. For example, Tobey Maguire's character, Nick, is very different to the character we know and love from the novel. Also, I didn't really see the point of the film being in 3D, as it gave some scenes a cartoonish and almost surreal feel.
I would recommend *The Great Gatsby* to anyone who wants to spend a couple of hours watching a visually stunning film, but if you are hoping for a film that is true to the novel, I'd probably tell you to give it a miss.

Useful Expressions

- Read the *Useful Expressions* to the students and ask them to repeat them. Correct their pronunciation and intonation if necessary.
- Remind students that they can use these expressions in their reviews in order to deal with each point appropriately.

4 Skin Mask

General Note

Please see the information about the National Geographic videos on page 18 of this Teacher's Book.

Background Information

Masks have been around for almost as long as humans have and still have the ability to scare, mystify or entertain those who see them. Once an important part of religious ceremonies and rituals, masks are now more commonly seen in a less-serious light and are popular around the world at festivals and occasions such as Carnival and Halloween. Todays' masks are mostly mass-produced and often take the form of popular cartoon characters, political and sports figures, or super heroes.

Before you watch

A

- Explain to students that in this lesson they are going to watch a video about a special effects studio in London. Ask them to look at the globe to see where London is (UK). Elicit what they know about London, and ask them what they know about the theatre there.
- Ask students to look at the photo and the caption and ask them how they think the mask was made *(perhaps by a special effects expert)*.
- Ask them how the picture makes them feel and why.
- Ask students to work in pairs to answer the question to encourage discussion.
- Go round the class monitoring students to make sure they are carrying out the task properly. Don't correct any mistakes at this stage, but make a note of any problems in structure and pronunciation.
- As a class, ask students at random to answer the question and ask the others if they agree or if they have anything else to add.
- Write any structural mistakes that students made on the board without saying who made them, and ask them to correct them. Deal with any problems in pronunciation that came up.

Answers

Students' own answers

While you watch

B

- Explain to students that they are now going to watch the video and do a task based on the information they hear.
- Ask students to read sentences 1–6 and explain anything they don't understand. Read the words in red to the students and ask them to repeat them. Correct their pronunciation where necessary.
- Ask them to think about which words may be correct before watching.
- Play the video all the way through without stopping and ask students to circle their answers. Ask students to compare their answers with a partner's and to justify any answers they have that are different. Play the video once more so that they can check their answers and circle any missing answers.
- Ask students to do the task individually, but check as a class.

Answers

1 studio (00:08)   4 series (01:38)
2 cap (00:29)   5 one eyebrow (02:23)
3 takes (01:05)   6 completed (02:28)

After you watch

C

- Explain to students that this is a summary of the information they heard on the video.
- Read the words in the yellow box to the students and ask them to repeat them. Ask them to write N, V or Adj beside each of the words depending on whether it is a noun, a verb or an adjective.
- Explain to students that they should read the whole summary through before filling in any answers to work out what part of speech is missing in each gap.
- Tell students to re-read the text once they have finished to check their answers.
- Ask students to do the task individually, but check as a class.

Answers

1 artists   6 master
2 brush   7 shade
3 motionless   8 face
4 bandages   9 life
5 mould   10 feel

Ideas Focus

- Ask students to read the two questions and answer any queries they might have.
- Ask students to work in pairs and explain that they should both give their opinions on both questions.
- Go round the class monitoring students to make sure they are carrying out the task properly. Don't correct any mistakes at this stage, but make a note of any problems in structure and pronunciation.
- Ask each pair to answer one of the questions and repeat until each pair has had a turn.
- Write students' opinions on special effects and lifelike masks on the board.
- Deal with any problems in structure or pronunciation that came up.

Answers

Students' own answers

Review 2 — Units 3 & 4

Objectives
- To revise vocabulary and grammar from Units 3 and 4
- To practise exam-type tasks

Revision
- Explain to students that Review 2 revises the material they saw in Units 3 and 4.
- Remind students that they can ask you for help with the exercises or look back at the units if they need help with an answer. Stress that the review is not a test.
- Decide how you will carry out the review. You could ask students to do one task at a time and then correct it immediately, or ask students to do all the tasks and correct them together at the end. If you do all the tasks together, let students know every now and again how much time they have got left to finish the tasks.
- Ask students not to leave any answers blank and to try to find any answers they aren't sure about in the units.
- When checking students' answers to the review tasks, make a note of any problem areas in vocabulary and grammar that they still have. Try to do extra work on these areas so that your students will progress well.

Vocabulary Revision
- Write these words on the board and ask students what part of speech they are: *thirst (n), respond (v), balance (n, v), body (n), dehydrate (v), press (v), delirious (adj)* and *parch (v)*. Ask students to write down any other parts of speech of these words that they know. Make sure they revise the parts that they will need to complete B.
- Play a word association game with words from the vocabulary section in Unit 3. Say one word related to health and ask each student in turn to say another word which they associate with the previous word, for example, *bodily – functions; failing – eyesight*.
- Ask students to explain the difference between the following pairs of words: *heal/recover, injure/wound, damage/harm*.
- Say the words *showbiz, a hitch, character, profession, the set, the background* and *a moment's notice* one by one to the students and ask them which prepositions come before them.
- Ask students to work in pairs to tell each other about what their favourite film in each genre is and why.

Grammar Revision
- Write these sentences on the board and ask students what type of pronoun is underlined in each sentence. Then revise all the kinds of pronouns students learnt in Unit 3 and elicit other pronouns that they know for each type of pronoun.
  - <u>This</u> medicine here is for headaches, and <u>that</u> medicine over there is for toothache. *(demonstrative; these those)*
  - They decided to start working out <u>themselves</u>; nobody told them to do it. *(reflexive; myself, yourself, herself, himself, etc.)*
  - Let's go out for a meal; there's <u>nothing</u> in the fridge. *(indefinite pronouns; any, all, anything, something, etc.)*
  - My parents call <u>each other</u> at least once a day. *(reciprocal; one another, each other's, one another's)*
- Write sentences a–d below on the board and elicit what is underlined in each one *(adverbs and adverb phrases)*. Then ask students at random the following questions:
  - Which sentence uses a prepositional phrase as an adverb phrase? *(c)*
  - Which sentence uses an adverb clause? *(d)*
  - Which sentence uses an infinitive phrase as an adverb phrase? *(b)*
  - Which sentence uses a single adverb? *(a)*
  - a He will be examined <u>now</u>.
  - b He will be examined <u>to see what is wrong with him</u>.
  - c He will be examined <u>in an hour</u>.
  - d He will be examined <u>when the doctor is ready</u>.
- Write the two sentences below on the board and ask a student to come to the board and underline the adverbs in each one. Ask students what the adverbs mean in the sentences. Remind students that adverbs can have more than one form and elicit that sometimes adverbs end with *-ly* and sometimes they don't.
  - The students were studying hard. *(busily)*
  - The students were hardly studying. *(almost not at all)*
  Ask students if they can think of any other adverbs like this *(late/lately; high/highly; slow/slowly)* and ask students at random to use them in sentences of their own.
- Write the sentence below on the board. Ask a student to read the sentence aloud and elicit from the class what adverb is used in the sentence *(totally)*. Ask students what word follows *totally (ridiculous)* and elicit what part of speech *ridiculous* is *(an adjective)*. Revise with students that *totally* is an intensifying adverb and remind them that in Unit 3 they learnt that adverbs of this type modify adjectives and adverbs.
  - You ate an entire box of chocolates? What a totally ridiculous thing to do!

- Write the sentences below on the board and ask students to complete them using the gerund, bare infinitive or full infinitive form of the verbs in brackets. Then revise the rules for gerunds and infinitives they learnt in Unit 4.
  - Julia doesn't like _____ (watch) scary films. *(watching)*
  - Is Tina good enough _____ (be) in the school play? *(to be)*
  - It's not worth _____ (try) to get tickets for the concert. *(trying)*
  - He didn't remember _____ (bring) his wallet so he couldn't pay. *(to bring)*
  - I don't feel like _____ (study) for the exam right now. *(studying)*
  - I hate to say it but that director can't _____ (direct) to save his life! *(direct)*

- Say the discourse markers *by the way, surely, obviously, all in all* and *as a matter of fact* one by one to the students and ask them to say a sentence using each one. Elicit how the discourse marker is used in each one. Ask students what other discourse markers they can remember from Unit 4.

A

- Ask students to read the instructions and check that they understand what they have to do.
- Ask students what they know about classic films and if they have a favourite, ask what it is called.
- Ask students to skim read the text, without filling in any answers at this stage, to find out what genre of classic films is described in the text *(action films)*.
- Encourage students to pay particular attention to the words immediately before and after each gap to work out what part of speech is missing. However, remind them that they have to take into consideration the general context of the sentence so that they understand what structure is being used.
- Remind students to re-read the text once they have finished to check their answers.

Answers

1	It	9	familiar
2	other	10	something
3	teach	11	replaced
4	themselves	12	many
5	a	13	some
6	In	14	all
7	they	15	again
8	This/The		

B

- Ask students to read the instructions and check that they understand what they have to do.
- Ask students to read the title of the text and ask them what it might mean. Then ask them to skim read the text, without filling in any answers, to find out why we feel thirsty. Ask students what can happen if we experience excessive loss of body fluids.
- Read the words in capital letters at the side of the text to the students and ask them to repeat them. Correct their pronunciation where necessary.
- Ask students to re-read the text and to decide which part of speech is missing from each gap, and to complete the gaps using the correct form of the words given.
- Remind students to re-read the text once they have finished to check their answers.

Answers

16	thirsty	22	pressure
17	survival	23	delirium/deliriousness
18	response(s)	24	sensation
19	imbalance	25	parched
20	bodily		
21	dehydration/dehydrating		

C

- Ask students to read the instructions and check that they understand what they have to do.
- Encourage students to read all three sentences before filling in any answers.
- Explain to students that the missing word in each set of sentences will be a fairly common one and that students should not spend time trying to find overly-difficult words.
- Tell students that the missing word in each set of sentences will be the same part of speech and that the word will have a different meaning in each sentence.
- Remind students to re-read the completed sentences once they have finished to check their answers.

Answers

26	cold	29	still
27	fact	30	age
28	set		

D

- Ask students to read the instructions and check that they understand what they have to do.
- Ask students to read both sentences in each item and to underline the information in the first sentence that is missing from the second sentence. Then ask them to look at the word given to decide how the missing information could be inserted into the second sentence using this word. Remind students that they will have to use a different structure in order to keep the meaning the same.
- Stress that they mustn't change the word given in bold in any way.
- Encourage students to re-read the completed sentences once they have finished to check their answers.

Answers

31	on the tip of my
32	little is known about the
33	oddly enough, she passed out
34	suffers from stage fright
35	saw the patient eating
36	the director himself advised me
37	can hardly hear

5 Eat Up!

Reading:	multiple texts, understanding the context in multiple texts
Vocabulary:	food-related vocabulary, phrasal verbs, collocations & expressions, word formation
Grammar:	transitive & intransitive phrasal verbs, separable & inseparable phrasal verbs, same-way question tags, question tags for polite requests, reinforcement tags
Listening:	multiple-choice questions, identifying distractors
Speaking:	talking about food and eating, follow-up questions, answering follow-up questions, adding ideas, contrasting, involving your partner
Writing:	proposal, understanding the purpose of a proposal, stating purpose, introducing, talking about positives & negatives, recommending

Unit opener

- Write *Eat Up!* on the board and explain to students that this is the title of Unit 5. Elicit that the title is a phrasal verb which means to eat all of something. Give students a minute to write down as many food related-words in English as they can. Then write the headings *savoury* and *sweet* on the board and ask students to call out the words they have written down and say which column they should go in. Elicit the words *rice* and *noodles* if the students don't mention them.
- In small groups, ask students, to look at the picture and read the caption. Then ask them to discuss where the picture was taken, what is going on in the picture and what the boys might be eating. Then ask each group to tell the class what they decided about the questions.
- Ask students what is unusual about the way the boys are eating *(they are using chopsticks)* and if they have ever eaten food in this way. If students seem interested, give them more information about eating with chopsticks using the Background Information box below.

Background Information

Many find the thought of eating with chopsticks somewhat daunting, but in fact it is quite easy once you get the hang of it! When eating with chopsticks, hold the upper chopstick with your index finger, middle finger and thumb. Put the other chopstick between the bottom of your thumb and the tip of your ring finger. Move the upper chopstick only when you pick up food.

Reading

A

- Ask students to look at the pictures in A and to name as many of the foods shown as possible. Ask them to look back at the list of foods they made for the Unit opener to see if any of the foods they had written down are shown in the pictures.
- Ask students to read the instructions and check that they understand what they have to do.
- Read the words in the yellow box to students and ask them to repeat them. Correct their pronunciation where necessary.
- As a class, ask students which picture shows savoury food and which shows sweet food.
- Ask students to read the four questions below the pictures and answer any queries they may have about them.
- Ask students to work in pairs and to take it in turns to ask and answer the questions about themselves.
- Go round the class monitoring students to make sure they are carrying out the task properly. Don't correct any mistakes at this point, but make a note of any problems in structure or pronunciation.
- Ask each pair to ask and answer one question and repeat until each student has had a turn.
- Write any structural mistakes made by students on the board without saying who made them, and ask them to correct them. Deal with any problems in pronunciation that came up.

Answers

1 savoury
2 sweet
Students' own answers

B

- Ask students to look at the title of the first text and the picture beside it. Elicit how they are related *(they both have to do with sugar)*. Then ask them to do the same for the second text *(they are both about foods that people crave)*. Ask them if they have ever craved a particular type of food, and if they have, what kind of food was it.
- Ask students to read the instructions for B and check that they understand what they have to do.
- Ask them to skim read the texts to find relevant information regarding the main ideas in each. Explain that they don't have to read in detail as they will have another opportunity to do that later.
- Ask students to do the task individually, but check answer as a class.

Suggested answers

Can Sugar Make You Stupid?:
Research has shown that diets high in sugar can negatively affect our ability to learn.
Stop Food Cravings through Imaginary Eating:
Imagining yourself eating a specific food can help reduce cravings for that food.

Word Focus

- Ask students to look at the words in red in the text and to re-read the sentences they are found in. Ask students to work in pairs to decide what each word means in the *Word Focus* box and to then find synonyms, if any, for each word.
- Ask students to compare their answers with another pair. Explain anything they don't understand.

C

- Ask students to read the *Exam Close-up* and then ask one to explain what it says in his or her own words. Explain that when reading multiple texts they should always skim the texts first to get a general idea of what they are about before answering any questions.
- Remind students to always read the *Exam Task* carefully and underline any key words.
- Ask students to read the *Exam Task* and the questions. Explain anything the students don't understand.
- Ask students to underline any key words in the questions, and also to underline the parts in the texts that refer to each of the items.
- Ask students to do the task individually, but check as a class.

Answers

1. B
2. A
3. A
4. B

D

- Ask students to read the instructions and check that they understand what they have to do.
- Point out that the verbs they are looking for must complete the expressions in italics in the sentences. Stress that the verbs may be in a different form in the text and might need to be changed.
- Encourage students to read all the sentences in D before scanning the texts for the missing verbs.
- Ask students to do the task individually, but check as a class.

Answers

1. pile
2. play
3. quench
4. run
5. shed
6. resist

Ideas Focus

- Explain to students that they are going to complete a week's menu and that they have to include only the healthy foods that they enjoy.
- Ask students to read the instructions and explain anything they don't understand.
- Ask students to complete the menu individually and to then compare their menu with a partner's.
- Go round the class monitoring students to ensure they are carrying out the task properly. Don't correct any mistakes at this point, but make a note of any problems in structure or pronunciation.
- Ask students at random to read out their menu for one day of the week, repeating until every student has had a turn. Ask the others if they agree with the menu selections or if they have anything else to add.
- Write any structural mistakes made by students on the board without saying who made them, and ask them to correct them. Deal with any problems in pronunciation that came up.

Answers

Students' own answers

Vocabulary

A

- Ask students to look at the picture to the right of the text in A and ask them to describe what they see (*a Japanese flag and sushi*). Ask them if they like to cook and to say why or why not.
- Read the words in the yellow box to students and ask them to repeat them. Correct their pronunciation where necessary.
- Ask students to read the title of the text and ask what they think a *junior chef* is. Ask them to skim read the text, without filling in any answers, to find out (*a young person who is very good at preparing/cooking food*). Ask students if they, or anyone they know, are good at cooking or would like to be a chef in the future.
- Ask students to do the task individually, but check as a class.

Answers

1. feed
2. culinary
3. cuisines
4. simmered
5. appetite

B

- Ask students to read the instructions and check that they understand what they have to do.
- Read the sets of words 1–8 to the students and ask students to repeat them after you. Correct their pronunciation where necessary.
- Ask students to work in pairs to encourage discussion, but check the answers as a class. Then ask them to explain why one of the words is the odd one out in each item.

5 Eat Up!

Answers

1 sip *(The others are ways of describing ways of eating, but 'sip' refers to taking a small amount of a drink.)*
2 salty *(The others mean when something tastes bitter, but 'salty' means when something has too much salt in it.)*
3 stunted *(The others are ways of saying someone is very hungry, but 'stunted' means when something is smaller in size than it should be.)*
4 supper *(The others are ways of describing a huge meal with multiple courses, but 'supper' means a light meal you have in the evening.)*
5 bake *(The others are ways of cooking something in boiling water, but 'bake' means to cook something inside the oven.)*
6 fizzy *(The others describe food that is past its best and possibly inedible, but 'fizzy' usually refers to drinks that contain bubbles.)*
7 bland *(The others are ways of saying that food or drink is appealing, but 'bland' describes something with little flavour.)*
8 platter *(The others are ways of describing an amount of food which is enough for one person, but 'platter' means a large shallow dish used for serving food.)*

C

- Ask students to read the instructions and check that they understand what they have to do. Explain that they are now going to do a food-related quiz.
- Elicit how many things they have to do in this task *(two)* and what they are *(circle the correct words and answer the questions)*.
- Ask students to read the sentences without circling any words or answering any questions at this stage.
- Read the words in red to students and ask them to repeat them. Correct their pronunciation where necessary. Point out that the task tests words that are often confused so the correct answers will depend on how naturally each option fits in with the context of the sentence.
- Ask students to circle their answers individually, but check as a class.

Answers

1 napkins	5 edible
2 cultivated	6 extracted
3 toppings	7 ethnic
4 staple	8 consume

- Then, ask students to write their answers to the eight questions individually, and once they have finished to discuss their answers with a partner.
- Ask students to look at the bottom of the page to see which answers are correct.
- As a class, discuss which answers surprised them the most.

Extra Class Activity

If time allows, ask students to write sentences of their own using the wrong words in each of the sentences from C and swap with a partner.

D

- Ask students to read the instructions and check that they understand what they have to do. Explain that they have to decide where the two words should go in each sentence.
- Read the words in the yellow boxes and ask students to repeat them after you. Correct their pronunciation where necessary.
- Encourage students to read the whole sentence before filling in any answers.
- Ask students to do the task individually, but check as a class.

Answers

1 scraps, leftovers	3 bitter, sharp
2 drink, beverage	4 crack, beat

E

- Read phrasal verbs 1–8 to the students and ask them to repeat them. Correct their pronunciation where necessary.
- Ask students to read definitions a–h without filling in any answers at this stage.
- Ask students to do the task individually, but check as a class.
- Encourage students to copy the phrasal verbs and their meanings into their notebooks.

Answers

1 h 2 d 3 f 4 a 5 g 6 b 7 e 8 c

F

- Ask students to read the instructions and check that they understand what they have to do. Stress that they have to use the phrasal verbs from E in the correct form to fill in the gaps.
- Ask students to first read the sentences for gist to work out which phrasal verb might be missing from each one. Remind them to pay attention to the subject and also other tenses used in the sentences to help them write the verbs in the correct form.
- Ask students to do the task individually, but check as a class.

Answers

1 tuck in	5 warm up
2 whipped up	6 polished off
3 picked at	7 dine out
4 lives on	8 pack away

G

- Ask students to read the instructions and check that they understand what they have to do.
- Ask students to read the sentences without circling any answers at this stage.
- Read the words in red to students and ask them to repeat them. Correct their pronunciation where necessary. Point out that the task tests collocations so the correct answers will depend on how naturally each option goes with the following word or phrase.
- Ask students to do the task individually, but check as a class.

Answers

1 smell	5 egg
2 cake	6 toast
3 sliced	7 beans
4 spilt	8 hot

H

- Ask students to read the instructions and check that they understand what they have to do.
- Read the words in capital letters to the students and ask them to repeat them. Correct their pronunciation where necessary. Ask students which part of speech each word is *(verbs: skim, diet, digest, act; nouns: gene, diet, nutrition, act)* and which other parts of speech of these words they know.
- Ask students to read the sentences, without filling in any answers, to work out what part of speech is missing from each gap.
- Remind students to re-read the sentences once they have finished to check their answers.
- Ask students to do the task individually, but check as a class.

Answers

1 skimmed	4 indigestion
2 genetically	5 malnutrition
3 dietary	6 inactive

Ideas Focus

- Explain to students that they are going to answer some questions about food and health. Ask students to read the questions and explain anything they don't understand.
- Ask students to answer the questions in pairs. Then go round the class monitoring students to ensure they are carrying out the task properly. Don't correct any mistakes at this point, but make a note of any problems in structure or pronunciation.
- Write any structural mistakes made by students on the board without saying who made them, and ask them to correct them. Deal with any problems in pronunciation that came up.

Answers

Students' own answers

Grammar

- Write the sentences below on the board and elicit from students where they have seen them before *(in the Reading texts on pages 58 and 59 about food)*. Ask students to identify the phrasal verb and object in each sentence. Ask students if the phrasal verbs are transitive or intransitive and elicit or explain why. Ask students which of the two phrasal verbs is separable and which is inseparable and elicit or explain why.
  - As well as making us pile on the pounds, products laced with corn sugar may also be affecting our brains. *(pile on; transitive because it is followed by an object (the pounds) after the particle, intransitive phrasal verbs are not; separable because the object could come between the verb and the particle, with inseparable phrasal verbs the object comes after the particle).*
  - The researchers hope that the findings from this study can help them come up with an anti-overeating technique. *(come up with; transitive because it is followed by an object (an anti-overeating technique) after the particle, intransitive phrasal verbs are not; inseparable because the object comes after the particle, with separable phrasal verbs the object could come between the verb and the particle. Generally, phrasal verbs with two particles are inseparable.)*
- Explain to students that in this lesson they will concentrate on transitive and intransitive phrasal verbs and separable and inseparable phrasal verbs.

Extra Class Activity

If time allows, ask students to look back at the Reading texts on pages 58 and 59 to find other phrasal verbs and to say if they are transitive or intransitive; separable or inseparable.

A

- Ask students to read the instructions and check that they understand what they have to do.
- Ask students to read sentences 1, 2 and 3 carefully before underlining or circling any answers.
- Ask students to do the task in pairs to encourage discussion, but check as a class.

Answers

1 phrasal verb: picked at, object: her food
2 phrasal verb: looks down on, object: the pastry cook
3 phrasal verb: pulled through, no object

B

- Ask students to read the rules carefully and to refer back to sentences 1, 2 and 3 before circling their answers.
- Ask students to do the task individually, but check as a class.

Answers

1 followed
2 not followed

5 Eat Up!

C
- Ask students to read the instructions and check that they understand what they have to do.
- Ask students to read the sentences carefully and to focus on the words in bold before moving on to D.

D
- Ask students to read the rules carefully and to refer back to the sentences in C before circling their answers.
- Ask students to do the task individually, but check as a class.

Answers
1. inseparable
2. can
3. cannot

Be careful!
- Read the information in *Be Careful!* to the students and explain anything they don't understand.
- Ask students to write a few sentences of their own using separable and inseparable phrasal verbs with personal pronouns and objects.

Now read the Grammar Reference on page 165 (5.1 & 5.2) with your students.

E
- Read the phrasal verbs in the yellow box to the students and ask them to repeat them. Correct their pronunciation where necessary.
- Tell students that they have to consider the meaning of the verb and the particle together and not just focus on the verb.
- Ask students to read the instructions and check that they understand what they have to do.
- Ask them to read the sentences on their own to work out the meaning of the missing phrasal verb. Also encourage them to underline the subject of each sentence so that they write the verbs in the correct form.
- Ask students to do the task individually, but check as a class.
- Encourage students to copy the phrasal verbs and their meanings into their notebooks.

Answers
1. picked something up
2. tuck in
3. dine out
4. picking at it
5. fight it off
6. pass out
7. threw it up/threw up
8. pull it off

F
- Ask students to read the instructions and check that they understand what they have to do.
- Point out that they have to pay attention to the phrasal verbs and the objects in each sentence to work out which sentences are correct and which are incorrect.
- Encourage students to look back at the *Grammar points* and *Be Careful!* if they need help as they do the task.
- Ask students to do the task individually, but check as a class.

Answers
1. incorrect; … polished them off …
2. correct
3. incorrect; … came up against some problems …
4. incorrect; … gulp it down …
5. correct
6. incorrect; … coming down with it too
7. incorrect; … our plans fell through …
8. incorrect; … get ahead as a chef.

- Write the sentences below on the board and elicit from students what they all have in common *(they all contain some kind of tag)*.
  – We're eating out tonight, aren't we?
  – We're eating out tonight, are we?
  – We couldn't eat out tonight, could we?
  – We could eat out tonight, we could.
- Ask students what they know about question-question tags *(Question-question tags are added to the end of a sentence. An affirmative statement is followed by a negative question tag, and a negative statement is followed by an affirmative question tag.)* and what these tags are normally used for *(to confirm or check information or ask for agreement)*.
- Elicit from students which of the sentences on the board is a question-question tag and ask what it is being used for *(the first one; it is being used to confirm or check information)*.
- Explain to students that in this lesson they will learn about other kinds of tags and what they are used for.
- Ask a student to read out the second sentence and as class discuss what is different about the tag it contains. *(It is a positive statement followed by an affirmative question tag.)*
- Explain to students that this is called a same-way question tag and that these tags are used to express emotions like interest, surprise, joy, anger, etc. and are not real questions. Read the sentence aloud again and ask the students what they think it expresses *(interest, surprise)*.
- Read the third sentence aloud to the students and elicit that it contains a negative statement followed by a positive question tag. Ask students what the tag expresses *(a polite request)* and explain that these kinds of tags are structured in the same way as question-question tags *(an affirmative statement is followed by a negative question tag, and a negative statement is followed by an affirmative question tag)*.
- Read the last sentence aloud and explain that it contains something called a reinforcement tag and that this kind of tag is used to reinforce what the speaker has said.
- Elicit from students that a reinforcement tag takes the form subject + auxiliary/modal verb and that this is the opposite of questions tags.

Teaching Tip
These structures will make more sense to students and sound more natural if they are given the opportunity to use them. Create cards with the situations below on them to give to each student. Then ask students to stand up and wander around the class until they 'meet' one of their classmates. They should then ask or inform them about the situation on their card using one of the structures from G, H or I.
- You want to go out for a meal.
- You want to act surprised that your classmate's mum won a cooking contest.
- You want to check that your classmate wants to go out for dinner that night.
- You want to stress that you and your classmate had fun at a barbecue at the weekend.
- You want to show surprise at how much food your classmate's brother can eat in one sitting.

G
- Ask students to read the instructions and check that they understand what they have to do.
- Ask students to read sentences a and b and underline the question tags.
- Elicit from students that the tags in these sentences are same-way question tags.
- Read 1–4 with the students and explain anything they don't understand.
- Ask students to do the task individually, but check as a class.

Answers

a have you?
b won't you?
1 A positive tag is used with a positive statement, and a negative tag is used with a negative statement. This is not the normal structure for question tags.
2 no
3 surprise/interest
4 anger/warning

H
- Ask students to read through the information on Question Tags for Polite Requests and the example sentences. Then ask them if they can think of any further examples.
- Check students understand how they are used.

Answers

Both sentences include a negative statement followed by a positive question tag (*couldn't borrow ... could I?*, *don't suppose I could, could I?*).

I
- Read the information on reinforcement tags to the students and explain anything they don't understand.
- Ask them to read the instructions and check that they understand what they have to do.
- Ask students to read the example sentences, focusing on the tags in bold.
- Ask students to do the task in pairs to encourage discussion, but check as a class.

Answers

The reinforcement tags take the form subject + auxiliary/modal verb, i.e. the opposite of question tags.

Now read the Grammar Reference on page 165 (5.3 to 5.5) with your students.

J
- Ask students to read the instructions and check that they understand what they have to do.
- Encourage students to read the whole sentence before circling any answers to look for clues to the right answer. Tell them they should pay particular attention to the verbs in the statements to see what they are and whether they are positive or negative.
- Remind students to re-read the sentences once they have finished to check their answers.
- Ask students to do the task individually, but check as a class.

Answers

1 shall we	5 is it
2 did he	6 would you
3 will you	7 am I
4 have they	8 could you

K
- Ask students to read the instructions and check that they understand what they have to do.
- Encourage students to read the whole sentence before writing any answers to look for clues to the right answer. Tell them they should pay particular attention to the verbs in the statements to see what they are and whether they are positive or negative.
- Encourage students to look back at G, H and I if they need help when doing the task.
- Remind students to re-read the sentences once they have finished to check their answers.
- Ask students to do the task individually, but check as a class.

Answers

1 did	4 does
2 would	5 have
3 am	6 do

L
- Ask students to read the instructions and check that they understand what they have to do.
- Encourage students to read the whole sentence before writing any answers to look for clues to the right answer. Tell them they should pay particular attention to the subject and any auxiliary or modal verbs in the statements.
- Encourage students to look back at I if they need help when doing the task.
- Remind students to re-read the sentences once they have finished to check their answers.
- Ask students to do the task individually, but check as a class.

5 Eat Up!

> **Answers**
>
> 1 he has   4 they would
> 2 that is   5 we had
> 3 she does   6 you are

Listening

A

- Ask students to read the instructions and make sure they understand what they have to do.
- Ask students to read the questions and underline any key words.
- Remind students that in multiple-choice listening tasks, ideas are often paraphrased and that it is a good idea to get into the habit of reading questions before listening and to think of other words and phrases that they might hear on the recording.
- Play the recording once all the way through and ask students to write down their answers. Ask students to compare their answers with a partner and to justify any answers they have that are different.
- Play the recording again to check their answers and fill in any missing answers.
- Check answers as a class and ask students to justify their answers using the words and expressions they heard on the recording.

> **Answers**
>
> a 1 cuttlefish and a green salad
>   2 the woman, because they ate octopus the day before
>   3 because the cuttlefish will go off otherwise
> b 1 the man
>   2 he is in great shape
>   3 for sticking to the diet

B

- Ask students to read the instructions and make sure they understand what they have to do.
- Explain that students will hear the same two conversations again. Ask them to read the statements and underline any key words. Explain anything they don't understand.
- Play the recording once all the way through and ask students to tick their answers. Ask students to compare their answers with a partner and to justify any answers they have that are different.
- Play the recording again to check their answers or to fill in any missing answers.
- Check answers as a class and ask students to justify their answers using the words and expressions they heard on the recording.

> **Answers**
>
> a 3 b 1

C

- Ask students to read the instructions and make sure they understand what they have to do.
- Ask students to read the statements again focusing on the answers that they did not tick.
- Ask the students to work with a partner to discuss what changes could be made to the statements to make them correct.
- Check the answers as a class and ask students to justify their answers using the words and expressions they heard on the recording.

> **Answers**
>
> a 1 The man gives the woman one option for lunch (made up of two foodstuffs – cuttlefish and a green salad).
>   2 The woman points out that they had seafood the previous day. **OR,** The man points out the cuttlefish will go off if they don't eat it soon.
> b 2 The woman reckons the man is in peak condition.
>   3 The woman wouldn't find it easy to cut out carbs. **OR,** The man has found it easy to cut out carbs.

D

- Ask students to read the Exam Close-up and ask a student to explain what it says in his or her own words.
- Elicit from students how this type of multiple-choice listening task is different to other multiple-choice listening tasks that they have come across in the past. (They won't be asked any specific questions. They will be given three options and they must choose the correct one based on what a speaker says during the conversation.)
- Remind students of any differences in any answers they might have had in the second part of B and explain that this task shows how important it is to read and understand the options properly in this type of listening task.
- Point out that in this kind of listening task, the distractors will be carefully worded wrong answers that use words and ideas from the conversation, so it is essential that they underline any key words in the options, and listen very carefully so as not to select wrong options.

E

- Ask students to read the instructions and check they understand what they have to do.
- Explain that they will hear eight short conversations and they must choose the correct option based on what they hear on the recording.
- Give students time to read 1–8 and to underline any key words in the options. Answer any questions they might have about them.
- Play the first conversation on the recording once and ask students to circle their answer to question 1 before playing the conversation again. Check the answer to the question and ask students to justify it before playing the rest of the recording.

- Play the recording once all the way through and ask students to circle their answers. Then ask students to discuss their answers with a partner and to justify any answers they have that are different.

F
- Play the recording again and ask students to check their answers and to circle any missing answers.
- Check the answers as a class and ask students to justify their answers.

Answers

1 b 2 c 3 b 4 b 5 a 6 a 7 c 8 b

Teaching Tip

If students run into problems while listening, play the recording again once you have checked their answers. Stop after each conversation and ask students what question was asked and to summarise the conversation in their own words.

Speaking

A
- Ask students to read the four questions and answer any queries they may have about them.
- Ask students to work in pairs and to take it in turns to ask and answer the questions about themselves.
- Go round the class monitoring students to make sure they are carrying out the task properly. Don't correct any mistakes at this point, but make a note of any problems in structure or pronunciation.
- Ask each pair to ask and answer one question and repeat until each student has had a turn.
- Write any structural mistakes made by students on the board without saying who made them, and ask them to correct them. Deal with any problems in pronunciation that came up.

Answers

Students' own answers

B
- Ask students to read the instructions and check that they understand what they have to do.
- Read the phrases to the students and ask them to repeat them. Correct their pronunciation where necessary.
- Ask the students to work in pairs to discuss the difference between the phrases in each set.
- If students are totally unfamiliar with these phrases, write the pairs of sentences below on the board to help them.
  - I don't like *eating on the hoof*, but some days I'm so busy that I've no choice but to eat as I walk or drive.
  - No matter how busy we are, my husband and I always make time for a long, leisurely *sit-down meal* in the evening.
  - I rather enjoy *working lunches*; you can deal with important business matters and have something to eat at the same time!
  - What a day! I didn't have a moment to myself and I even had to *work through lunch*. Now, I'm starving!
  - I think factory farming that raises *battery hens* should be banned; forcing an animal to spend its entire life in a tiny cage is simply wrong.
  - My grandfather raises *free-range hens* on his farm; they are happy and healthy because they spend lots of time outside.
  - *Mass production* has been the norm for many decades now; almost everything we buy is made in huge quantities.
  - *Subsistence farming* may not provide a farmer with any profit, but at least he can grow enough food to feed his family.
  - I'm not much of a cook, so I pretty much live on *ready meals* that I get from the local supermarket.
  - I always like going home; mum always has a hot *freshly cooked meal* on the table.
  - *Genetically-modified produce* indeed! Who would want to eat a square tomato!
  - My family eats only *organic produce*; it's delivered to the house once a week by the farmer himself.
- Go round the class monitoring students to make sure they are carrying out the task properly. Don't correct any mistakes at this point, but make a note of any problems in structure or pronunciation.
- Ask each pair to talk about one of the sets of phrases until each pair has had a turn. Ask the others if they agree or if they have anything else to add.
- Write any structural mistakes made by students on the board without saying who made them, and ask them to correct them. Deal with any problems in pronunciation that came up.

Answers

1 *eating on the hoof* means eating while doing other things usually walking; *a sit-down meal* is a formal meal, served at a table
2 *a working lunch* is where people meet to discuss business or work matters while having lunch; *to work through lunch* means that you keep on working despite it being your lunch break
3 *battery hens* are hens that are kept in a confined space; *free-range hens* are hens that are allowed to roam freely in the farmyard
4 *mass production* is when food is produced in extremely large quantities; *subsistence farming* is when you produce food for your own consumption
5 *a ready meal* is a pre-prepared and pre-cooked meal bought in a container; *a freshly cooked meal* is a dish prepared using only fresh produce for immediate consumption
6 *genetically-modified produce* is food that has been grown from seeds whose genes have been altered to make them more resistant to pests and diseases; *organic produce* is food that has been grown without or with very small amounts of pesticides and other chemicals

5 Eat Up!

C

- Ask students to read the instructions again and ask them how many things they have to do *(two)* and what they are *(talk about how the photos show various approaches to food nowadays and decide which picture best reflects modern attitudes to eating)*.
- Explain to students that in collaborative tasks, like this, they should listen carefully to their partner and try to naturally link their ideas with theirs.
- As a class, elicit what approach to food is shown in the pictures and encourage students to think about which picture best reflects modern attitudes to eating.
- Ask students to do the task in pairs and to use the structures from the *Useful Expressions* box to present their opinions and reach a decision.
- Go round the class monitoring students to make sure they are carrying out the task properly. Don't correct any mistakes at this point, but make a note of any problems in structure or pronunciation.
- Ask each pair to tell the rest of the class which option(s) they chose and say why.
- Write any structural mistakes made by students on the board without saying who made them, and ask them to correct them. Deal with any problems in pronunciation that came up.

Answers

Students' own answers

D

- Ask students to read the *Exam Close-up*.
- Point out that in this type of task, it is very important that students always listen to what their partner says. If they don't listen to their partner, they will be unable to link their ideas to his or hers.
- Explain to students that they will learn various structures for linking their ideas in the *Useful Expressions* box.
- Ask students to read through the rubric and the *Exam Task* and think about how they would answer the questions.

E

- In pairs, students should take turns answering the follow-up questions in the *Exam Task*.
- Go round the class monitoring students to make sure they are carrying out the task properly. Don't correct any mistakes at this point, but make a note of any problems in structure or pronunciation.
- Ask a student from each pair to answer one of the questions until each pair has had a turn. Ask the other students if they agree or if they have anything else to add.
- Write any structural mistakes made by students on the board without saying who made them, and ask them to correct them. Deal with any problems in pronunciation that came up.

Answers

Students' own answers

Useful Expressions

- Read the *Useful Expressions* to the students and ask them to repeat them. Correct their pronunciation and intonation where necessary.
- Point out to students that they should use some of these expressions when they do C and the *Exam Task*.

Ideas Focus

- Ask students to read the questions quickly and deal with any queries they may have.
- Ask students to work in pairs and to take it in turns to answer the questions.
- Go round the class monitoring students to make sure they are carrying out the task properly. Don't correct any mistakes at this point, but make a note of any problems in structure or pronunciation.
- Ask a student from each pair to answer one of the questions until each pair has had a turn. Ask the other students if they agree or if they have anything else to add.
- Write any structural mistakes made by students on the board without saying who made them, and ask them to correct them. Deal with any problems in pronunciation that came up.

Answers

Students' own answers

Writing: a proposal

- Ask students what a proposal is and why they are written. Ask students if they have ever written a proposal for anyone. If so, ask them who the person was, what the proposal was about and whether the reader of the proposal adopted the course of action they recommended.
- Explain to students that in this lesson they are going to deal with writing proposals.
- Read the *Learning Focus* on understanding the purpose of a proposal to the students and explain anything they don't understand. Ask students how a proposal is similar to a report *(organisation, register and target reader)* and how it differs from a report *(a report is to identify a problem, explain it and recommend action that will lead to a solution, while a proposal is to persuade the reader to adopt a course of action about a product, service or idea)*. Elicit from students when reports are usually written *(after something has been experienced)* and when a proposal is usually written *(before an action is carried out)*.

A

- Ask students to read the instructions and check that they understand what they have to do.
- Allow students time to look at the writing task and deal with any queries students might have about unfamiliar words.
- Ask students to do the task individually, but check as a class.

> **Answers**
>
> proposal (x2)

B

- Ask students to read the instructions and check that they understand what they have to do.
- Ask students to read the writing task in A again and questions 1–3 in B. Explain anything they don't understand.
- Ask students to work in pairs to encourage discussion, but check as a class.

> **Answers**
>
> 1 the social committee; same peer group; semi-formal (contractions acceptable)
> 2 probably all three, but describing one or two is also possible
> 3 one of the venues for the end-of-year event; by comparing the students' suggestions with the handwritten notes

C

- Ask students to read the instructions and check that they understand what they have to do.
- Ask students to read the writing task in A and the example proposal in C and explain anything they don't understand.
- Ask students to do the task individually, but check as a class. Encourage students to justify their answers using information from the example proposal.

> **Suggested answers**
>
> I agree that the river boat cruise would be the best option because it would be fun and also something that the students wouldn't have experienced before.

D

- Ask students how many things the task asks them to do (*two things: 1 to identify the language the writer has used instead of repeating the words from the input material; 2 to find where the writer reveals their choice of venue and identify the language used*).
- Ask students to work in pairs to encourage discussion, but check as a class.

> **Answers**
>
> 1 great food → delicious, affordable → reasonably priced, costs nothing to hire → free, fun → entertaining, unusual → original
> 2 In the conclusion; I strongly recommend

E

- Ask students to read the instructions and check that they understand what they have to do.
- Ask students to look at the writing task in A again, choose a different venue and use the notes to write a conclusion in their notebooks.
- Give students no more than five minutes to write their conclusions and go round the class offering help where necessary.
- Ask some students to read out their conclusions to the rest of the class. You could hang all the conclusions on the wall and ask students to read each other's work.

> **Answers**
>
> Students' own answers

F

- Ask the students to read the *Exam Close-up* and point out that the writer of the example proposal did all the things on the list.
- Remind students that they can use the information here as a checklist when writing their own proposals.
- Ask students to read the instructions and the *Exam Task* and ask them to underline any key words and phrases in the task. Explain anything they don't understand.
- Ask students to answer the questions in B about this writing task so that they know what they have to do.
- As a class, ask students who has asked them to write the proposal (*their principal*), what their proposal should be about (*improvements to the college canteen*) and what they should use when writing their proposal (*the principal's email and their notes*).
- Ask students to read the paragraph plan and to make notes for each paragraph, if time allows. Ask students how many paragraphs they will have in their proposals (*six, introduction, one paragraph for each of the four suggestions, conclusion*).
- Set the *Exam Task* for homework.
- Encourage students to use the Writing Reference and checklist for proposals on page 179.

5 Eat Up!

Suggested answers

Proposal for improvements to the college canteen

Introduction

The purpose of this proposal is to recommend improvements that could be made to the college canteen.

Food

Regarding food, at the moment there are only sandwiches available. There could be a wider range of food. For example, vegetarian students could be catered for and also ethnic foods, such as Chinese, Italian and Indian cuisine could be introduced.

Décor

In terms of décor, at the moment the walls of the canteen are a dull shade of grey. Maybe painting it a nice bright colour would help.

Queues

At the moment students have to queue for a long time to pay for their food which eats into their break time. Perhaps another cashier could be employed although this would be very expensive.

Hygiene

With so many students using the canteen every lunchtime it often gets messy. If there were more cleaning staff on hand to tidy up it would probably be a nicer place to spend time. Again this may cost a lot of money.

Conclusions

I strongly recommend introducing a wider variety of food. At the moment the vegetarian students are not being catered for and have to bring in packed lunches. Also, many students said that they would use the canteen if the food was more varied.

Useful Expressions

- Read the words and phrases in *Useful Expressions* to the students and ask them to repeat them. Correct their pronunciation and intonation if necessary. Explain anything they don't understand.
- Ask them to circle words and phrases from the list that are in the example proposal *(The purpose of this proposal is to recommend …, On the minus side, …, I strongly recommend …)*
- Elicit in which part of their proposal they can use each category of expressions and tell them to use them when writing their proposal for the *Exam Task*.

5 The Smelliest Fruit

General Note

Please see the information about the National Geographic videos on page 18 of this Teacher's Book.

Background Information

Borneo, which lies on the equator, is the third largest island in the world and its territory spreads across Malaysia, Indonesia and Brunei. It is a beautiful place with white sandy beaches and the oldest rainforest on the planet. It is a large region and has many distinct traditional foods which vary from place to place. Fruit is often eaten raw in large salads. Some of the stranger-looking Borneo fruit include the rambutan, which is red and hairy, and the jackfruit, which is yellow and prickly.

Before you watch

A

- Explain to students that in this lesson they are going to watch a video about a special fruit. Ask them to look at the globe and to tell you in which part of the world the fruit grows *(Malaysian Borneo)*. Elicit what they know about Malaysian Borneo and the food that people eat there.
- Ask students to read the instructions and the three questions and explain anything they don't understand.
- Ask students to answer the questions in pairs. Encourage them to draw on their own personal experiences involving foods from other cultures.
- Go round the class monitoring students to make sure they are carrying out the task properly.
- Ask each pair to answer one of the questions and repeat until each pair has had a turn.
- Deal with any problems in pronunciation that came up.

Answers

Students' own answers

While you watch

B

- Explain to students they are now going to watch the video and do a task based on the information they hear.
- Ask students to read statements 1–6 and ask them what the documentary will be about *(the durian fruit)*.
- Ask them to think about which answers might be true and which might be false before watching. Explain anything in the statements that the students don't understand.
- Play the video all the way through without stopping and ask students to mark their answers. Ask students to compare their answers with a partner's and to justify any answers they have that are different. Play the video again so that they can check their answers.
- Ask students to do the task individually, but check as a class.

Answers

1	F (00:28)	4	T (01:30)
2	T (00:40)	5	F (01:36)
3	T (01:05)	6	F (02:14)

After you watch

C

- Explain to students that this is a summary of the information they heard on the video.
- Read the words in the yellow box to the students and ask them to repeat them. Correct their pronunciation where necessary. Ask them to write N, V, Adj, Adv or Prep beside each of the words depending on whether it is a noun, a verb, an adjective, an adverb or a preposition.
- Explain to students that they should read the whole summary through before writing any answers first, to work out what part of speech is missing.
- Tell students to re-read the text once they have finished to check their answers.
- Ask students to do the task individually, but check as a class.

Answers

1	rotten	6	smuggle
2	strongly	7	bedspreads
3	Despite	8	slowly
4	bear	9	long
5	constant	10	fresh

Ideas Focus

- Ask students to read the three questions and answer any queries they might have.
- Ask students to work in pairs and explain that they should both give their opinions on all questions.
- Go round the class monitoring students to make sure they are carrying out the task properly. Don't correct any mistakes at this stage, but make a note of any problems in structure and pronunciation.
- Ask each pair to answer one of the questions and repeat until each pair has had a turn.
- Write the foods that students think have an unpleasant smell and what foods they think it is totally unacceptable to consume on the board.
- Deal with any problems in pronunciation that came up.

Answers

Students' own answers

6 Living Planet

Reading:	missing paragraphs, understanding the text structure
Vocabulary:	environment- and weather-related vocabulary, word formation, phrasal verbs, prepositions, gapped texts, dealing with gapped texts
Grammar:	modal verbs, perfect modal verbs
Listening:	multiple-choice questions, identifying opinion and attitude
Speaking:	talking about nature, natural disasters, comparing photographs, selecting photographs, starting and finishing
Writing:	contribution, using the appropriate register, writing a contribution, engaging the reader, describing a problem, explaining effects, recommending a course of action

Unit opener

- Ask students to look at the title of the unit and to guess what it might mean (*a planet that supports and maintains life*). Start a discussion about how the Earth supports and maintains life (*it supplies plants and animals with food, water, heat and shelter*).
- Ask them to look at the picture and read the caption. Then ask students to say how the picture might relate to the unit (*the picture is of the planet as it looks from space with the major air routes illuminated to show how interconnected we all are*).
- Ask students to tell the rest of the class how the picture makes them feel and why.

Reading

A

- Ask students to look at the picture in the top right-hand corner of the page and ask them if they know what it is of. If they mention volcanoes, ask them what they know about them and how they might be linked to the theme of the unit.
- Ask students to read the instructions for A and check that they know what they have to do.
- Ask students to work in pairs to encourage discussion, but don't check answers yet.

B

- Ask students to look at the picture to the left of the article and to describe it.
- Ask students to read the title of the text and elicit how it relates to the picture (*the photo shows magma flowing from a volcano, and magma contributed to starting life on the planet*).
- Ask students to read the instructions for B and check that they understand what they have to do. Tell them to skim read the text to find relevant information about the statements in A. Explain that they should only concentrate on these details and that they don't have to read in detail as they will have another opportunity to do that later.

- Ask students to do the task individually, but check answer as a class.
- Ask students which information surprised them the most and why.

Answer

1F 2T 3T

Word Focus

- Ask students to look at the words in red in the text and to re-read the sentences they are found in. Ask students to work in pairs to decide what each of the words means in the *Word Focus* box and to then find synonyms, if any, for each word.
- Ask students to compare their answers with another pair. Explain anything they don't understand.

C

- Ask students to read the *Exam Close-up* and ask a student to explain what it says in his or her own words. Explain that there will be times when they do missing paragraph tasks that they will have to deal with a scientific text. Explain that in these types of texts it is not so important that they understand individual words or specific ideas, but that they understand the structure of the text and how one idea flows on from the previous one.
- Elicit from students how a person is usually referred to the first time they are mentioned in a text (*by their full name and title*). Point out that any following references to the same person may use only the person's first or last name and that this could be very important when they are trying to decide where to place a missing paragraph.
- Encourage students to underline the names and titles of people in the missing paragraphs that relate to the ideas in the text, but remind them that after the first reference to a person is made, they may be referred to by only their first or last name.
- Ask students to read the instructions and check that they understand what they have to do.
- Elicit that this is a missing paragraph task and that five paragraphs have been removed from the text. and that students must choose from seven paragraphs (*there are two extra paragraphs which they do not need to use*) the one which fits each of the five gaps in the text.

- Ask students to read paragraphs A–G and to underline the names and titles which might help them decide where to place the missing paragraphs *(Para D – Keller, and Para E – C. Brenhin Keller of Princeton University)*. Point out that the paragraphs should also make sense before the paragraph that follows after the gap.
- Ask students to read the text again and to decide where each paragraph goes. Tell them to pay attention to the paragraphs before and after each gap.
- When they have finished tell them to re-read the text to make sure the paragraphs they have chosen make sense in the gaps and to check that the paragraph they haven't used doesn't fit anywhere.
- Ask students to do the task individually, but check as a class.

Answer

1F 2A 3E 4D 5B

Teaching Tip

Point out to students that a good way to practise for this type of reading task is to find an article and cut it up according to paragraphs. Tell students they should number the back of each paragraph as paragraph 1, paragraph 2, etc. as it appeared in the article. Students must then read the paragraphs and try to piece the article back together. Once students have finished putting the article back together, they can see if they were correct by looking at the numbers on the back of the paragraphs.

D

- Ask students to look at the words in the yellow box and to scan the text again to find and underline them. Remind them that they may appear in a different form in the text. Ask them to say each of the words after you and elicit that they are all verbs. Correct their pronunciation where necessary.
- Remind them that they should always try to work out the meaning of the word from its context and ask them to read the sentences in the text in which each word is contained to get an idea.
- Ask students to read the instructions and check that they understand what they have to do. Encourage them to read all the definitions in D once before writing any answers. Ask students to do the task individually, but check as a class.

Answer

1 endure   5 emit
2 thrive   6 harness
3 spew   7 consume
4 trigger   8 absorb

Ideas Focus

- Ask students to read the question quickly and deal with any queries they may have.
- Ask students to work in pairs and to take it in turns to answer the question.
- Go round the class monitoring students to make sure they are carrying out the task properly. Don't correct any mistakes at this point, but make a note of any problems in structure or pronunciation.

- Write any structural mistakes made by students on the board without saying who made them, and ask them to correct them. Deal with any problems in pronunciation that came up.

Answer

Students' own answers

Vocabulary

Teaching Tip

Point out to students that a good way to improve their vocabulary is by learning words in the context of groups. Tell them that they should go through their vocabulary notebooks from time to time and categorise the words in there under group headings such as weather, animals, environment, etc.

A

- Ask students to read the instructions and check that they understand what they have to do.
- Read the words in the yellow box and ask students to repeat them after you. Correct their pronunciation where necessary.
- Ask students to read the sets of words 1–6 and elicit how they are connected *(they are all weather-related words)*.
- Ask students to do the task individually, but check as a class.
- Then read a–f to the students and explain anything they don't know.
- In pairs, allow students time to match a–f with word sets 1–6.
- As a class, ask each pair to give one answer.

Answer

1 pouring   4 overcast
2 roasting   5 sticky
3 clear   6 gusty
1e 2c 3d 4f 5a 6b

B

- Ask students to read the instructions and check that they understand what they have to do. Ask students to read the sentences without circling any words at this stage. Explain anything they don't understand.
- Read the words in red to students and ask them to repeat them. Correct their pronunciation where necessary. Point out that the task tests words that are often confused so the correct answers will depend on how naturally each option fits in with the context of the sentence.
- Ask students to do the task individually, but check as a class.

Answer

1 soil   4 landfill
2 drill   5 spill
3 pollutant   6 landslide

6 Living Planet

C

- Ask students to read the title of the text and to look at the accompanying picture. Ask them how the people – do not reveal who they are at this stage – in the picture might relate to the title *(they are hunters)*.
- Read the words in capital letters to the students and ask them to repeat them. Correct their pronunciation where necessary. Ask students which part of speech each word is *(verbs: rely, suffice, migrate, surround; nouns: nomad, element)* and which other parts of speech of these words they know.
- Ask students to read the text, without filling in any answers, to find out how the person in the picture is related to the title *(as above)*.
- Ask students to read the instructions and check that they understand what they have to do. Ask students to work out what part of speech is missing from each gap before they write their answers.
- Remind students to re-read the text once they have finished to check their answers.
- Ask students to do the task individually, but check as a class.

Answers

1 reliance
2 sufficient
3 nomadic
4 migration
5 surroundings
6 elements

D

- Ask students to read the instructions and check that they understand what they have to do.
- Read the phrasal verbs in the yellow box to the students and ask them to repeat them. Correct their pronunciation where necessary. Ask students if they know what any of the verbs mean.
- Tell students that they have to consider the meaning of the verb and the particle together and not just focus on the verb.
- Ask them to read the definitions on their own to work out the meaning of the missing phrasal verb. Also encourage them to underline the subject of each definition so that they write the verbs in the correct form.
- Remind students to re-read the sentences once they have finished to check their answers.
- Ask students to do the task individually, but check as a class.
- Encourage students to copy the phrasal verbs and their definitions into their notebooks before moving on to E.

Answers

1 dries up
2 bucketing down
3 blows up
4 clears up
5 beats down
6 blows over

E

- Ask students to read the instructions and check that they understand what they have to do. Stress that they have to use the phrasal verbs from D in the correct form to fill the gaps.
- Ask students to first read the sentences for gist to work out which phrasal verb might be missing from each one. Remind them to pay attention to the subject and also other tenses used in the sentences to help them write the verbs in the correct form.
- Ask students to do the task individually, but check as a class.

Answers

1 clears up
2 dried up
3 beat down
4 blew over
5 blew up
6 bucketing down

F

- Ask students to read the instructions and check that they understand what they have to do. Encourage them to read the sentences carefully and to pay attention to the words before and after the options before circling any answers.
- Remind students to re-read their answers once they have finished to check their answers.
- Ask students to do the task individually, but check as a class.

Answer

1 of
2 to
3 against
4 to
5 with
6 on

G

- Write the words *pack* and *herd* on the board and say the word *dog*. Ask students which word on the board goes with *dog* (*pack*). Repeat for the word *sheep* (*herd*). Explain that words like *pack* and *herd* are an example of collective nouns and that they are used to refer to groups of the same animal. Ask students to come up with at least two more collective nouns and animals *(flock of birds, swarm of bees)*.
- Read the words to the students and ask them to repeat them. Correct their pronunciation where necessary.
- Ask the students to work in pairs to match the collective nouns with the animals.
- As a class, ask each pair to give one answer.

Answer

an army of ants
a tower of giraffes
a pride of lions
a parliament of owls
a bed of snakes
a drove of cattle

H

- Ask students to look at the picture at the bottom of the page and ask them to describe what they can see. Ask them if it looks like a place that they would like to visit and ask why or why not.

- Ask students to read the *Exam Close-up* and check that they understand it.
- Ask students to read the title of the text and ask if they know where Death Valley is located. Ask them to skim read the text, without filling in any answers, to find out *(Death Valley National Park, United States)*.
- Ask students to do the *Exam Task* individually, but check as a class.

Answer

1 located
2 sits
3 one
4 to
5 It
6 event
7 taking
8 starts

Grammar

- Before students open their books, ask them the questions below at random round the class, making sure all students answer at least one question.
  - Do you have to take your rubbish to a landfill site or is it collected from your house?
  - Do you think people should do more to help the planet?
  - Can charities like the World Wildlife Fund really help save animals?
  - What must governments do to stop global warming?
  - What is bound to happen if we don't start looking after the Earth better?
- Elicit from students that all these questions contain modal verbs. Elicit that these verb forms are often followed by the bare infinitive form of a verb, and that with the exception of *be able to* and *have to*, we use the same form for all persons. Stress that we don't use *to* after affirmative or negative forms of *can, could, should, must, may* or *might*.

A

- Ask students to read the instructions and check that they understand what they have to do.
- Ask students to read sentences 1–14, focusing on the modals in bold in each sentence.
- Read uses a–n to the students and explain anything they don't understand.
- Ask students to do the task individually, but check as a class.

Answer

1e 2j 3d 4a 5h 6n 7b
8g 9k 10c 11m 12f 13i 14l

Teaching Tip

You could extend this task by asking students to write sentences of their own for each of the functions in the Grammar box.

Now read the Grammar Reference on pages 165 & 166 (6.1) with your students.

B

- Ask students to read the instructions and check that they understand what they have to do. Encourage students to read the sentences carefully and to pay attention to the options within the context of the sentence before circling any answers.
- Remind students to look back at A if they need help when they do the task.
- Remind students to re-read the sentences once they have finished to check their answers.
- Ask students to do the task individually, but check as a class.

Answer

1 might
2 don't have to
3 will
4 could
5 ought to
6 must
7 won't
8 should

C

- Ask students to read the instructions and check that they understand what they have to do. Explain that they mustn't change the word in bold.
- Ask students to read the two sentences in item 1. Then ask them to underline the part in the first sentence that is missing from the second sentence.
- Explain to students that in order to complete the second sentence they will have to make a structural change.
- Ask students to complete the first item and correct it before they move on to the rest of the task.
- Ask students to do the task individually, but check as a class.

Answers

1 must be
2 have to pay
3 are bound to have/get
4 will not work
5 ought to be of interest
6 do not have/need to buy

D

- Write the sentences below on the board and ask students what they refer to.
  - We can cut down on rubbish by recycling. *(present/general)*
  - They must clean up the polluted river next year. *(future)*
  - You mustn't throw that on the ground! *(present)*
  - We have to pass a law against poaching by March. *(present/future)*
- Elicit from students that in order to talk about the past using modals verbs, we must use perfect modals.
- Read the information on perfect modals and the instructions to the students and check that they understand what they have to do.
- Ask students to read the sentence in item 1 and to explain what it means in their own words. Elicit that the sentence deals with the past so they have to use the correct perfect modal form and the verb given.
- Give students a minute to complete item 1 individually, but check as a class.
- Remind students to read the whole sentence before writing their answer and to pay attention to time expressions, adverbs of frequency and the tenses of other verbs in the sentence.
- Encourage them to look back at the Grammar box if they need help as they do the task. Ask students to do the task individually, but check as a class.

6 Living Planet

Answer

1. would/could have lent
2. may/might/could have missed
3. must have cleaned
4. should/ought to/might/could have told
5. needn't have brought
6. can't have eaten
7. should/ought to have returned

Now read the Grammar Reference on page 166 (6.2) with your students.

E

- Ask students to read the title and then skim read the text to find out how the title relates to the picture *(The text is about Lonesome George, the tortoise that is shown in the picture).*
- Explain to students that they should think about which form and use of each perfect modal is being used in each item and to refer back to the Grammar box when they are choosing their answers.
- Remind students to re-read the text once they have finished to check their answers.
- Ask students to do the task individually, but check as a class.

Answers

1. could
2. can't
3. may
4. might
5. must
6. should

Listening

A

- Ask students to work in pairs to describe the pictures on page 76. One student should describe the picture in the top right-hand corner and the other should describe the one in the bottom left-hand corner of the page. Ask them to describe the scenes and the situations as well as to guess why someone might have taken the picture.
- Ask students what animal they can see in the picture in the top-right hand corner *(tropical fish)* and explain that in this part of the lesson they are going to deal with synonymous words and phrases.
- Ask students to read the instructions and make sure they understand what they have to do.
- Ask students to do the task on their own and then to compare their answers with a partner.
- Check answers as a class and ask students to justify their answers.

Answers

1. laid-back, unrushed
2. look like, be similar to
3. bizarre, weird
4. in adulthood
5. commemorate, be named after
6. composed of, constructed using
7. be absolutely sure
8. have little time to spare, work against the clock

Teaching Tip

You could expand this task further by asking students to tell a partner about a relaxing or laid-back experience they have had recently. In pairs, ask students to discuss a situation where they were pushed for time, or a time when they had to work around the clock in order to complete something, etc.

B

- Ask students to read the *Exam Close-up*.
- Remind them of any differences in any answers they might have had in A and explain that this task shows how important it is to read and understand the questions and options properly in this type of listening task.
- Point out the options will paraphrase the ideas and information they will hear on the recording, so before listening they should always read the questions and the options, underline the key words and phrases and think about other ways of expressing these main ideas.
- Stress that the speakers on the recordings rarely, if ever, use the exact same words that are written in the options.
- Ask students to read the *Exam Task* and make sure they understand what they have to do.
- Read the questions and options to the students and explain anything they don't understand. Elicit from students which picture goes with which extract *(Extract One, goes with the picture in the top right-hand corner; Extract Two, goes with the picture in the bottom left-hand corner).*
- Give students time to underline the key words and phrases individually, but check as a class.
- Ask students to work in pairs and discuss other ways in which they might hear the information they have underlined.
- Go round the class monitoring students to make sure they are carrying out the task properly. Don't correct any mistakes at this point, but make a note of any problems in structure or pronunciation.
- Ask each pair to talk about one of the options and repeat until each student has had a turn.
- Write any structural mistakes made by students on the board without saying who made them, and ask them to correct them. Deal with any problems in pronunciation that came up.

Answer

Students' own answers

C

- Ask students to read the instructions and check they understand what they have to do.
- Explain that they will hear two different extracts and that there are two questions for each extract.
- Remind students that in this type of listening task, the situation is always given and that they should read it carefully so they will be able to predict, to a degree, what might be said in each extract.
- Give students time to read questions 1–4 and their options again focusing on the key words that they underlined.
- Play the recording once all the way through and ask students to circle their answers. Then ask students to discuss their answers with a partner and to justify any they have that are different.

D

- Play the recording again and ask students to check their answers and to complete any answers they haven't already marked.
- Check the answers as a class and ask students to justify their answers.

Answer

1 b 2 c 3 a 4 c

Speaking

A

- Ask students to read the four questions and answer any queries they may have about them.
- Ask students to work in pairs and to take it in turns to ask and answer the questions about themselves.
- Go round the class monitoring students to make sure they are carrying out the task properly. Don't correct any mistakes at this point, but make a note of any problems in structure or pronunciation.
- Ask each pair to ask and answer one question and repeat until each student has had a turn.
- Write any structural mistakes made by students on the board without saying who made them, and ask them to correct them. Deal with any problems in pronunciation that came up.

Answer

Students' own answers

B

- Ask students to read the instructions and check that they understand what they have to do. Explain that during their long turn in the *Exam Task*, they will have to speak for one minute, but they should try not to use any words in the rubric. Explain that they need to paraphrase these words.
- Ask students to read the six ideas and answer any queries they may have about them.
- Ask students to take it in turns to come up to the front of the class and talk about one of the ideas in B without using any of the words written. The others should listen with their books closed and try to guess which idea their classmate is talking about.

- Don't correct any mistakes at this point, but make a note of any problems in structure or pronunciation.
- Repeat until all students have had a turn.
- Write any structural mistakes made by students on the board without saying who made them, and ask them to correct them. Deal with any problems in pronunciation that came up.

Answer

Students' own answers

C

- Ask students to read the *Exam Close-up*.
- Ask students to quickly read the instructions for the *Exam Task* and elicit that students will have one long turn and one short turn and that during both they will talk separately as this is a non-collaborative task.
- Point out that in this task type, they should not be tempted to add to what their partner is saying or to ask them further questions related to their photos or task.

Useful Expressions

- Read the *Useful Expressions* to the students and ask them to repeat them. Correct their pronunciation and intonation where necessary.
- Explain to students that all these expressions can be used when they refer to the two of the three photos they have selected to talk about.
- Point out to students that they should use some of these expressions when they do the *Exam Task*.

D

- Ask students to read the instructions again and check that they understand what they have to do.
- Ask students to work in pairs and to decide who will be Student A and who will be Student B. Ask them to read the instructions for their role and to spend a few minutes looking at their own set of photos.
- Remind students again that this kind of task isn't a discussion and that each student is expected to speak for one minute on his or her photos answering the questions provided or to respond briefly (30 seconds) to the follow-up questions about his or her partner's photos.
- Ask Student A to begin answering the questions about the two photos they have chosen from the three and for Student B to answer the follow-up question once Student A has finished. Then ask Student B to answer their questions about the two photos they have chosen from the three and Student A answers the follow-up question.
- Go round the class monitoring students to make sure they are carrying out the task properly. Don't correct any mistakes at this point, but make a note of any problems in structure or pronunciation.
- Ask one pair of students to carry out the task in front of the class and ask the other students if they have anything to add.
- Write any structural mistakes made by students on the board without saying who made them, and ask them to correct them. Deal with any problems in pronunciation that came up.

Answer

Students' own answers

6 Living Planet

Ideas Focus

- Ask students to read the questions quickly and deal with any queries they may have.
- Ask students to work in pairs and to take it in turns to answer the questions.
- Go round the class monitoring students to make sure they are carrying out the task properly. Don't correct any mistakes at this point, but make a note of any problems in structure or pronunciation.
- Ask a student from each pair to answer one of the questions until each pair has had a turn. Ask the other students if they agree or if they have anything else to add.
- Write any structural mistakes made by students on the board without saying who made them, and ask them to correct them. Deal with any problems in pronunciation that came up.

Answers

a 1 The target reader is someone interested in environmental issues who would like to learn more about them.
  2 You do not know the reader or anything about them other than they are interested in conservation.
  3 A discursive style with a formal register should be used because it is a serious topic.

b 1 The target reader is your peer and they are most likely to be reading because they are interested in going on an eco-holiday in your country.
  2 You do not know the reader personally but are likely to be similar to them in age and tastes.
  3 Factual information in a semi-formal register should be used.
  4 For topic b, you may have to persuade the reader about the value of 1) an eco-holiday 2) in your country.

Answer

Students' own answers

Writing: a contribution

- Ask students what a contribution is and why they are written. Ask if they have ever written a contribution before. If so, ask them what topic it gave information or an opinion on, and in which type of larger document it appeared.
- Explain to students that in this lesson they are going to deal with writing contributions.
- Read the *Learning Focus* on using the appropriate register to the students and explain anything they don't understand. Ask students what determines the register and style of the contribution (*the purpose and target reader of the main document*) and elicit what a contribution must always include (*an introduction and a conclusion*).

A

- Ask students to read the instructions and check that they understand what they have to do.
- Ask students to underline the key words in the contribution topics.
- Explain that students should answer the questions as if they were planning to write the contributions.
- Point out that they should ask themselves questions like these when they are asked to write a contribution so that they can work out exactly what they are going to write and how they will write it before they start.
- Ask students to do the task individually and then to discuss their answers with a partner to compare how they would write their contribution.
- As a class, ask several students to read their answers and ask the other students if they agree or if they have anything else to add.

B

- Ask students to read the instructions and check that they understand what they have to do.
- Ask students to read the writing task and explain anything they don't understand.
- Ask students to underline the key words in the writing task.
- Ask students to do the task individually, but check as a class.

Answers

1 three, one for each bullet point
2 description of a place, explanation of activities and learning opportunities, discussion of the importance of eco-friendly tourism
3 to provide information that will convince the reader to visit an eco-friendly destination

C

- Ask students to read the instructions and check that they understand what they have to do.
- Then ask students to read the example contribution and to underline information that relates to questions in the instructions. Ask them to compare the parts they underlined with a partner.
- As a class, ask students the two questions and repeat until all the students have had a turn. Ask students to justify their answers and ask the other students if they agree or have anything else to add.

Answer

Students' own answers

D

- Ask students how many things the task asks them to do (*two – look at the example contribution again and answer the four questions*).

72

- Read questions 1–4 to the students and explain anything they don't understand.
- Ask students to work in pairs to encourage discussion, but check as a class.

Answers

1. begins with a question; uses the phrase 'spectacular setting' which creates interest
2. by using plenty of positive adjectives (*picturesque, stunning, fragrant, wonderful*, etc.)
3. yes, all three bullets in the task are addressed
4. yes, after reading the contribution the reader is fully informed and in a position to make a decision about visiting the resort

E

- Ask students to read the instructions and check that they understand what they have to do.
- Remind students that they have to write both an introduction and a conclusion for the example contribution and that both should begin with a question to engage the reader.
- Give students no more than ten minutes to write their paragraphs and go round the class offering help where necessary.
- When students have finished their paragraphs, remind them that when they have finished a piece of writing they should always proofread it to check for spelling, grammatical and punctuation errors.
- Ask students to swap notebooks with a partner and give them a few minutes to read and underline any mistakes they find in their partner's work. Explain that they don't have to correct them.
- Ask students to hand the paragraphs back to their partners and to correct any mistakes that have been noted down.
- As a class, ask several students to read out their paragraphs.

Answer

Students' own answers

Teaching Tip

Some students might be reluctant to let another student look at their work. Explain that swapping work with a partner is a good idea because it will make them more likely to pick up on their own mistakes if they are encouraged from time to time to check another student's work.

F

- Ask the students to read the *Exam Close-up* and point out that the writer of the example contribution did all the things on the list.
- Remind students that they can use the information here as a checklist when writing their own contributions.
- Ask students to read the *Exam Task* and ask them to underline any key words and phrases in the task. Explain anything they don't understand.
- Ask students to answer the questions in A and B about this writing task so that they know what they have to do.
- As a class, ask students where their contribution will appear (*in an international magazine*) and what their contribution will be about (*environmental problems around the world*).
- Ask students to read the paragraph plan and to make notes for each paragraph, if time allows.
- Ask students in which paragraph they will recommend one solution to the problem (*main paragraph 3*).
- Set the *Exam Task* for homework.
- Encourage students to use the Writing Reference and checklist for contributions on page 180.

Suggested answer

Environmental Issues in the UK

Imagine if we lived in a world where there were no environmental problems. It seems unlikely, but there are many things we can do to minimise the existing problems. In my country, there is a problem that comes from an unlikely source, … cows!

In the UK, there are lots of cows which are kept for meat and dairy produce. Unfortunately, these cows are contributing to global warming in their own unique way. Each cow produces around 100-200 litres of methane every day, which has caused greenhouse gas pollution levels to soar.

This problem is responsible for higher levels of pollution. Methane is around twenty-three times more powerful than carbon dioxide gas which comes from cars. So with around 10 million cows in the UK chewing away in our fields, it is important we think of ways to reduce this greenhouse gas.

By changing the cows' diet we can effectively deal with the problem, or at least reduce the amount of methane produced. Scientists have said that by feeding cows grass that is high in sugar it will change the way the bacteria in the stomach breaks down the plant material into waste gas.

So it seems there is a relatively simple way that farmers can limit or even solve this problem. All they need to do to help the problems associated with climate change is to make a slight change to the cows' diet. I really hope this environmental problem will be solved soon leaving us all cleaner air to breathe.

Useful Expressions

- Read the *Useful Expressions* to the students and ask them to repeat them. Correct their pronunciation and intonation if necessary.
- Elicit in which part of their contribution they can use each category of expressions and tell them to use them when writing their contribution for the *Exam Task*.

6 Holland Water

General Note

Please see the information about the National Geographic videos on page 18 of this Teacher's Book.

Background Information

As a country with two thirds of its area vulnerable to flooding, the subject of flood control is one that people in the Netherlands take very seriously. In order to keep their land above the water, inhabitants of the Netherlands make use of sand dunes, dikes, dams and floodgates. River dikes keep the waters of the Rhine and Meuse Rivers back and ditches, canals and pumping stations are used to keep residential areas and farmland dry.

Before you watch

A

- Explain to students that in this lesson they are going to watch a video about how global warming is affecting Holland, the Netherlands. Ask them to look at the globe to see where Holland is. Elicit what they know about Holland and ask them why it might be especially at risk from global warming.
- Ask students to read questions 1–3 and explain anything they don't understand. Tell students to work in pairs and encourage them to draw on their own knowledge of global warming and how it affects their country when answering the questions.
- Go round the class monitoring students to make sure they are carrying out the task properly. Don't correct any mistakes at this stage, but make a note of any problems in structure and pronunciation.
- Ask each pair to answer one of the questions and repeat until each pair has had a turn.
- Deal with any problems in pronunciation that came up.

Answer

Students' own answers

While you watch

B

- Explain to students that they are now going to watch the video and do a task based on the information they hear. Ask them to read sentences 1–6 and explain anything they don't understand.
- Ask them to think about which words might be correct before watching.
- Play the video all the way through without stopping and ask students to circle their answers. Ask students to compare their answers with a partner's and to justify any answers they have that are different. Play the video again so that they can check their answers and fill in any missing answers.
- Ask students to do the task individually, but check as a class.

Answer

1 war	(00:25)	4 million	(01:51)
2 sink	(00:35)	5 wildlife	(02:32)
3 man	(01:40)	6 younger	(03:34)

After you watch

C

- Explain to students that this is a summary of the information they heard in the video.
- Read the words in the yellow box to the students and ask them to repeat them. Ask them to write N, V, Adj or Adv beside each of the words depending on whether it is a noun, a verb, an adjective or an adverb
- Explain to students that they should read the whole summary before writing any answers first to work out what part of speech is missing.
- Tell students to re-read the text once they have finished to check their answers.
- Ask students to do the task individually, but check as a class.

Answer

1 worried	6 constant
2 rise	7 radical
3 surprisingly	8 resistance
4 preserve	9 Regardless
5 marshlands	10 shift

Ideas Focus

- Ask students to read the three questions and answer any queries they might have. Then ask them to read the three questions and explain anything they don't understand.
- Ask students to work in pairs and explain that they should both give their opinions on all three questions.
- Go round the class monitoring students to make sure they are carrying out the task properly. Don't correct any mistakes at this stage, but make a note of any problems in structure and pronunciation.
- Ask each pair to answer one of the questions and repeat until each pair has had a turn.
- Write how the students' country is affected by global warming and how they think we should deal with global warming on the board.
- Deal with any problems in structure or pronunciation that came up.

Answer

Students' own answers

Review 3

Units 5 & 6

Objectives
- To revise vocabulary and grammar from Units 5 and 6
- To practise exam-type tasks

Revision
- Explain to students that Review 3 revises the material they saw in Units 5 and 6.
- Remind students that they can ask you for help with the exercises or look back at the units if they need help with an answer. Stress that the review is not a test.
- Decide how you will carry out the review. You could ask students to do one task at a time and then correct it immediately, or ask students to do all the tasks and correct them together at the end. If you do all the tasks together, let students know every now and again how much time they have got left to finish.
- Ask students not to leave any answers blank and to try to find any answers they don't know in the units.
- When checking students' answers to the review tasks, make a note of any problem areas in vocabulary and grammar that they still have. Try to do extra work on these areas so that your students will progress well.

Vocabulary Revision
- Ask students to write down as many adjectives related to food and drink as they can think of. Then ask them to write down whether these adjectives are positive or negative.
- Ask students to explain the difference between the following pairs of words: *dishcloths/napkins, cultivated/harvested, coverings/toppings, stable/staple, eatable/edible, dissolved/extracted, ethnic/cultural, consume/swallow.*
- Elicit from students the phrasal verbs they learnt in Unit 6 that are related to the weather *(beat down, blow up, bucket down, clear up, blow over, dry up)* and ask them to write sentences of their own using these phrasal verbs.
- Say the words *unaware, indifferent, advised, alternative, interfere* and *insistence* one by one to the students and ask them which prepositions come after them.
- Ask students to work in pairs to write down as many collective nouns as they can. Then ask them to say which group of animals the collective nouns refer to.

Grammar Revision
- Write the sentences below on the board and ask students to identify the phrasal verb and object in each sentence. Ask students if the phrasal verbs are transitive or intransitive and separable or inseparable and elicit or explain why. Then revise the rules for transitive/intransitive and separable/inseparable phrasal verbs that students learnt in Unit 5.
  - As well as making you pile on weight, fatty foods may also be affecting your heart. *(pile on; transitive because it is followed by an object [weight] after the particle, intransitive phrasal verbs are not; separable because the object could come between the verb and the particle, with inseparable phrasal verbs the object comes after the particle)*
  - Scientists hope that the new data can help them come up with an anti-aging therapy. *(come up with; transitive because it is followed by an object [an anti-aging therapy] after the particle, intransitive phrasal verbs are not; inseparable because the object comes after the particle, with separable phrasal verbs the object could come between the verb and the particle).*
- Write the following sentences on the board and ask students to complete the tags and to say what type of question tag each one is. Then revise the types and forms they learnt in Unit 5.
  - So you've started a diet, _____? *(have you, same-way question tag)*
  - 'I'm not tired. I won't go to bed, Dad!' 'Oh, _____? *(won't you, same-way question tag)*
  - I couldn't borrow a cup of flour, _____? *(could I, question tag for polite requests)*
  - That's a nice steak, _____. *(that is, reinforcement tag)*
  - My sister really likes that café, _____. *(she does, reinforcement tag)*
- Write the following on the board and elicit that they are the uses of the modal verbs that students learnt in Unit 6: *ability, certainty, possibility, advice and suggestions, necessity and obligation, habit, refusal, impossibility, certainty in the future, lack of necessity or obligation, inability, expectation, prohibition, permission and requests.* Ask students which modals can be used with each use and ask them to write sentences to demonstrate their use. Encourage students to write sentences using modals with a present or future meaning and others with perfect modals.

A
- Ask students to read the instructions and check that they understand what they have to do.
- Ask students to read the title of the text and ask them what they think it means. Then ask them to skim read the text, without circling any answers, to find out what *it* means in the context of the text *(a kind of energy involving the direct conversion of light into electricity inside an atom).*

- Point out to students that they should read all four options for each item before deciding which word best fits each gap. Remind them to pay attention to the whole sentence each gap is in as the general context will help them understand what word is missing.
- Remind students to re-read the text once they have finished to check their answers.

Answer

1 D	5 A	9 B
2 A	6 D	10 B
3 C	7 C	11 D
4 B	8 C	12 A

B

- Ask students to read the instructions and check that they understand what they have to do.
- Ask students what they know about the history of salt and when people first began using it on their food. Ask students to skim read the text, without filling in any answers, to find out (since the earliest recorded times).
- Encourage students to pay particular attention to the words immediately before and after each gap to work out what part of speech is missing. However, remind them that they have to take into consideration the general context of the sentence so that they understand what structure is being used.
- Remind students to re-read the text once they have finished to check their answers.

Answers

13 or	21 every	
14 must	22 has	
15 such	23 there	
16 the	24 to	
17 to	25 had	
18 since	26 all	
19 as	27 one	
20 enough		

C

- Ask students to read the instructions and check that they understand what they have to do.
- Encourage students to read all three sentences before filling in any answers.
- Explain to students that the missing word in each set of sentences will be a fairly common one and that students should not spend time trying to find overly-difficult words.
- Tell students that the missing word in each set of sentences will be the same part of speech and that the word will have a different meaning in each sentence.
- Remind students to re-read the completed sentences once they have finished to check their answers.

Answer

28 bright
29 off
30 sharp
31 sign
32 thin

D

- Ask students to read the instructions and check that they understand what they have to do.
- Ask students to read both sentences in each item and to underline the information in the first sentence that is missing from the second sentence. Then ask them to look at the word given to decide how the missing information could be inserted into the second sentence using this word. Remind students that they will have to use a different structure in order to keep the meaning the same.
- Remind students that they mustn't change the word given in bold in any way.
- Encourage students to re-read the completed sentences once they have finished to check their answers.

Answer

33 unaware of the danger
34 must have known
35 put up with companies dumping
36 use crying over spilt milk
37 have lost my appetite
38 shouldn't have eaten
39 did they

7 Eureka!

Reading: multiple-matching, looking for specific information
Vocabulary: technology- and inventions-related vocabulary, compound nouns, idioms
Grammar: conditionals, unreal past, inversion
Listening: sentence completion, making notes
Speaking: talking about inventions and inventors, modern technology, decision making, giving opinions with reasons & examples, justifying choices
Writing: nomination, nominating someone for achievement, writing an effective nomination, talking about reputations, influence & achievements

Unit opener

- Ask students to look at the title of the unit and to guess what it might mean (I found it! – an exclamation attributed to Archimedes, the great Greek inventor) and ask what emotion it expresses (excitement, joy, pride, etc.). If students seem interested give them more information using the Background Information box below.
- Ask them to look at the picture and read the caption. Then ask students to say how the picture might relate to the unit (lightbulbs commonly link to good ideas and Eureka will sometimes be said at the same time).
- Ask students to come up with as many names of great inventors and their inventions as they can and write them on the board.

Background Information

It is said that the ancient Greek scholar Archimedes shouted 'Eureka!' after he stepped out of his bathtub and realised that the level of water in the tub had gone down. He was excited because he realised that the volume of water displaced must be the same as the volume of the part of his body he had submerged in the bath water. It has been rumoured that Archimedes was so pleased about his discovery, and so eager to share what he had learnt, that he jumped out of the tub and ran through the streets naked.

Reading

A

- Ask students to look at the list of inventions in A and ask them to discuss with a partner which of the inventions they use. Go through the inventions as a class and discuss which they use and which they don't. If students aren't sure about some of the inventions you can explain what they do in this part of the exercise.
- Ask students to read the instructions and the list of inventors and inventions. Ask them to look at the board to see if any of the inventors or inventions they came up with in the unit opener are also in the list in A. Answer any questions they might have about them.
- Ask students to do the task in pairs to encourage discussion, but check answers as a class.

- Ask students at random round the class which of the inventions listed is the most impressive. Encourage students to justify their answers.

Answers

Archimedes – the irrigation screw (for raising water from the ground) – pre **211** BC
John Logie Baird – the television – **1925**
Josephine Cochran – the dishwasher – **1886**
Martin Cooper – the mobile phone – **1973**
Mary Anderson – windscreen wipers – **1905**
Thomas Edison – the phonograph – **1877**

Extra Class Activity

If time allows, ask students to rank the inventions in order of importance. Then do a class survey to see which invention they think affects our lives the most. Encourage students to justify their answers.

B

- Ask students to look at the pictures in the article and ask them what all the scenes in the picture have in common (they show great inventions and modern technology).
- Ask students to read the title of the article and elicit how it relates to the picture (Thomas Edison was a great inventor).
- Ask students to read the instructions in B and check that they understand what they have to do. Elicit from students which of the inventions in A is attributed to Edison (the phonograph).
- Tell students to skim read the article to find which other of Edison's inventions are mentioned. Remind them that they don't have to read in detail as they will have another opportunity to do that later.
- Ask students to do the task individually, but check answers as a class.
- If students seem interested give them more information using the Background Information box on the next page.

Answer

the long kiln

77

7 Eureka!

Background Information

Thomas Alva Edison was born on February 11, 1847 in Ohio, United States. Thomas's first invention was an electric vote recording machine. He also worked on a telegraph that had the ability to send up to four messages simultaneously. In 1876, he set up the laboratory where two of his greatest inventions, the phonograph and the light bulb, were developed and perfected.

Word Focus

- Ask students to read the words in red in the text and to re-read the sentences they are found in. Ask students to work in pairs to decide what each of the words means in the *Word Focus* and to then find synonyms, if any, for each word.
- Ask students to compare their answers with another pair. Explain anything they don't understand.

C

- Ask students to read the *Exam Close-up* and then ask a student to explain what it says in his or her own words.
- Explain that in multiple-matching tasks, it is very important that they read the questions and underline the key words before they read the text as this will help them identify which sections contain information related to what they've underlined in the questions.
- Point out that they should then re-read the questions before looking back at the parts they have underlined to find their answers.
- Remind students that the questions will paraphrase the ideas in the text so they should pay attention to synonyms and other ways that the key ideas have been expressed.
- Explain to students that this is a multiple matching task and that they should answer A, B, C, D, E or F to show which part of the article they found the information in.
- Ask students to read the questions before reading the text again and to underline any key words so that they know what information to pay attention to.
- Encourage students to guess the meaning of any unfamiliar words from the context they're in before looking them up in their dictionaries. Explain any problem words and correct their pronunciation where necessary.
- Ask students to read the text again and to underline any sentences or phrases that correspond to the questions, in pencil, while reading.
- Ask students to do the task individually, but check as a class.

Answers

1C (*His prediction came true – but was short-lived.*)
2F (*When it came to flying, Edison was spot on.*)
3C (*One of Edison's own inventions … which revolutionised the cement industry.*)
4E (*… he proclaimed, 'that there will be no poverty in the world a hundred years from now.'; If only this were the case!*)
5A (*But it's not all good news … no longer fully employ people … has proved more cost effective.*)
6A (*He even realised that when this revolution in industry took place, certain jobs would disappear.*)
7F (*… he informed himself by observing nature – in particular, the agility of the bumblebee.*)
8E (*As a firm believer in the power of the brain and technological progress to transform the human condition, …*)
9B (*… if paper was replaced by nickel, books would be made of a cheaper, stronger and more flexible material.*)
10F (*Eight years after the Wright brothers' triumphant first flight in a flying machine, …*)
11D (*'The babies of the next generation will sit in steel high-chairs … They will not know what wooden furniture is.'*)
12A (*The car industry wouldn't be able to produce cars at the rate it does today if it wasn't for technological developments.*)

D

- Ask students to read the instructions and check that they understand what they have to do.
- Point out that they have to replace the words and phrases in bold in the sentences with others from the text that have the same meaning.
- Encourage students to read all the sentences in D before scanning the texts for synonymous words and phrases.
- Ask students to do the task individually, but check as a class.

Answers

1 prophecies
2 mundane
3 more cost effective
4 was short-lived
5 spot on
6 artificial

Ideas Focus

- Explain to students that they are now going to answer some questions about inventions. Ask students to read the questions and explain anything they don't understand.
- Ask students to answer the questions in pairs and encourage them to draw on personal experience as much as possible.
- Go round the class monitoring students to ensure they are carrying out the task properly. Don't correct any mistakes at this point, but make a note of any problems in structure or pronunciation.

- Ask students at random to answer each of the questions and encourage the other students to give their opinions.
- Write any structural mistakes made by students on the board without saying who made them, and ask them to correct them. Deal with any problems in pronunciation that came up.

Answers

Students' own answers

Vocabulary

A

- Ask students to read the instructions and check that they understand what they have to do.
- Read the sets of words 1–6 to the students and ask them to repeat them after you. Correct their pronunciation where necessary.
- Ask students to work in pairs to encourage discussion, but check the answers as a class. Ask them to explain why one of the words is the odd one out in each item.

Answers

1. stimulate (*The others are ways of describing change, but 'stimulate' means to excite.*)
2. substance (*The others are words used to refer to work equipment, but 'substance' means the tangible matter of which a thing consists.*)
3. manual (*The others are ways of saying something is controlled by a machine, but 'manual' means something that is controlled by hand.*)
4. assumption (*The others are ways of saying what you think will happen, but 'assumption' means to take something for granted.*)
5. discard (*The others are ways of describing the removal of impurities, but 'discard' means to throw something away.*)
6. rectangle (*The other words describe rounded shapes, but 'rectangle' is a shape with four sides.*)

B

- Ask students to read the instructions and check that they understand what they have to do. Ask students to read the sentences without circling any words at this stage. Explain anything they don't understand.
- Read the words in red to students and ask them to repeat them. Correct their pronunciation where necessary. Point out that the task tests words that are often confused so the correct answers will depend on how naturally each option fits in with the context of the sentence.
- Ask students to do the task individually, but check as a class.

Answers

1. displaced
2. conductors
3. elements
4. phenomenon
5. corrode
6. explosives
7. expands
8. molten

C

- Ask students to look at the picture to the right of the text in C and ask them to describe what they can see. Ask them who the man in the picture is and what he might be doing (*he may be a jeweller/gemstone dealer/ valuer who is checking a diamond for flaws*).
- Read the words in the yellow box to students and ask them to repeat them. Correct their pronunciation where necessary.
- Ask students to read the title and ask how they think it is related to the text. Then ask them to skim read the text, without filling in any answers, to find out (*the text is about how diamonds are so long-lasting*).
- Ask students what they know about diamonds and encourage a short class discussion on the topic.
- Ask students to do the task individually, but check as a class.

Answers

1. hardness
2. gemstone
3. material
4. property
5. purity
6. industry
7. instruments
8. devices

D

- Ask students to read the instructions and check that they understand what they have to do.
- Read the words to the students and ask students to repeat them after you. Correct their pronunciation where necessary.
- Explain that they will match words from the two columns to form compound nouns. Elicit what all the compound nouns have in common (*they are all related to computers*).
- Ask students to do the task individually, but check as a class.

Answers

1. control panel
2. password
3. home page
4. hard drive
5. laser printer
6. memory stick
7. recycle bin
8. search engine

Teaching Tip

You could extend this task by asking students to put the compound nouns from the task under the headings 1) Physical Parts of a Computer, 2) Terms Related to Computing, or 3) Other.

E

- Ask students to read the instructions and check that they understand what they have to do. Stress that they have to use the compound nouns from E to complete the sentences.
- Ask students to first read the sentences for gist to work out which compound noun might be missing from each one.
- Ask students to do the task individually, but check as a class.
- Encourage students to copy the compound nouns and their meanings into their notebooks.

7 Eureka!

Answers

1 home page	5 password
2 search engine	6 laser printer
3 memory stick	7 recycle bin
4 hard drive	8 control panel

F

- Ask students to look at the picture and ask them to describe what they can see *(a car plant)*.
- Read the words in the yellow box to students and ask them to repeat them. Correct their pronunciation where necessary.
- Ask students to tell you what the method, by which the cars are being made in the picture, is called. Ask them to skim read the text, without filling in any answers, to find out *(an assembly line)*.
- Ask students to do the task individually, but check as a class.

Answers

1 assembly	5 innovation
2 process	6 stations
3 sequence	7 components
4 plant	8 fraction

Extra Class Activity

If time allows, ask students what they know about assembly lines and encourage a short class discussion on what is good and bad about them.

G

- Ask students to read the instructions and check that they understand what they have to do.
- Read the words in the yellow box to students and ask them to repeat them. Correct their pronunciation where necessary.
- Ask students to look quickly at the definitions in italics and the sentences below each one. Explain to students that in English there are lots of colourful expressions and that some of these expressions are called idioms. Tell them that in this task they will be dealing with idioms related to technology.
- Ask students to work in pairs to encourage discussion, but check as a class.
- Point out that they will be better able to remember idioms if they write them down in their notebooks and include their definitions as well as a sentence demonstrating their use.

Answers

1 wheel	4 years
2 edge	5 button
3 wires	6 science

H

- Read the information about the longest word to ever appear in an English language dictionary to the students and explain anything they don't understand.
- Ask students to read the instructions and check that they understand what they have to do.
- Ask students to work in pairs to write down as many medical and health words as they can, using the letters of the coloured word.
- Go round the class monitoring students to make sure they are carrying out the task properly. Don't correct any mistakes at this point, but make a note of any problems in structure or pronunciation.
- Ask each pair to call out one of the words they have written down and write it on the board beside the names of the students in the pair. Repeat until the pairs have said all their words. The pair with the most words wins.
- Write any structural mistakes made by students on the board without saying who made them, and ask them to correct them. Deal with any problems in pronunciation that came up.

Answers

Student's own answers

Grammar

- Write the sentences below on the board and ask students what kind of structures they are.
  - If Henry Ford hadn't loved automobiles, he wouldn't have invented the assembly line. *(Third Conditional)*
  - If you heat water to 100 degrees Celsius, it boils. *(Zero Conditional)*
  - If machines could do all our work, people would be rather bored. *(Second Conditional)*
  - If we take this course, we will learn all about technology. *(First Conditional)*
  - If Alexander Graham Bell hadn't invented the telephone, I wouldn't be on the phone with you right now. *(Mixed conditional)*
- Elicit the verb tenses used in the *if* clause and in the result clause of each conditional. *(Zero: Present Simple, Present simple; First: Present Simple, Future Simple; Second: Past Simple, would + bare infinitive; Third: Past Perfect Simple, would have + past participle; Mixed: there are many types of mixed conditionals, but the two most commonly used types follow this pattern - Third Second Mixed: Past Perfect, would + bare infinitive (this is the one focussed on in this book) and Second Third Mixed: Past Simple, would have + Past Participle).* Point out that conditionals can be formed with modal verbs instead of *will* or *would*.
- Explain that students are going to revise the use and forms of these conditionals in this part of the lesson.

A

- Ask students to read the instructions and check that they understand what they have to do. Elicit how many things they have to do *(two)* and say what they are *(underline the verb forms in the sentences and identify the verb forms)*.
- As a class, ask different students to read out one of the sentences and say which verb forms are used in the *if* clause and in the result clause in each one.

Answers

Zero: split, release (Present Simple in both clauses)
First: study, will learn (Present Simple, Future Simple)
Second: could answer, would be (Past Simple, would + bare infinitive)
Third: hadn't become, would have been (Past Perfect, would + have + Past Participle)
Mixed: wouldn't be cleaning, hadn't exploded (Present Continuous, Past Perfect)

B

- Ask students to read the instructions and check that they understand what they have to do.
- Read questions 1–5 to the students and elicit that the questions focus on the use of each of the conditionals.
- Point out that they should write the type of conditional on the lines provided to the right of the questions.
- Ask students to do the task in pairs to encourage discussion, but check as a class.

Answers

1 second
2 zero
3 mixed
4 first
5 third

- Once the answers have been checked, ask students to look back at the Reading text on pages 84 and 85 to find conditional sentences. Ask them to identify the type of conditional sentences they find *(Section A: ...when this revolution in industry took place, certain jobs would disappear [second]; The car industry wouldn't be able to produce cars at the rate it does today if it wasn't for ... [second]; Section B: if paper was replaced by nickel, books would be made ... [second]; Section C: If his kiln hadn't been invented, modern construction would be very different [mixed] Section D: If Edison's prediction about household furniture had come true, then today we'd all furnish ... [third])*.
- Ask students which sentence is slightly different from the ones they looked at in A *(... when this revolution in industry took place, certain jobs would disappear)*. Elicit that when has been used in this sentence instead of *if* but that it is still a conditional sentence. Explain that there are several ways of forming the conditional without using *if*.
- Write the sentence below on the board and ask students what *unless* means *(if not)*. Explain that *unless* can be used in first and second conditional sentences.
  - Unless you study hard, you won't get into university.

- Call out the following words one at a time and ask students at random round the class to re-write the sentence on the board using the word you have called out in their notebooks.
  - Otherwise (Study hard, <u>otherwise</u> you won't get into university.)
  - Provided that (<u>Provided that</u> you study hard, you will get into university.)
  - As long as (<u>As long as</u> you study hard, you will get into university.)
  - Supposing (<u>Supposing</u> I study hard, will I get into university?)
  - Should (<u>Should</u> you study hard, you will get into university.)
- Ask students in pairs to compare their answers. Encourage students to justify their answers. Ask each pair, to read out one of their sentences. Ask the others if they agree or have anything else to add.
- Elicit that all these words can take the place of *if* and that they will be revising other conditionals in this part of the lessons.

C

- Ask students to read the instructions and check that they understand what they have to do.
- Ask students to read sentences 1–7 and explain anything they don't understand.
- Ask students to do the task individually, but check as a class.

Answers

1 Provided = If
2 As long as = If
3 Supposing = What if?
4 But for = If it hadn't been for his support
5 unless = if you don't show them
6 otherwise = if you don't
7 Help (imperative) = If you help

Now read the Grammar Reference on pages 166 & 167 (7.1 to 7.6) with your students.

D

- Ask students to read the instructions and check that they understand what they have to do.
- Ask students to read the first fact and elicit that the verb is missing from the result clause. Ask students if the sentence at the beginning of the fact talks about something in the present, past or future *(present)*. Elicit that the situation in the *if (But for)* part of the sentence is an imaginary one. Ask students what this tells us about the result clause that follows *(it needs to use Second Conditional)*. Ask students to fill in the answer and check it before moving on.
- Explain that they should analyse facts 2–5 in this way to help them decide which verb forms should be used in each gap.
- Ask students to do the task individually, but check as a class.
- Ask students which of the facts surprised them the most and why.

81

7 Eureka!

> **Answers**
> 1 wouldn't be
> 2 turns, corrodes
> 3 hadn't noticed, wouldn't have
> 4 put, would circle
> 5 look, can/will see

E

- Ask students to read the instructions and check that they understand what they have to do.
- Encourage students to read the whole sentence before circling any answers to look for any clues to the right answer.
- Encourage them to look back at C if they need help while doing the task.
- Remind students to re-read the sentences once they have finished to check their answers.
- Ask students to do the task individually, but check as a class.

> **Answers**
> 1 as long as
> 2 provided
> 3 unless
> 4 But for
> 5 otherwise

Extra Class Activity

For further practice of conditionals, you might like to ask students to work in small groups to make conditional sentences about inventing something important. Encourage them to form a chain story in their groups with one conditional sentence linking to another. For example, one student could start by saying: If I was really intelligent, I would invent a ... . Then the next student would continue by saying: If I invented a ..., I would ... . And so on around the group until each student has made two conditional sentences

F

- Ask students to read the instructions and check that they understand what they have to do.
- Ask students to look at the sentences and to focus on the words in bold, then ask them about each of the sentences in order.
- Does the person know how to cure all diseases? *(no)*
- Did the person tell you last night? *(no)*
- Does the person interrupt you all the time? *(yes)*
- Does the person want to be an astronaut on the next space mission? *(yes)*
- Do the people have to leave tomorrow? *(yes)*
- Ask students what they notice about the verb tenses in the sentences and how they are different in the questions above.
- Ask students to do the task individually, but check as a class.

> **Answers**
> 1 present
> 2 past
> 3 present
> 4 future
> 5 future

Be careful!

- Read the information in *Be careful!* to the students and explain anything they don't understand.
- Ask students to write sentences of their own using *I wish* + *(you/he/she, etc.)* + *would(n't)* to talk about other people's annoying habits.

G

- Ask students to read the instructions and check that they understand what they have to do.
- Ask students to look at the sentences and to underline the verb forms that follow the negative adverbs.
- Ask students to work in pairs to encourage discussion, but check as a class.
- Once the answers have been checked, ask students to look back at the Reading text about Thomas Edison on pages 84 and 85 and to find an example of inversion *(Paragraph B – Never could he have imagined that ...)*

> **Answer**
> They are all in question word order.

Be careful!

- Read the information in the *Be careful!* to students and explain anything they don't understand.
- Ask students to write sentences of their own using an inverted form to replace the if-clause in conditional sentences.

Now read the Grammar Reference on page 167 (7.7 & 7.8) with your students.

H

- Ask students to read the instructions and check that they understand what they have to do.
- Encourage students to read the whole sentence before circling their answers to look for any clues to the right answer. Tell them they should pay particular attention to the verb tense in each sentence.
- Encourage them to look back at F if they need help while doing the task.
- Remind students to re-read the sentences once they have finished to check their answers.
- Ask students to do the task individually, but check as a class.

> **Answers**
> 1 wouldn't give
> 2 had phoned
> 3 didn't have to learn
> 4 wouldn't bite
> 5 had paid
> 6 hadn't come

I

- Ask students to read the instructions and check that they understand what they have to do.
- Encourage students to read the whole sentence before writing any answers to look for any clues to the right answer. Tell them they should pay particular attention to the verb forms in the sentences and the word after the gap.
- Point out that they must use the negative adverbs from G to complete the sentences.

82

- Remind students to re-read the sentences once they have finished to check their answers.
- Ask students to do the task in pairs to encourage discussion, but check as a class.

Answers

1. Little
2. Never/Rarely/Seldom
3. Only then
4. Not until
5. Under no circumstances
6. Not only
7. Nowhere
8. No sooner, than
9. Not once

Listening

A

- Ask students to work in pairs to describe the pictures on page 90. One student should describe the one in the top right-hand corner and the other should describe the one at the bottom of the page. Ask them to describe the person, what he is doing and how the pictures might be related *(the man is installing solar panels on a building; perhaps it is the same building that is in the picture at the bottom of the page)*.
- Ask students to read the instructions and make sure they understand what they have to do.
- Read the terms to the students and ask them to repeat them. Correct their pronunciation where necessary.
- Ask students to work in pairs to discuss what the terms mean.
- If students are totally unfamiliar with these terms, write the sentences below on the board to help them.
  - Since we had solar panels installed on the roof of our house, our energy bills have halved.
  - The main principle behind sustainable technologies is to affect the environment as little as possible and to connect people with the natural environment.
  - There are large windmills on many of the Greek islands; they were put there to harness the energy of the wind.
  - We shouldn't be using fuels like coal and oil to heat our homes; we should be using clean energy sources like the sun, wind and water.
- As a class, ask each pair to give their definition of one of the terms.

Answers

solar panels – boards fitted to buildings to collect energy from the sun
sustainable technology – using forms of energy which are renewable and don't harm the environment as much
to harness energy – to control energy so that it can be used
clean energy – a means of power that is generated without harming the environment

B

- Ask students what kind of technology they have read about so far in the unit. Ask them to think about some of the latest technologies and ask them what they are used for. Explain that they are now going to listen to someone talking about solar panels.
- Ask students to read the instructions and make sure they understand what they have to do.
- Then ask students to read sentences 1–5 and to underline any key words and phrases. Elicit from students that it is often a good idea to make notes at the side of each item while they are listening to the recording.
- Play the recording once all the way through and ask students to make brief notes beside each item. Point out that it is not necessary for them to mark all the statements true or false. Ask students to compare their answers with a partner and to justify any answers they have that are different.
- Play the recording again and ask students to check their answers or to fill in any missing answers.
- Check answers as a class and ask students to justify their answers.

Answers

1F (They wanted the solar panels to help pay the mortgage.)
2T
3F (They underestimated the kilowatt-hours of electricity they'd be able to produce.)
4T
5T

C

- Ask students to read the *Exam Close-up*.
- Remind them of any differences in any answers they might have had for B and explain that this task shows how helpful it can be to make brief notes beside each item in this type of listening task.
- Point out that sometimes they will have to listen to a long recording which will require them to take in a lot of information at one time.
- Stress that taking brief notes beside each item will help them to remember which points, made by the speaker, relate to the missing information in each item.
- Ask students to read the instructions and check they understand what they have to do.
- Explain that they will hear a presentation about a new way to generate electricity.
- Explain that in this type of listening task, the situation is always given and that they should read it carefully so that they will be able to predict, to a degree, what might be said on the recording.
- Give students time to read questions 1–8 and to underline any key words in the situation and the sentences. Answer any questions they might have about them.
- Encourage students to take brief notes beside each item as they listen.
- Play the recording once all the way through and ask students to complete the sentences they can. Then ask students to discuss their answers with a partner and to justify any answers they have that are different.

83

7 Eureka!

D

- Play the recording again and ask students to check their answers and to fill in any missing answers.
- Check the answers as a class and ask students to justify their answers.

Answers

1. revolutionary new
2. Kinetic energy
3. green rubber
4. clean energy
5. excellent condition
6. sustainable technology
7. 200 times
8. reduce

Speaking

A

- Ask students to read the three questions and answer any queries they may have about them.
- Ask students to work in pairs and to take it in turns to ask and answer the questions about themselves.
- Go round the class monitoring students to make sure they are carrying out the task properly. Don't correct any mistakes at this point, but make a note of any problems in structure or pronunciation.
- As a class, ask each pair to ask and answer one question and repeat until each student has had a turn.
- Write any structural mistakes made by students on the board without saying who made them, and ask them to correct them. Deal with any problems in pronunciation that came up.

Answers

Students' own answers

B

- Ask students to read the instructions and check that they understand what they have to do.
- Then ask students to read the six statements and answer any queries they have about them.
- Point out to students that in this task they have to tick how far they agree with each statement (*completely agree, partly agree or completely disagree*).
- Give students time to tick their answers and then ask them to discuss their views on each statement in pairs.
- Go round the class monitoring students to make sure they are carrying out the task properly. Don't correct any mistakes at this point, but make a note of any problems in structure or pronunciation.
- As a class, ask each pair to discuss their views on one statement until each pair has had a turn. Ask the others if they agree or have anything else to add.
- Write any structural mistakes made by students on the board without saying who made them, and ask them to correct them. Deal with any problems in pronunciation that came up.

Answers

Students' own answers

C

- Ask students to read the *Exam Close-up*. Explain that they will now take part in a discussion and decision-making task.
- Ask students to quickly read the *Exam Task* and ask them what they will have to discuss (*which invention has had the greatest impact on our lives*).
- Point out to students that one of the most important parts of this type of task is to keep the discussion flowing. Explain to students that they should always listen carefully to their partner.
- Explain to students that they will learn some vocabulary to justify their choices in the *Useful Expressions* box.

Useful Expressions

- Read the *Useful Expressions* to the students and ask them to repeat them. Correct their pronunciation and intonation where necessary.
- Point out to students that they should practise using some of this topic vocabulary when they are discussing the photos in C.
- Ask students to read the instructions again and ask them how many things they have to do here (*two*) and what they are (*talk together about the inventions the photos show and decide which picture best reflects the role technology plays in our lives today*).
- As a class, elicit what aspects of inventions are shown in each of the pictures and encourage students to think about which picture best reflects the role technology plays in our lives today.
- Ask students to do the task in pairs and to use the vocabulary in *Useful Expressions* to discuss the photos and to justify their decision.
- Go round the class monitoring students to make sure they are carrying out the task properly. Don't correct any mistakes at this point, but make a note of any problems in structure or pronunciation.
- Ask each pair to tell the rest of the class which option(s) they chose and to say why.
- Write any structural mistakes made by students on the board without saying who made them, and ask them to correct them. Deal with any problems in pronunciation that came up.

Answers

Students' own answers

Ideas Focus

- Ask students to read the questions quickly and deal with any queries they may have.
- Ask students to work in pairs and to take it in turns to answer the questions.
- Go round the class monitoring students to make sure they are carrying out the task properly. Don't correct any mistakes at this point, but make a note of any problems in structure or pronunciation.

- Ask a student from each pair to answer one of the questions until each pair has had a turn. Ask the other students if they agree or if they have anything else to add.
- Write any structural mistakes made by students on the board without saying who made them, and ask them to correct them. Deal with any problems in pronunciation that came up.

Answers

Students' own answers

Writing: a nomination

- Ask students what a nomination is and why they are written. Ask if they have ever written a nomination for a competition entry before and what type of competition entry it was. If the competition entry was to nominate themselves or someone else for something, ask students what the nomination was for.
- Explain to students that in this lesson they are going to deal with writing a nomination for a competition.
- Read the *Learning Focus* on nominating someone for achievement to the students and explain anything they don't understand. Ask students what the purpose of this type of competition entry is (*to persuade the reader that their choice is best*) and what else they must include aside from their choice and a description of the person's achievements (*the reasons why they have nominated them*).

A

- Ask students to read the instructions and check that they understand what they have to do.
- Remind them that they must make notes about the achievements of a famous scientist, inventor or entrepreneur and that their choice should be someone that their classmates have probably heard of.
- Once students have made their notes, ask for a volunteer to read their notes out to the rest of the class and ask the other students to try to guess who the notes are about.
- Let as many students as possible read out their notes.

Answers

Students' own answers

B

- Ask students to read the instructions and check that they understand what they have to do.
- Ask students to read the writing task and explain anything they don't understand.
- Ask students to do the task individually, but check as a class.

Answers

1 b, d, e **2** c

C

- Ask students to read the instructions and check that they understand what they have to do.
- Then ask students to read the example competition entry and to underline any information that relates to the nominated person and the things he may have done that might make him one of the most influential people of all time. Then ask them to compare the parts of the competition entry they underlined with a partner.
- As a class, ask students if they have ever heard of the person before. Then discuss whether they agree that he is one of the most influential people of all time. Ask students to justify their answers.

Answers

Students' own answers

D

- Ask students how many things the task asks them to do (*two – look at the example competition entry again and answer the questions*).
- Read questions 1–6 to the students and explain anything they don't understand.
- Ask students to work in pairs to encourage discussion, but check as a class.

Answers

1 the writer names the nominee and gives a brief, but general, summary of his achievements, and the writer grabs the reader's attention
2 by emphasising the enormity of his accomplishment ('radically changed')
3 a list of specific, and impressive, achievements
4 it's very strong; it not only summarises the writer's view, but also makes Thales' achievements relevant to us today because without him, we would be living in a very different world
5 to avoid copying from the task input and to show a range of vocabulary; Introduction: greatest thinkers, revolutionised, laid the foundations for 1st main paragraph: founder of, father of, radically changed, 2nd main paragraph: made the first known mathematical discovery, first to notice static electricity, Final paragraph: groundbreaking, paved the way, if not for him …
6 yes; questioning, experimenting, propose theories, mathematics, geometry, calculate, discovery, theorem, static electricity, record his findings, hypotheses, scientific method, observation, scientific discovery

Eureka!

E

- Ask students to read the instructions and check that they understand what they have to do.
- Remind students that they should use their notes from A to write their short paragraph. Explain that they should use the second paragraph in the example competition entry as an example.
- Give students no more than five minutes to write their paragraph and go round the class offering help where necessary.
- Ask some students to read out their paragraphs to the rest of the class. You could hang all paragraphs on the wall and ask students to read each other's work.

Answers

Students' own answers

Teaching Tip

When students have finished their paragraphs remind them that when they have finished a piece of writing they should always proofread it to check for spelling, grammatical and punctuation errors. Ask students to swap notebooks with a partner and give them a few minutes to read and underline any mistakes they find in their partner's paragraphs. Explain that they don't have to correct them. Ask students to hand the paragraphs back and to correct any mistakes their partner has noted.

F

- Ask the students to read the information in the *Exam Close-up* and point out that the writer of the model competition entry (nomination) did all the things on the list.
- Remind students that they can use the information here as a checklist when writing their own competition entries (nomination).
- Ask students to read the *Exam Task* and ask them to underline any key words and phrases in the task. Explain anything they don't understand.
- Ask students to answer the questions in B about this task so that they know what they have to do.
- As a class, ask students what kind of person they have to nominate (*someone who has made the most important contribution to science or business in their country*) and where the best entries will be published (*in the next issue of an international magazine*).
- Ask students to read the paragraph plan and to make notes for each paragraph, if time allows.
- Set the *Exam Task* for homework.
- Encourage students to use the Writing Reference and checklist for competition entries (nomination) on page 181.

Suggested answer

Richard Branson – Best of British Business
When you hear the name Richard Branson what springs to mind? Airlines? Record Companies? Mobile Phones? Cola? Or even Space tourism. Richard Branson is regarded as one of Britain's best-known businessmen and entrepreneurs.
Branson is the founder and chairman of the Virgin Group which consists of more than 400 companies making him a billionaire and the 4th richest man in the UK according to the Forbes 2012 Rich list. His first successful business venture was in 1966, when he produced a popular Student Magazine. He then went on to open his first charity 'The Student Advisory Centre' which was also a huge success. Then, over the past forty years or so, his business ventures have got bigger and bigger.
Of his many businesses his greatest success is probably his airline, Virgin Atlantic Airways, or simply Virgin Atlantic as it's known today. Since launching in 1984, Virgin Atlantic has become the 8th largest UK airline carrying 5.3 million passengers a year. Now, his radical new venture Virgin Galactic aims to offer flights into space starting in the next few years.
Richard Branson is without a doubt one of the greatest entrepreneurs that Britain has and possibly will ever have in its history. If it wasn't for him a lot of things wouldn't be how they are today, such as the music we listen to, the charities we support, and quite possibly, in the near future, space travel.

Useful Expressions

- Read the *Useful Expressions* to the students and ask them to repeat them. Correct their pronunciation and intonation if necessary.
- Elicit in which part of their competition entry (nomination) they can use each category of expressions and tell them to use them when writing their competition entry (nomination) for the Exam Task.

 7 Lighting the Dark

General Note

Please see the information about the National Geographic videos on page 18 of this Teacher's Book.

Background Information

Suruga Bay, one of Japan's deepest bays, lies on the Pacific coast of Honshu, Japan. The Fuji, Oi and Abe Rivers all empty into the west part of the bay while the Kano River flows into a section of the bay at Numazu. In this area the water is very clear and the seabed is even and flat. Much of the coast of Suruga Bay is sandy and therefore very popular for those wanting to fish, do water sports or conduct research on the many unique deep-sea creatures that inhabit the waters of the bay.

Before you watch

A

- Explain to students that in this lesson they are going to watch a video about a special invention. Ask them to look at the globe and tell you in which part of the world the invention has been used *(Suruga Bay, Japan)*. Elicit what they know about Suruga Bay, Japan and the sea life that lives there.
- Read words 1–4 to the students and ask them to repeat them. Correct their pronunciation where necessary.
- Then ask students to read meanings a–d and explain anything they don't understand.
- Ask students to do the task individually, but check as a class.

Answers

1 c 2 d 3 a 4 b

While you watch

B

- Explain to students that they are now going to watch the video and do a task based on the information they hear.
- Ask students to read statements 1–6 and ask them what the documentary will be about *(Suruga Bay)*.
- Explain anything in the statements that the students don't understand. Then ask them to think about which ones may be true and which ones may be false before watching.
- Play the video all the way through without stopping and ask students to mark their answers. Ask students to compare their answers with a partner's and to justify any answers they have that are different. Play the video again so that they can check their answers.
- Ask students to do the task individually, but check as a class.

Answers

1 T (00:07)	4 F (01:11)
2 T (00:31)	5 T (01:31)
3 F (00:52)	6 T (01:51)

After you watch

C

- Explain to students that this is a summary of the information they heard on the video.
- Read the words in the yellow box to the students and ask them to repeat them. Ask them to write N or Adj beside each of the words depending on whether it is a noun or an adjective.
- Explain to students that they should read the whole summary before writing any answers first to work out what part of speech is missing.
- Tell students to re-read the text once they have finished to check their answers.
- Ask students to do the task individually, but check as a class.

Answers

1 situated	6 submarine
2 floor	7 images
3 depths	8 existence
4 glimpse	9 occurrence
5 victims	10 scientists

Ideas Focus

- Ask students to read the three questions and answer any queries they might have.
- Ask students to work in pairs and explain that they should both give their opinions on all three questions.
- Go round the class monitoring students to make sure they are carrying out the task properly. Don't correct any mistakes at this stage, but make a note of any problems in structure and pronunciation.
- As a class, ask each pair to answer one of the questions and repeat until each pair has had a turn.
- Write what the students think is the most important technological advance of this decade and the ways they think technology has enabled them to increase their knowledge on the board.
- Write any structural mistakes that students made on the board without saying who made them, and ask them to correct them. Deal with any problems in structure or pronunciation that came up.

Answers

Students' own answers

87

8 Money Mad

Reading: multiple-choice questions, understanding opinion & attitude
Vocabulary: money-related vocabulary, phrasal verbs, collocations & expressions, word formation
Grammar: relative clauses, participle clauses, cleft sentences
Listening: multiple-choice questions, dealing with specific questions
Speaking: talking about money, shopping, poverty, comparing photos, answering follow-up questions, linking ideas
Writing: article (1), making an article interesting, using appropriate language, engaging the reader, expressing positives & negatives, giving your opinion

Unit opener

- Ask students to look at the title of the unit and to guess what it might mean (*being obsessed with money*).
- Ask them which other words they know that can mean money mad in this context (*materialistic, money-hungry, greedy, etc.*).
- Ask students to tell the rest of the class one positive and one negative thing about being very wealthy.
- Ask students to look at the picture and read the caption. Ask them what is being depicted in the picture. Ask them how the picture corresponds to the theme of the unit (*they are both about money*).

Reading

A

- Ask students to read the instructions and make sure they understand what they have to do.
- Read the words and phrases to the students and ask them to repeat them. Correct their pronunciation where necessary.
- Ask the students to work in pairs to discuss what the words and phrases mean.
- If students are totally unfamiliar with these words, write the sentences below on the board to help them.
  - We've got no money. How about bartering? I'll give you some apples if you walk my dog.
  - My grandfather has got government bonds; when he sells them, he'll get the money he paid for them back plus interest.
  - If you go to the bank, you can convert dollars into pounds at today's exchange rate.
  - The government is giving out food vouchers to people who haven't got much money; they can be used at any supermarket.
  - In some countries, traders expect you to haggle over a price; you almost always pay less than what it says on the price tag.
  - The euro is the legal tender used in many European countries.
  - I don't have any cash on me, so I'll use my credit card – thank goodness for plastic money!
- As a class, ask each pair to give their definition of one of the words.

Answers

bartering – exchanging goods and services for other goods and services instead of paying for them with money
bond – a document containing an agreement with a government or company agreeing to pay you interest on money you have lent them
exchange rate – the price at which currencies are bought and sold for other currencies
food voucher – a ticket or coupon which can be used to buy food instead of money
haggling – negotiating a price for goods or services with the trader or provider
legal tender – official currency
plastic money – credit cards

Background Information

The Eurozone crisis is a financial crisis being suffered in many countries in Europe. It has made the repayment of debts difficult or impossible for some countries. The causes of the crisis differ according to which country is being discussed. In Greece, the crisis can be blamed somewhat on the larger global financial crisis. What this crisis meant for Greece was that its main industries went into decline, removing large amounts of money from the country's economy. In order to keep the country afloat, the government spent large amounts of money, therefore increasing the already large Greek debt.

B

- Ask students to read the title of the article and elicit how it relates to the pictures (*they are about bartering*).
- Ask students to read the instructions for B and check that they understand what they have to do. Tell them to skim read the text to find the three alternatives to the euro that are described. Remind them that they don't have to read in detail as they will have another opportunity to do that later.
- Ask students to do the task individually, but check answer as a class.
- Ask students at random round the class whether they feel that the three alternatives to the euro described in the text are a good way to deal with the financial crisis, or not. Encourage students to justify their answers.

Answers

TEM – an alternative currency used in Volos, Greece
Ovolos – an alternative currency used throughout Greece
Peliti – an organisation which uses bartering instead of money to exchange goods and services

Word Focus

- Ask students to look at the words in red in the text and to re-read the sentences they are found in.
- Ask students to work in pairs to decide what each of the words mean in the Word Focus box and to then find synonyms, if any, for each word.
- Ask students to compare their answers with another pair.

C

- Ask students to read the *Exam Close-up* and ask a student to explain what it says in his or her own words.
- Explain that it's important to underline key words or expressions when looking for sections where the writer expresses his or her opinions or the opinion of others.
- Ask students to read the instructions and items 1–7 with their options. Explain anything the students don't understand.
- Encourage students to guess the meaning of any unfamiliar words from the context before looking them up in their dictionaries. Explain any problem words and correct their pronunciation where necessary.
- Ask students to underline any key words in the items and options and to underline the parts in the text that refer to each of the items and options as they read.
- Remind students of the ways that the distractors can be wrong and stress they should be very careful when choosing their answers.
- Ask students to do the task individually, but check as a class.

Answers

1 d (*Struggling Greeks find alternatives to euro in recession-hit times*)
2 a (*… residents of the small town of Volos found themselves struggling to afford even essential items in euros, what they did was come up with an alternative currency.*)
3 c (*But it's not only at the local market that TEM is accepted. … local shops in Volos will accept both TEM and euros.*)
4 b (*This kind of exchange system is not unique to Volos. … other communities and social networks have come up with a similar system using an alternative currency called ovolos.*)
5 b (*The name is apt …*)
6 c (*…ovolos has a major advantage over the euro. … not affected by inflation or downgrading in the way the official currency is.*)
7 a (*Peliti differs from the TEM and ovolos systems as it works purely by bartering.*)

D

- Ask students to look at the phrases in the yellow box and to scan the text and options again to find and underline them. Ask them to say each of the words after you and elicit that they are all verbs. Correct their pronunciation where necessary. Stress that the verbs may be in a different form in the text and might need to be changed to fit the sentences.
- Remind them that they should always try to work out the meaning of the word from its context and ask them to read the sentences in the text and options in which each word is contained.
- Ask students to read the instructions and check that they understand what they have to do. Encourage them to read all the sentences in D once before writing any answers. Ask students to do the task individually, but check as a class.

Answers

1 gain   4 took
2 make   5 cover
3 brings   6 Opening

Ideas Focus

- Explain to students that they are going to discuss a money-related saying. Ask students to read the statement and explain anything they don't understand.
- Ask students to discuss in pairs and encourage them to draw on their personal opinions as much as possible.
- Go round the class monitoring students to ensure they are carrying out the task properly. Don't correct any mistakes at this point, but make a note of any problems in structure or pronunciation.
- Ask each pair to give their opinions.
- Write any structural mistakes made by students on the board without saying who made them, and ask them to correct them. Deal with any problems in pronunciation that came up.

Answers

Students' own answers

Vocabulary

A

- Ask students to look at the picture at the bottom of the page and ask them to describe it. Ask them if they can identify any of the legal tender shown and what country each is used in.
- Read the words in the yellow box to students and ask them to repeat them. Correct their pronunciation where necessary.
- Ask students to look at the title of the text and elicit what 'plastic' means in this context (*credit cards*). Ask them if they, or their parents, have a credit card and if so, what they tend to use it for.
- Ask students if they can think of any disadvantages of using credit cards and encourage a short class discussion on the topic.
- Ask students to do the task individually, but check as a class.

8 Money Mad

Answers

1 currency	6 coins
2 pound	7 denominations
3 circulation	8 notes
4 dollar	9 counterfeit
5 cents	10 forgeries

Extra Class Activity

You could extend this task by asking students to write a similar paragraph to the one in A about the currency used in their country.

B

- Ask students to read the instructions and check that they understand what they have to do. Ask students to read the sentences without circling any words at this stage. Explain anything they don't understand.
- Read the words in red to students and ask them to repeat them. Correct their pronunciation where necessary.
- Point out that this task tests words that are often confused so the correct answers will depend on how naturally each option fits in with the context of the sentence.
- Ask students to do the task individually, but check as a class.

Answers

1 crash	4 owe
2 shares	5 invested
3 fund	6 teller

C

- Ask students to read the instructions and check that they understand what they have to do.
- Read the words in the yellow box to students and ask them to repeat them. Correct their pronunciation where necessary.
- Ask students to look at the title of the text and elicit what 'The City' means in this context (the heart of London).
- Point out that they have to replace the words in bold in the text with synonymous words from the yellow box.
- Encourage students to read the whole text in C before trying to replace the words in bold.
- Ask students to do the task individually, but check as a class.
- Encourage students to write the synonymous words in their notebooks.

Answers

1 leading	4 bustling
2 financial	5 prosperous
3 advantageous	6 mutual

D

- Read the verbs in the yellow box to the students and ask them to repeat them. Correct their pronunciation where necessary.
- Ask students to read the instructions and check that they understand what they have to do.
- Tell students that they have to consider the meaning of the verb in the yellow box and the particle after the gap together and not just focus on the verb.
- Ask students to read the sentences on their own to work out the meaning of the missing phrasal verb. Also encourage them to underline the subject of each sentence so that they write the verbs in the correct form.
- Ask students to do the task individually, but check as a class.
- Encourage students to copy the phrasal verbs and their meanings into their notebooks.

Answers

1 splashed	4 chipped
2 lived	5 set
3 fork	6 put

E

- Write *food* and *voucher/bond* on the board and ask students which noun completes the expression (*voucher*). Remind students that in English we call this a collocation, which means when certain words are used together to form a common expression.
- Ask students to read the instructions and check that they understand what they have to do. Make sure they realise that one word in each item cannot be used to form a collocation.
- Ask students to do the task in pairs to encourage discussion, but check as a class.

Answers

1 buffalo (the correct terms are bear market – shares falling in price; bull market – shares increasing in price)
2 fluid (the correct term is liquid assets)
3 return (the correct term is tax return)
4 debt (the correct term is run up a debt; get into debt)
5 chat (the correct term is sales talk)
6 crush (the correct term is credit squeeze; credit crunch)

Extra Class Activity

If time allows, ask students to write sentences of their own using these collocations. Encourage them to use the topic vocabulary and the theme of money when they write their sentences.

F

- Read the phrases in the yellow box to the students and ask them to repeat them. Correct their pronunciation where necessary.
- Ask students to read the instructions and check that they understand what they have to do.

- Tell students that they have to consider the meaning of the phrases in the yellow box and the phrases in italics at the end of the sentences when choosing their answers.
- Ask them to read the sentences on their own to work out the meaning of the missing phrases and what form they will take.
- Ask students to do the task individually, but check as a class.

Answers

1 throws his money around
2 're/are in the money
3 throw money at
4 our money's worth
5 for my money

G

- Ask students to read the instructions and make sure they understand what they have to do.
- Read the expressions to the students and ask them to repeat them. Correct their pronunciation where necessary.
- Ask the students to work in pairs to discuss what the expressions mean.
- If students are totally unfamiliar with these expressions, write the sentences below on the board to help them.
  - If you only earn a low salary, you'll have to tighten your belt and cut down your expenses.
  - Did you know that Mr James, the bank manager, was sent to prison? I heard he was lining his pockets with money from the safe.
  - Mrs March may have lots of money but she's got deep pockets; I've never heard her offer to pay for anything in my life.
  - I travelled to Thailand on a shoestring; I may not have had much money to spend but I had the time of my life.
- As a class, ask each pair to give their definition of one of the expressions.

Answers

If you *tighten your belt*, you have to economise.
If you *line your pockets*, you earn money by using dishonest or illegal means.
If someone *has deep pockets*, they are wealthy, yet very frugal with money.
If you *do something on a shoestring*, you try to spend the absolute minimum amount of money possible on it.

H

- Ask students to read the instructions and check that they understand what they have to do.
- Read the words in capital letters to the students and ask them to repeat them. Correct their pronunciation where necessary. Ask students which part of speech each word is (*verbs: save, beg, break, withdraw; nouns: penny, economy, fraud, laundry, trade; adjectives: poor*) and which other parts of speech of these words they know.
- Ask students to read the sentences, without filling in any answers, to work out what part of speech is missing from each gap.

- Remind students to re-read the sentences once they have finished to check their answers.
- Ask students to do the task individually, but check as a class.

Answers

1 penniless
2 savings
3 beggar
4 broke
5 economical
6 poverty
7 fraudulent
8 laundering
9 withdrawal
10 traders

Ideas Focus

- Ask students to read both questions and answer any queries they might have.
- Ask students to work in pairs and explain that they should both give their opinions on each question.
- Go round the class monitoring students to make sure they are carrying out the task properly. Don't correct any mistakes at this stage, but make a note of any problems in structure and pronunciation.
- Ask various pairs to answer one of the questions.
- Write any structural mistakes that the students made on the board without saying who made them, and ask them to correct them. Deal with any problems in structure or pronunciation that came up.

Answers

Students' own answers

Grammar

- Write the sentence below on the board.
  - Kevin was the one who won the money.
- Ask students what kind of word *who* is in this sentence (*a relative pronoun*) and elicit other relative pronouns and adverbs that they know (*pronouns: who, that, which, whom, whose; adverbs: where, when, why*). Explain that in this part of the lesson, they are going to revise relative clauses.

A

- Ask students to read the instructions and check that they understand what they have to do.
- Read the information about relative clauses to the students and explain anything they don't understand.
- Ask students to do the first part of the task in pairs to encourage discussion. Check the answers to this part before moving on to the sentence completion part of the task.
- Ask students to read the sentences and to underline the words that the missing relative pronouns refer to without writing any answers at this stage.
- Remind students to re-read the sentences once they have finished to check their answers.
- Ask students to do the task individually, but check as a class.

Answers

1 who/that, who/that/-
2 whose, whom/who
3 who/that/-, which

91

8 Money Mad

B

- Ask students to read the instructions and check that they understand what they have to do.
- Read the information about defining and non-defining relative clauses to the students and explain anything they don't understand.
- Elicit from students that they will read the sentences in A again and identify which sentences contain a defining relative clause and which contain a non-defining relative clause.
- Ask students to do the task individually, but check as a class.

Answers

1. defining, defining
2. non-defining, non-defining
3. defining, non-defining

C

- Write the sentence below on the board.
  – People use their credit cards for everything, which means they often accumulate a lot of debt.
- Ask students to identify the relative pronoun in the sentence (*which*) and elicit whether it refers to a noun or a situation (*situation – people use their credit cards for everything*). Explain to students that a relative clause can qualify a whole sentence.
- Ask students to read the instructions and check that they understand what they have to do.
- Ask students to do the task individually, but check as a class.

Answer

a situation (*people not spending*)

D

- Ask students to read the instructions and check that they understand what they have to do.
- Read the two sentence stems and explain anything the students don't understand. Encourage students to look back at the sentence in C if they need help while completing the task.
- Ask students to do the task in pairs to encourage discussion, but check as a class.

Answers

Students' own answers
– Petra's purse was stolen while she was on holiday, which was quite an inconvenience.
– When Nigel retired he bought a Ferrari, which was somewhat ridiculous for a man of his age.

Be careful!

- Read the information in *Be careful!* and explain anything the students don't understand.
- Read out the three sentences and ask students to focus on the relative adverbs in bold.
- Elicit in which sentence the adverb can't be omitted (*the last sentence*).

- If time allows, ask students to write sentences of their own using the relative adverbs *where*, *why* and *when*.

Now read the Grammar Reference on pages 167 & 168 (8.1 to 8.4) with your students.

E

- Ask students to read the title of the text and to look at the picture to the right of the text. Elicit how they are related (*they both have to do with the British pound*) and ask students what they know about the origin of the pound sign.
- Ask students to read the text, without filling in any answers, to find out where the pound sign originated (*it comes from the letter L, for libra*).
- Ask students to read the instructions and check that they understand what they have to do.
- Remind students to underline the words the relative pronouns refer to before filling in their answers.
- Tell students to re-read the text once they have finished to check their answers.
- Ask students to do the task individually, but check as a class.

Answers

1. which
2. which/that
3. from
4. where
5. when/that
6. whose
7. in
8. who

F

- Read the information on participle clauses to the students and explain anything they don't understand. Elicit that there are two kinds of participles and ask students what they are (*the present participle – verb + -ing and the past participle -verb + -ed or irregular form*).
- Ask students to read the instructions and check that they understand what they have to do.
- Ask students to read the sentences and underline the participle clauses. Check answers as a class.

Answers

The participle clauses are 'Founded in **1817**', 'Holding a gun', 'Being both generous and wealthy' and 'released last month'.

G

- Ask students to answer the questions individually, but check as a class.

Answers

1. a and d have past participles, b and c have present participles
2. a the New York Stock Exchange, b a masked man, c Stavros, d the sales figures
3. a and d are passive, b and c are active
4.
   a The New York Stock exchange, <u>which was founded</u> in 1817, is located in Wall Street.
   b A masked man <u>who was holding a gun</u> walked into the bank and began shooting.
   c Stavros, <u>who is both generous and wealthy</u>, donates huge sums to charity.
   d The sales figures <u>which were released</u> last month were very good.

H

- Ask students to read the instructions and check that they understand what they have to do.
- Ask students to do the task individually, but check as a class.

Answers

1. Having mugged me, Having been stolen – perfect constructions
2. sentence a is active, sentence b is passive

I

- Read the rules to the students and explain anything they don't understand.
- Ask students to do the task individually, but check as a class.

Answers

1. present
2. past
3. perfect

J

- Read the information about cleft sentences to the students and elicit that they are used to add emphasis to a particular part of a sentence.
- Ask students to read the five sentences and find the structures which add emphasis.
- Ask students to do the task individually, but check as a class.

Answers

1. The reason (why)
2. What impressed us
3. The thing (that)
4. the year (when)
5. It was my brother who

Now read the Grammar Reference on page 168 (8.5 & 8.6) with your students.

K

- Read the verbs in the yellow box to the students and ask them to repeat them. Correct their pronunciation where necessary.
- Ask students to read the instructions and check that they understand what they have to do.
- Ask them to read the sentences on their own to decide which verb fits best in each sentence.

- Encourage students to underline the subject of each sentence and to pay attention to the verb tense in the sentence so that they write the verbs in the correct participle form.
- Ask students to do the task individually, but check as a class.

Answers

1. Introduced/Having been introduced
2. Being
3. wiped out
4. Not being/Not having been
5. restored
6. Borrowing/Having borrowed

L

- Ask students to read the instructions and check that they understand what they have to do. Point out that they may have to make other changes so that the new sentence makes sense.
- Explain to students that they have to use the words given when writing their new sentences.
- Ask students to do the task individually, but check as a class.

Answers

1. What he did was to buy stocks in FaceMask, but they fell in value.
2. It is his low-paid job that is really getting him down.
3. All you need to do is invest 10% of your salary each month.
4. It was on Monday when the fraud was discovered.
5. The thing (that) you should do first is open a bank account./The first thing you should do is open a bank account.
6. The place where they have the best prices is Woolywarts Supermarket.

Listening

A

- Ask students to read the instructions and make sure they understand what they have to do.
- Ask students to read the questions and underline the key words.
- Remind students that in multiple-choice listening tasks, the correct reply is the one that provides a logical answer to the focus of the question.
- Ask students to read the questions again and to tick their answers. Ask them to compare their answers with a partner and to justify any answers they have that are different.
- Check answers as a class and ask students to justify their answers.

8 Money Mad

Answers

1a b is wrong because it doesn't answer how much in any way. It answers a question like Where do you have a bank account?
2a b is wrong: it seems to be responding to the time (next week) rather than the question (Do you mind?).
3b a is wrong: Monday comes before Tuesday, which is what is meant by by Tuesday so it should be a yes answer rather than no.

B

- Ask students to read the instructions and make sure they understand what they have to do.
- Explain to the students that they will listen to some questions and then they have to write a suitable answer to each one.
- Play the recording once all the way through and ask students to write their answers. Ask students to compare their answers with a partner and to justify any answers they have that are different.
- Play the recording again and ask students to check their answers or to fill in any missing answers.
- Check answers as a class and ask students to justify their answers.

Suggested answers

1 I'm afraid not.
2 At Herald College.
3 Not a lot.
4 The owner's name should be on it.
5 I needed some money to pay for my new bike.
6 At the end of the month if I'm not mistaken

C

- Ask students to read the *Exam Close-up*.
- Remind students of any differences in the answers they might have had in A and B, and explain that these tasks show how important it is to choose the reply that provides a logical answer to the focus of the question in this type of listening task.
- Point out that if a question word such as *where, why, who, when, how much/many* or *what* is used in the question, they have to make sure the reply mentions *a place, the reason, a person, a date/day/time, an amount/a number* or *an object/idea* respectively. This will help them to choose the correct reply to the question.
- Ask students to read the instructions and check they understand what they have to do.
- Explain that they will hear 14 questions and that they must choose the best reply to each question.
- Give students time to read 1–14 and to underline the key words in the options. Answer any questions they might have about them.
- Play the recording once all the way through and ask students to circle their answers. Then ask students to discuss their answers with a partner and to justify any they have that are different.
- Play the recording again and ask students to check their answers and to fill in any missing answers.
- Check the answers as a class and ask students to justify their answers.

Answers

1b 2c 3a 4a 5b 6b 7c 8c 9b 10c 11a 12b 13b 14a

Speaking

A

- Ask students to read the four questions and answer any queries they may have about them.
- Ask students to work in pairs and to take it in turns to ask and answer the questions about themselves.
- Go round the class monitoring students to make sure they are carrying out the task properly. Don't correct any mistakes at this point, but make a note of any problems in structure or pronunciation.
- Ask each pair to ask and answer one question and repeat until each student has had a turn.
- Write any structural mistakes made by students on the board without saying who made them, and ask them to correct them. Deal with any problems in pronunciation that came up.

Answers

Students' own answers

B

- Ask students to read the instructions and check that they understand what they have to do.
- Read the sets of words 1–6 to the students and ask students to repeat them after you. Correct their pronunciation where necessary.
- Ask students to work in pairs to encourage discussion, but check the answers as a class. Ask students to explain why one of the words is the odd one out in each item.

Answers

1. chauffeur ('beggar' and 'down-and-out' mean someone who has very little money and may live on the streets, but a 'chauffeur' is someone whose job it is to drive other people from place to place)
2. boutique ('flea market' and 'second-hand store' refer to places where you can buy used clothes and goods, but a 'boutique' is a shop selling expensive clothes and goods)
3. budgeting ('spending spree' and 'splashing out' mean when someone spends a lot of money in a short period of time, but 'budgeting' means to keep a close eye on your finances in order to spend as little as possible)
4. have money to burn ('make ends meet' and 'be on the breadline' mean to get by on very little money, but 'have money to burn' means to have a surplus amount of money which you can spend as you wish)
5. make a living ('make a fortune' and 'make a killing' mean to earn/make a large amount of money, but 'make a living' means to work in return for a standard wage/salary)
6. down-to-earth ('extravagant' and 'lavish' mean when something is very over the top and has lots of money spent on it, but 'down-to-earth' means to be very practical and sensible)

C

- Read words 1–4 to the students and ask them to repeat them. Correct their pronunciation where necessary.
- Then ask students to read words a–d without filling in any answers at this stage.
- Ask students to do the task individually, but check as a class before asking students to write sentences using each word pair in their notebooks.
- Give students no more than five minutes to write their sentences and go round the class offering help where necessary.
- Ask some students to read out their sentences to the rest of the class. You could hang all sentences on the wall and ask students to read each other's work.

Answers

1 c 2 d 3 b 4 a
Students' own answers

D

- Ask students to read the *Exam Close-up*.
- Then ask students to quickly read the instructions for the *Exam Task* and elicit that they will have one long and one short turn and that during their short turn they will have to answer a follow-up question about their partner's photos.
- Stress that they do not have to talk about the photos that their partner chose to talk about in their long turn. Explain that they can talk about the photo that wasn't chosen if they feel it is the best answer to their short turn follow-up question.

Useful Expressions

- Read the *Useful Expressions* to the students and ask them to repeat them. Correct their pronunciation and intonation where necessary.
- Explain that these expressions are ways they can link their ideas and that they should use some of these expressions when they do the *Exam Task*.

E

- Ask students to read the instructions again and check that they understand what they have to do.
- Ask students to work in pairs and to decide who will be Student A and who will be Student B. Ask them to read the instructions for their role and to spend a few minutes looking at their own set of photos.
- Remind students that this kind of task isn't a discussion and that each student is expected to speak for one minute on his or her photos *(two photos)* or to respond briefly *(30 seconds)* to the follow-up question about his or her partner's photos.
- Ask Student A to begin answering the questions about the two photos they have chosen from the three and for Student B to answer the follow-up question once Student A has finished. Then ask Student B to answer their questions about the two photos they have chosen from the three and Student A answers their follow-up question.
- Remind students that they do not have to talk about the photos that their partner chose to talk about in their long turn. Stress that they can talk about the photo that wasn't chosen if they feel it is the best answer to the follow-up question.
- Go round the class monitoring students to make sure they are carrying out the task properly. Don't correct any mistakes at this point, but make a note of any problems in structure or pronunciation.
- Ask one pair of students to carry out the task in front of the class and ask the other students if they agree or they have anything to add.
- Write any structural mistakes made by students on the board without saying who made them, and ask them to correct them. Deal with any problems in pronunciation that came up.

Answers

Students' own answers

Ideas Focus

- Ask students to read the questions quickly and deal with any queries they may have.
- Ask students to work in pairs and to take it in turns to answer the questions.
- Go round the class monitoring students to make sure they are carrying out the task properly. Don't correct any mistakes at this point, but make a note of any problems in structure or pronunciation.
- Ask a student from each pair to answer one of the questions until each pair has had a turn. Ask other students if they agree or if they have anything else to add.
- Write any structural mistakes made by students on the board without saying who made them, and ask them to correct them. Deal with any problems in pronunciation that came up.

8 Money Mad

> **Answers**
>
> Students' own answers

Writing: an article (1)

- Ask students what an article is and where they usually appear (*magazines or newspapers*). Ask if they have ever written an article before. If so, ask them what their article was about and ask them what title they gave their article.
- Explain to students that in this lesson they are going to deal with writing articles.
- Read the *Learning Focus* about making an article interesting to the students and explain anything they don't understand. Ask students what the main purpose of an article is (*to interest and engage the reader while expressing their view on a given topic*) and what they can do to 'speak' to the reader (*ask questions*).

A

- Ask students to read the instructions and check that they understand what they have to do.
- Ask students in pairs to imagine they are going to write an article about Internet shopping and allow them time to make a list of what the advantages and disadvantages of shopping online might be in their notebooks.
- As a class, discuss the points raised by each pair and make a list on the board of suitable ideas.

> **Suggested answers**
>
> Advantages – convenience, easy price comparisons, choice, reviews, no sales pressure
> Disadvantages – can't check before purchase that the item is in working order or good condition, can't try clothes on, can't have your questions answered immediately, security risks, could be lost in the post, may have problems returning an incorrect or damaged item

B

- Ask students how many things the task asks them to do (*three – look at their list from A, choose the two advantages and two disadvantages they have the most to say about, write notes about each one to support their view*).
- Give students no more than ten minutes to write their notes and go round the class offering help where necessary.
- Ask students at random round the class to read out their notes to the rest of the class.

> **Answers**
>
> Students' own answers

C

- Ask students to read the instructions and check that they understand what they have to do.
- Ask students to read the writing task and explain anything they don't understand.
- Ask students to do the task individually, but check as a class.

> **Answers**
>
> 1 like/dislike about online shopping, explain how you think it affects conventional shops
> 2 three main paragraphs: (1) what you like about online shopping (2) what you dislike about online shopping (3) how it affects conventional shops (*there will also be an introduction and conclusion*)
> 3 target reader is a fellow reader of the magazine; semi-formal, slightly chatty style

D

- Ask students to read the instructions and check that they understand what they have to do.
- Ask students to read the example article and to underline the information that relates to the advantages and disadvantages that the writer has chosen to focus on. Then ask them to compare the parts they underlined with a partner.
- As a class, ask students if the writer has fully supported the advantages and disadvantages that they chose to focus on. Then discuss how the writer did this. Ask students to justify their answers.

> **Answers**
>
> Yes, the writer has fully supported the advantages and disadvantages by expanding on the points and providing examples.

E

- Ask students to read the instructions and check that they understand what they have to do.
- Ask students to read the example article again and to underline the topic sentences in the three main paragraphs. Then ask them to compare the parts they underlined with a partner.
- As a class, ask students if they are good topic sentences (*yes*). Then discuss why they are good topic sentences (*because they give a clear idea about the type of information that is to follow in that paragraph*). Ask students to justify their answers.

Answers

The topic sentences are:
- Nothing beats the Internet for convenience and choice.
- Internet shopping sounds ideal, but it has some major minuses too.
- Internet shopping is causing headaches for shop owners too.

Yes, they are good topic sentences because they inform the reader fully about what information will follow.

F

- Ask students to read the instructions and check that they understand what they have to do.
- Ask students how many things the task asks them to do (two – look at the notes they made in B on the two advantages and two disadvantages they have the most to say about, use the notes to write two topic sentences for an article).
- Give students no more than five minutes to write their topic sentences and go round the class offering help where necessary.
- Ask some students to read out their topic sentences to the rest of the class. Correct where necessary.

Answers

Students' own answers

G

- Ask students to read the instructions and check that they understand what they have to do.
- Ask students to read the example article and to underline the instances where the writer directly addresses the reader. Then ask them to compare the parts they underlined with a partner.
- As a class, elicit what grammatical form they take.

Answers

- Imagine how useful this is for busy people or those who are house-bound.
- What if the jeans you bought don't fit or are damaged?
- Worse still, what if the site you purchased from is a fake?
- … how much will our need for convenience cost us in the end?

The first is an imperative and the others are direct questions.

H

- Ask the students to read the Exam Close-up and point out that the writer of the example article did all the things on the list.
- Remind students that they can use the information here as a checklist when writing their own articles.
- Ask students to read the Exam Task and ask them to underline any key words and phrases in the task. Explain anything they don't understand.
- Ask students to answer the questions in C about this writing task so that they will know what they have to do.

- As a class, ask students what the topic of their article will be (the popularity of malls) and where their article will be published if it is chosen as one of the most interesting (in an English-language magazine).
- Ask students to read the paragraph plan and ask them to make notes for each paragraph if time allows. Ask them how many paragraphs their article will contain (five).
- Set the Exam Task for homework.
- Encourage students to use the Writing Reference and checklist for articles on page 182.

Suggested answers

The rise of the shopping mall … convenient or catastrophe?

When was the last time you popped round the corner to the butcher's, greengrocers or bought a dress from the high street? Can you remember? These days more and more people are shopping at malls which has caused local shops to suffer. Small business owners are understandably concerned about what the future may hold.

Nothing beats being able to go shopping and buy everything you need in one place, as many people find it tiresome going from shop to shop for hours on end. You also aren't affected by the weather as you park your car and then are sheltered as you browse. Also, the shops in malls are much bigger than local shops, which means there is more choice on offer.

Shopping in malls may sound ideal, but it does have its drawbacks. For example, malls are often a victim of their own success. By this I mean, you often have to queue for a long time for a space in the car park, which puts people off going to them.

Malls are causing a big headache for local shop owners too. They are unable to offer such a wide variety of products so people are often left disappointed when they visit. They also have trouble competing pricewise with malls as they sell less on the whole.

Despite the possible drawbacks of shopping in malls I would have to say that they are very convenient and fit in well with peoples' fast-paced modern lifestyles. That's probably why they are so popular.

Useful Expressions

- Read the Useful Expressions to the students and ask them to repeat them. Correct their pronunciation and intonation if necessary.
- Ask them to circle the words and phrases from the list that are used in the example article (Nothing beats …, Imagine …, sounds ideal …, is a serious drawback …, can be a headache …, I believe …)
- Elicit in which part of their article they can use each category of expressions. Tell them to use them when writing their article in the Exam Task, but that they should be careful not to overuse them.

8 Art of the Deal

General Note

Please see the information about the National Geographic videos on page 18 of this Teacher's Book.

Background Information

Souks, a kind of market, are an important part of life in Morocco. Most towns have a special section where there are weekly or daily souks and in the countryside there is a souk on a different day in the different villages of the area. Almost anything from leather goods to pets to clothing to food can be bought at these markets. It is common for customers to haggle over prices with the vendors who run the stalls until both parties can agree on a price for what is being purchased.

Before you watch

A

- Explain to students that in this lesson they are going to watch a video about a special way to shop in a market, called a souk. Ask them to look at the globe and tell you in which part of the world souks are located. Elicit what they know about Fes, Morocco and ask them to guess what kind of products can be bought in the souks there.
- Read words 1–4 to the students and ask them to repeat them. Then ask students to read meanings a–d and explain anything they don't understand.
- Ask students to do the task individually, but check as a class.

Answers

1 c   2 a   3 d   4 b

While you watch

B

- Explain to students that they are now going to watch the video and do a task based on the information they hear.
- Ask students to read sentences 1–6 and ask them what they think the documentary will be about (how shopping is conducted in souks).
- Explain anything in the sentences that the students don't understand. Then ask them to think about which words may be correct before watching.
- Play the video all the way through without stopping and ask students to circle their answers. Ask students to compare their answers with a partner's and to justify any answers they have that are different. Play the video again so that they can check their answers.
- Ask students to do the task individually, but check as a class.

Answers

1 oldest	(00:09)	4 carpet	(02:35)
2 bargaining	(01:07)	5 enjoy	(03:17)
3 cheat	(02:20)	6 make	(03:56)

After you watch

C

- Explain to students that this is a summary of the information they heard on the video.
- Read the words in the yellow box to the students and ask them to repeat them. Ask them to write N, V, Adj or Det beside each of the words depending on whether it is a noun, a verb, an adjective or a determiner.
- Explain to students that they should read the whole summary before writing any answers first to work out what part of speech is missing.
- Tell students to re-read the text once they have finished to check their answers.
- Ask students to do the task individually, but check as a class.

Answers

1 deals	6 thirty
2 shopper	7 pressure
3 jewellery	8 bargain
4 city	9 sixth
5 fixed	10 more

Ideas Focus

- Ask students to read the instructions and make sure they understand what they have to do. Then ask them to read the three questions and answer any queries they might have.
- Ask students to work in pairs and explain that they should both give their opinions on all three questions.
- Go round the class monitoring students to make sure they are carrying out the task properly. Don't correct any mistakes at this stage, but make a note of any problems in structure and pronunciation.
- Ask each pair to answer one of the questions and repeat until each pair has had a turn.
- Write about whether online auctions are a good way of shopping and what the advantages and disadvantages of fixed prices are on the board.
- Deal with any problems in structure or pronunciation that came up.

Answers

Students' own answers

Review 4

Units 7 & 8

Objectives
- To revise vocabulary and grammar from Units 7 and 8
- To practise exam-type tasks

Revision
- Explain to students that Review 4 revises the material they saw in Units 7 and 8.
- Remind students that they can ask you for help with the exercises or look back at the units if they need help with an answer. Stress that the review is not a test.
- Decide how you will carry out the review. You could ask students to do one task at a time and then correct it immediately, or ask students to do all the tasks and correct them together at the end. If you do all the tasks together, let students know every now and again how much time they have got left to finish.
- Ask students not to leave any answers blank and to try to find any answers they don't know in the units.
- When checking students' answers to the review tasks, make a note of any problem areas in vocabulary and grammar that they still have. Try to do extra work on these areas so that your students will progress well.

Vocabulary Revision
- Ask students to explain the difference between the following pairs of words: *displaced/replaced, conductors/monitors, components/elements, anomaly/ phenomenon, corrode/erode, bombs/explosives, expands/extends, liquefied/molten*.
- Play a word association game with vocabulary from Unit 7. Say one word related to computers and ask each student in turn to say another word which they associate with the previous word, for example, *laser – printer*.
- Say the words *market, money, a bank, make a, sales* and *credit* one by one to the students and ask them for words that collocate with each one.
- Write these words on the board and ask students what part of speech they are: *prosper (v), economy (n), penny (n), poor (adj), invest (v), speculate (v), fund (n, v), save (v), finance (n, v)* and *industry (n)*. Ask students to write down any other parts of speech of these words that they know. Make sure they revise the parts that they will need to complete 2 (Part 3).

Grammar Revision
- Ask students the questions below at random round the class. Then revise all forms of the conditional that they learnt in Unit 7.
    - What would you do if you discovered a star that nobody had seen before?
    - What happens if you boil water?
    - What will you learn about if you study science?
    - What would life have been like if cars hadn't been invented?
    - What would have happened if Alexander Graham Bell had never been born?
    - What activities would you be involved with if you had made the debate team?

- Ask students to write conditional sentences of their own using the words: *provided, as long as, supposing, but for, unless* and *otherwise*.
- Ask students to write sentences of their own using *I wish* and *If only*. Revise the meaning of these phrases and the various structures that they are followed by that students learnt about in Unit 7. Encourage students to write sentences about technology and inventions, or money.
- Write these sentences on the board and ask students to find and correct the mistakes.
    - No sooner than had he won the money, he spent it all. *(No sooner had he won the money than he spent it all.)*
    - Under any circumstances must you bother the inventor when she is working. *(Under no circumstances must you bother the inventor when she is working.)*
    - Then only did Edison realise that he had invented something that would change the world. *(Only then did Edison realise that he had invented something that would change the world.)*
    - Seldom I have seen a house with such beautiful furnishings. *(Seldom have I seen a house with such beautiful furnishings.)*
    - You can find nowhere such a fine collection of coins as the one at the local museum. *(Nowhere can you find such a fine collection of coins as the one at the local museum.)*
- Write these sentences on the board and ask students to correct them.
    - That is the mansion when the millionaire lives. *(where not when)*
    - That's the woman what invented a solar car. *(who/that not what)*
    - The banker, that used to be a lawyer, is a very clever person. *(who not that)*
- Revise the rules about relative clauses that students learnt in Unit 8 and ask them to write sentences of their own using relative pronouns and adverbs. Make sure that they remember when we can use *that* instead of *who* or *which* and when we can omit the relative pronoun or adverb.
- Write these sentences on the board and ask students to rewrite them using participle clauses.
    - The scientist, who was working in his lab, yelled loudly at the technician. *(Working in his lab, the scientist yelled loudly at the technician.)*
    - The bank manager was locked in the vault and started to panic. *(Locked in the vault, the bank manager started to panic.)*
    - The money which was stolen last week has been returned to its owners. *(The money stolen last week has been returned to its owners.)*
    - People who do their best always get ahead. *(People doing their best always get ahead.)*

- Write these sentences on the board and ask students to find the structures which add emphasis. Revise the other structures that can add emphasis that students learnt about in Unit 8.
  - It was the thief who took the painting. *(It was)*
  - The thing she doesn't understand is that she will have to pay the money back. *(The thing /is)*

A

- Ask students to read the instructions and check that they understand what they have to do.
- Ask students to read the title of the text and ask them what they think it will be about. Then ask them to skim read the text, without circling any answers, to find out who *Archimedes* was *(a mathematician and inventor)*.
- Point out to students that they should read all four options for each item before deciding which word best fits each gap. Remind them to pay attention to the whole sentence each gap is in as the general context will help them understand what word is missing.
- Remind students to re-read the text once they have finished to check their answers.

Answers

1 B	5 A	9 A
2 A	6 B	10 C
3 D	7 D	11 B
4 C	8 C	12 D

B

- Ask students to read the instructions and check that they understand what they have to do.
- Ask students to read the title of the text and ask them what it might mean. Ask students to skim read the text, without filling in any answers, to find out when the *Great Depression* started *(October 1929)*. Ask students if anything like that has ever happened in their country and if it did, ask them how it affected their country.
- Read the words at the side of the text to the students and ask them to repeat them. Correct their pronunciation where necessary.
- Ask students to re-read the text and to decide which part of speech is missing from each gap, and to complete the gaps using the correct form of the words given.
- Remind students to re-read the text once they have finished to check their answers.

Answers

13 prosperous	18 Speculation
14 economic	19 funds
15 penniless	20 savings
16 poverty	21 financial
17 investment	22 industrialised

C

- Ask students to read the instructions and check that they understand what they have to do.
- Encourage students to read all three sentences before filling in any answers.
- Explain to students that the missing word in each set of sentences will be a fairly common one and that students should not spend time trying to find overly-difficult words.
- Tell students that the missing word in each set of sentences will be the same part of speech and that the word will have a different meaning in each sentence.
- Remind students to re-read the sentences once they have finished to check their answers.

Answers

23 raise	26 pockets
24 bank	27 easy
25 ahead	

D

- Ask students to read the instructions and check that they understand what they have to do.
- Ask students to read both sentences in each item and to underline the information in the first sentence that is missing from the second sentence. Then ask them to look at the word given to decide how the missing information could be inserted into the second sentence using this word.
- Remind students that they will have to use a different structure in order to keep the meaning the same.
- Stress that they mustn't change the word given in bold in any way.
- Encourage students to re-read the sentences once they have finished to check their answers.

Answers

28 not until 1941 did
29 we got our wires crossed
30 being (both) trustworthy and reliable
31 we hadn't invested
32 if only you had told
33 if they had seen the proof/had they seen the proof
34 what concerned me was/what caused me concern was

9 All That Jazz!

Reading:	multiple-matching, understanding the overall message
Vocabulary:	music- and art-related vocabulary, compound nouns, prepositions, collocations & expressions
Grammar:	comparison of adjectives & adverbs, other ways of comparing, qualifiers, *too* & *enough*, *so*, *such*
Listening:	multiple-choice questions, listening again
Speaking:	talking about art and artists, decision making, speculating, evaluating & negotiating
Writing:	report, recognising the purpose of a report, structuring a report, introducing positives & negatives, making recommendations

Unit opener

- Ask students to look at the title of the unit and to guess what it might mean (*everything else related to a subject, or other similar things OR it could be referring to the song or the film of the same name*).
- Ask students to look at the picture and to read the caption. Ask them to say how the picture might relate to the unit (*the picture is of an electronic music concert*).
- Ask students to tell the rest of the class how the picture makes them feel and why.

Reading

A

- Ask students to look at the picture in the top right-hand corner of page 110 and to say what the man is doing and what he is in holding. If they mention the theatre or Shakespeare, ask them what they know about them and how they might be linked to the theme of the unit.
- Ask students to read the instructions for A and check that they know what they have to do.
- Ask students to work in pairs to encourage discussion, but don't check their answers yet.

B

- Ask students to look at the pictures contained in the leaflet and ask them what the pictures have in common (*they show outdoor performances*).
- Ask students to read the title of the leaflet and elicit how it relates to the picture (*it could be referring to a cultural event where people have a great time or a free cultural event*).
- Ask students to read the instructions for B and check that they understand what they have to do. Tell them to skim read the text to find relevant information about the statements in A. Explain that they should only concentrate on these details as they will have another opportunity to read the text in full later.
- Ask students to do the task individually, but check answer as a class.
- Ask students which information surprised them the most and why.

- If students seem interested, you might like to give them more information about Shakespeare using the Background Information box below.

Answers

1F 2T 3F 4T

Background Information

William Shakespeare was born in 1564, in Stratford-upon-Avon and died on April 23 1616. In November 1582, Shakespeare married a woman named, Anne Hathaway when he was eighteen and she was 26. They had three children together. Shakespeare was a playwright; as well as an actor who performed on stage in London, England. Shakespeare is buried in Holy Trinity Church in Stratford, England.

Word Focus

- Ask students to look at the words in red in the text and to re-read the sentences they are found in. Ask students to work in pairs to decide what each of the words means in the *Word Focus* box and to then find synonyms, if any, for each word.
- Ask students to compare their answers with another pair.

C

- Ask students to read the *Exam Close-up*, and check that they understand what it means.
- Explain to students that the task here is multiple matching and that they should answer A, B, C, D, E or F to indicate in which part of the leaflet they found the information.
- Ask students to read the questions before reading the text again so that they know what information to look out for.
- Encourage students to guess the meaning of any unfamiliar words from the context before looking them up in their dictionaries. Explain any problem words and correct their pronunciation where necessary.
- Ask students to read the text again and to underline any information related to the questions while reading.
- Ask students to do the task individually, but check as a class.

9 All That Jazz!

Answers

1A (*Obtain your tickets early to avoid disappointment.*)
2E (*Plays are held in a historic fire station in Minneapolis ...*)
3F (*... project is the result of the combined efforts of deprived inner-city youth and local theatre professionals.*)
4D (*... with an incredible seven performances a day ...*)
5D (*... treat yourself to one of the tastiest hot dogs you've ever tried, ...*)
6C (*Since 1923, the Miller has been running ... free performances ...*)
7C (*Come to Hermann Park's open air theatre.*)
8D (*Children's classic Hansel and Gretel will keep even the most demanding youngsters amused.*)
9A (*Shakespeare in the Park; New York July 23 to August 25*)
10E (*... but the cast also take the play on tour ...*)
11B (*... started out as a three-city pilot project ... soon mushroomed into a monster event.*)
12B (*... 1,800 performances in 19 states.*)
13E (*Each play is specially written for the event ...*)
14C (*... making it one of a kind in the US.*)
15F (*... that build their confidence and stimulate their intellect and imagination.*)

D

- Ask students to look at the words in the yellow box and to scan the text again to find and underline them. Ask them to say each of the words after you and elicit that they are all verbs. Correct their pronunciation where necessary.
- Remind them that they should always try to work out the meaning of the phrase from its context and ask them to read the sentences in the text in which each word is contained.
- Ask students to read the instructions and check that they understand what they have to do.
- Encourage them to read all the definitions in D once before writing any answers. Ask students to do the task individually, but check as a class.

Answers

1 exceed   4 culminate
2 erase   5 endeavour
3 stimulate

Ideas Focus

- Explain to students that they are going to answer the questions about the theatre.
- Ask students to answer the questions in pairs.
- Ask one student from each group to give their answers to one of the questions.

Answers

Students' own answers

Vocabulary

A

- Ask students to read the instructions and check that they understand what they have to do.
- Read the words in the yellow box to students and ask them to say them after you. Correct their pronunciation where necessary.
- Ask students to read all the sentences first to try to work out the meaning of the missing word.
- Remind students to re-read the sentences once they have finished to check their answers.
- Ask students to do the task individually, but check as a class.

Answers

1 single   4 downloads
2 pianist   5 chart
3 label   6 decibels

B

- Ask students to read the instructions and check that they understand what they have to do. Ask students to read the sentences without circling any words at this stage. Explain anything they don't understand.
- Read the words in red to students and ask them to repeat them. Correct their pronunciation where necessary. Point out that the task tests words that are often confused so the correct answers will depend on how naturally each option fits in with the context of the sentence.
- Ask students to do the task individually, but check as a class.

Answers

1 lyrics   4 beats
2 set   5 read
3 tastes   6 copies

C

- Ask students to read the instructions and check that they understand what they have to do.
- Read the sets of words 1–8 to the students and ask students to repeat them after you. Correct their pronunciation where necessary.
- Ask students to work in pairs to encourage discussion, but check the answers as a class. Ask students to explain why one of the words is the odd one out in each item.

Answers

1 stroke (*The others are ways of describing colours, but 'stroke' describes a particular method of using a brush or the mark that the brush makes.*)
2 carving (*The others are different words for creating drawings, but 'carving' means to cut or chip at wood, stone, etc. to form something.*)
3 clay (*The others are all things you need to paint a picture, but 'clay' is a material; made of earth that is soft when wet and hard when baked.*)
4 plaster (*The others are all types of paint, but 'plaster' is a paste which people put on walls and ceilings so that they look smooth.*)
5 auction (*The others are all words for artwork that's not authentic, but an 'auction' is a place where artwork is bought and sold.*)
6 fresco (*The others are different styles/types of paintings, but a 'fresco' is a wall painting.*)

D

- Ask students to look at the pictures either side of the text in D and to describe what they can see and what kind of art it might be (*pop art*). Encourage a short class discussion about pop art by asking students what they know about the movement and its artists.
- Ask students to read the instructions and check that they understand what they have to do.
- Read the words in the yellow box to students and ask them to repeat them. Correct their pronunciation where necessary.
- Ask students to read all the sentences first to work out the meaning of the missing word.
- Remind students to re-read the sentences once they have finished to check their answers.
- Ask students to do the task individually, but check as a class.

Answers

1 movement   4 controversy
2 concept   5 subjects
3 exhibition   6 commissions
The artist is Andy Warhol

Extra Class Activity

Ask students to write a text like the one in D about an artist from their own country. When they have finished ask students to read out their texts and encourage the others to guess who is being written about.

E

- Read the words in red to students and ask them to repeat them. Correct their pronunciation where necessary.
- Ask students to read the instructions and check that they understand what they have to do.
- Ask them to read all the sentences for meaning and underline the words that come after the red words. Explain that the correct word in each case can form a compound noun with these words.
- Remind students to re-read the sentences once they have finished to check their answers.
- Ask students to do the task individually, but check as a class.
- Encourage students to copy the compound nouns and their meanings into their notebooks.

Answers

1 highest   5 cover
2 backing   6 opening
3 lead   7 mainstream
4 performing   8 debut

Extra Class Activity

To extend this task ask students to write sentences of their own using the compound nouns from E in their notebooks. If time allows, ask students to read out a couple of their sentences to the rest of the class.

F

- Read the prepositions in the yellow box to the students and explain that they will use these to complete the sentences. Point out that they should use each preposition twice.
- Ask students to read the sentences carefully and to pay attention to the words before or after the gap and to try to think of a preposition which follows or precedes the words without filling in any answers at this stage.
- Ask students to do the task individually, but check as a class.

Answers

1 on   5 in
2 in   6 on
3 by   7 under
4 under   8 by

Teaching Tip

Point out to students that dependent prepositions must be memorised. Encourage them to copy the prepositional phrases into their vocabulary notebook and to study them for homework. In the next lesson, give students a quick quiz based on the phrases featured in F.

G

- Ask students to read the instructions and check that they understand what they have to do.
- Ask students to read the sentences without filling in any answers at this stage.
- Read the words in the yellow box to the students and ask them to repeat them. Correct their pronunciation where necessary. Point out that the task tests collocations and expressions so the correct answers will depend on how naturally each option goes with the word or phrase that comes before the gap.
- Ask students to do the task individually, but check as a class.

Answers

1 tune   5 trumpet
2 music   6 canary
3 song   7 praises
4 ears   8 dance

9 All That Jazz!

H

- Elicit from the class who their favourite girl or boy band is. Explain to students that they are going to have the opportunity to create a new girl or boy band of their own.
- Ask students to read the instructions and check that they understand what they have to do.
- Ask students to work in pairs to come up with an idea for a new girl or boy band and give them time to discuss the various aspects of the band (*name, number of members, style of music the band will sing/play, etc*).
- Go round the class monitoring students to make sure they are carrying out the task properly. Don't correct any mistakes at this stage, but make a note of any problems in structure or pronunciation.
- Ask each pair to tell the rest of the class about their new girl or boy band and give them time to describe the various aspects of their band. After all the pairs have described their bands you could do a class survey to see which band is the most popular. Write the names of the bands on the board and then call out the names and ask students to vote for their favourite.
- Write any structural mistakes made by students on the board without saying who made them, and ask them to correct them. Deal with any problems in pronunciation that came up.

Answers
Students' own answers

Grammar

- Ask students to look back at the extracts in the Reading text on pages 110 and 111 to find examples of comparative and superlative adjectives and adverbs (*B: one of the greatest events of the year; C: move closer; D: bigger and better than ever, most famous works, most distinguished theatre groups, the most demanding youngsters, one of the tastiest hot dogs you've ever tried; F: the most inspiring elements*).
- Ask students why the writer has included so many of these forms in the extracts (*they are all advertisements whose purpose is to attract people to go to these events, so comparatives and superlatives have been used to make the events sound more appealing to theatre-goers*).

A

- Ask students to read the instructions and check that they understand what they have to do.
- Ask students to read sentences 1–6 and to focus on the words in bold in each sentence.
- Ask students to do the task individually, but check as a class.

Answers
Comparatives: nicer than, less talented than, more loudly, the longer ... the less likely
Superlatives: the greatest, the most incredible

B

- Ask students to read the instructions and check that they understand what they have to do. Read out the information about other ways of comparing and explain anything they don't understand.
- Ask students to read sentences 1–8 and to underline the structures used for comparisons.
- Ask students to do the task individually, but check as a class.

Answers
1 as good as
2 as normal a life as
3 not as good a director as
4 not such a popular singer as
5 as much (money) as
6 as many paintings as
7 As few as
8 not so interesting as

Be careful!

- Read the *Be careful!* information to the class and explain anything they don't understand.
- Ask students to write sentences of their own using the comparison structures in the sentences on the theme of music.

C

- Write the sentences below on the board and ask students to find and correct the mistakes. Elicit why the words are wrong (*they've been collocated with the wrong kind of adjective*).
  - The music is sort of loud; I can't hear a word you're saying! (*sort of; the correct word is 'rather' or 'very'*)
  - Jazz is quite more enjoyable than rock if you ask me. (*quite; the correct word is 'a great deal' or 'far', etc*)
- Read the information on qualifiers to the students and explain anything they don't understand.
- Ask students to read the instructions and check that they understand what they have to do.
- Ask students to do the task individually, but check as a class.
- Once the answers have been checked, ask students to work in pairs to think of other qualifiers.
- As a class, ask each pair of students to call out a qualifier they found and write it on the board. Repeat until all the pairs have called out their qualifiers. The pair with the most qualifiers on the board wins.

Answers
1 a great deal
2 a bit

Now read the Grammar Reference on page 168 (9.1 to 9.3) with your students.

D

- Ask students to look at the title of the text and the picture. Then ask them what the text might be about (*a music festival*). Ask students how the people in the picture are probably feeling.

104

- Ask students to read the instructions and check that they understand what they have to do. Then ask them to read the words in the yellow box.
- Ask students to read the text all the way through without filling in any answers at this stage. Ask students to think about which word might fill each gap and to look for clues in the surrounding sentences as to which form of the word they should use.
- Remind students to re-read the text once they have finished to check their answers.
- Ask students to do the task individually, but check as a class.

Answers

1	the most famous	6	better
2	as little as	7	more popular than
3	smaller	8	more expensive
4	as many as	9	wettest
5	longer	10	most dramatic

- Write the sentences below on the board and elicit which one they have seen before and where (*the first one, in the Reading texts on pages 110 and 111 about theatre*). Ask students to complete each sentence using *too*, *enough*, *so* or *such*.
  - In Texas, there's no such thing as _____ much fun. (*too*).
  - There is _____ little money in the budget this year that we can't afford to buy instruments for the school band. (*so*).
  - The guitar player wasn't loud _____ for us to hear him. (*enough*).
  - The play was _____ a big hit that it will be performed on Broadway next year! (*such*).
- Explain to students that in this lesson they will revise *too* & *enough* and *so* & *such*.

E

- Ask students to read the instructions and check that they understand what they have to do.
- Ask students to read the sentences and focus on the words in bold before moving on to fill in the rules below.
- Ask students when we usually use *too* (*to show that something is more than we want or need*) and *enough* (*to show that something isn't as much as we want or need*).
- Ask students to read the rules carefully and to refer back to the sentences before writing their answers.
- Ask students to do the task individually, but check as a class.

Answers

1	nouns	3	too
2	enough	4	for

F

- Ask students to read the instructions and check that they understand what they have to do.
- Ask students to read the sentences and focus on the words in bold before moving on to fill in the rules below.
- Ask students to read the rules carefully and to refer back to the sentences before writing their answers.
- Ask students to do the task individually, but check as a class.

Answers

1	that	4	much
2	many	5	little
3	few	6	so

G

- Ask students to read the instructions and check that they understand what they have to do.
- Ask students to read the sentences and focus on the words in bold before moving on to fill in the rules.
- Ask students to read the rules carefully and to refer back to the sentences before writing their answers.
- Ask students to do the task individually, but check as a class.

Answers

1	adjective
2	noun

Now read the Grammar Reference on pages 168 & 169 (9.4 & 9.5) with your students.

H

- Ask students to read the instructions and check that they understand what they have to do. Explain that they mustn't change the word in bold in any way when completing the second sentence.
- Ask students to read the two sentences in item 1. Then ask them to underline the part in the first sentence that is missing from the second sentence. Explain to students that in order to complete the second sentence they will have to make a structural change.
- Ask students to complete the first item and correct it before they move on to do the rest of the task.
- Ask students to do the task individually, but check as a class.

Answers

1	the public response was such
2	too intellectual a play
3	interesting enough to catch
4	so famous as to have
5	so beautifully made that
6	too big to fail

9 All That Jazz!

Listening

Background Information

Andy Warhol – see text in task D, page 112 of the Student's Book.

Gustav Klimt – a 19th-century artist born in Austria in 1862. He is known for the highly decorative style of his works, which were seen as a rebellion against the traditional academic art of his time. Once a famed Naturalist painter, he turned to the Art Noveau style when he was at the height of his career. His most famous painting is *The Kiss*.

Pablo Picasso – a 20th-century Spanish painter and sculptor born in Malaga in 1881. He is best known for co-founding the Cubist movement and for the wide variety of styles he used in his works. Among his most famous paintings are *Les Demoiselles d'Avignon* and *Guernica*.

A

- Ask students to work in pairs to describe the picture on page 116. Also ask them to guess what kind of style it is (cubism).
- Ask students for their opinion on the picture, and styles of painting in general.
- Ask students to read the instructions and make sure they understand what they have to do.
- Ask students to do the task in pairs. Check answers as a class. Use the background information if students don't have much knowledge on the painters.

Answers

Andy Warhol - Pop art
Gustav Klint - Art Nouveau
Pablo Picasso - Cubism
Students' own answers

Teaching Tip

You could expand this task further by asking students to tell a partner about an art gallery they have been to. In pairs, ask students to discuss what kind of gallery it was and whether it had any examples of art nouveau, pop art or cubism in it.

B

- Explain that students will hear two people talking about funny art stories. Ask students to read the instructions and make sure they understand what they have to do.
- Ask students to read the questions and underline any key words.
- Remind students that in multiple-choice listening tasks, ideas are often paraphrased and that it is a good idea to get into the habit of reading the questions before listening and to think of other words and phrases that they might hear on the recording.
- Play the recording once all the way through and ask students to write down their answers. Ask students to compare their answers with a partner and to justify any answers they have that are different.
- Play the recording again to check their answers or complete any missing answers.
- Check answers as a class and ask students to justify their answers using the words and expressions they heard on the recording.

Answers

1 five paintings
2 he found an Andy Warhol sketch behind it
3 whether the story is true or not
4 because he asked a famous artist to sign a sketch he had done, which would make it very valuable

C

- Ask students to read the instructions and make sure they understand what they have to do.
- Explain that students will hear the same conversation again.
- Ask students to read the questions and the options and to underline any key words.
- Point out to students that when they listen to a recording for a multiple-choice listening task for the first time, that it is a good idea to get into the habit of trying to answer the questions in their own words and to make notes at the side of each question.
- Play the recording all the way through and ask students to make notes and circle their answers. Then ask students to discuss their notes with a partner and to justify any answers they have that are different.
- Play the recording again and ask students to check why the options, other than the option they chose, are incorrect.
- Check the answers as a class and ask students in pairs to discuss why the other options were incorrect. Ask students to justify their answers using the notes they made as well as the words and expressions they heard on the recording.

Answers

1 c 2 c 3 a 4 c

D

- Ask students to read the *Exam Close-up*.
- Remind students of any differences in any answers they might have had in C and explain that this task shows how important it is to make notes at the side of each question in this type of listening task.
- Point out that they should then choose the option that is closest to their own answer.
- Stress that students should use the second listening to check that the other options are incorrect.
- Ask students to look at the *Exam Task* and underline any key words.

E

- Ask students to read the instructions and check they understand what they have to do.
- Elicit that the interview topic is lost works of art.
- Give students time to read questions 1–6 and their options carefully. Remind them to underline any key words and phrases. Explain anything they don't understand.

- Play the recording once all the way through and ask students to make notes and circle their answers. Then ask students to discuss their notes with a partner and to justify any answers they have that are different.

F
- Play the recording again and ask students to check why the options, other than the option they chose, are incorrect.
- Check the answers as a class and ask students to justify their answers using the notes they made as well as the words and expressions they heard on the recording.

Answers

1c 2a 3d 4a 5b 6c

Speaking

A
- Ask students to read the three questions and answer any queries they may have about them.
- Ask students to work in pairs and to take it in turns to ask and answer the questions about themselves.
- Go round the class monitoring students to make sure they are carrying out the task properly. Don't correct any mistakes at this point, but make a note of any problems in structure or pronunciation.
- Ask each pair to ask and answer one question and repeat until each student has had a turn.
- Write any structural mistakes made by students on the board without saying who made them, and ask them to correct them. Deal with any problems in pronunciation that came up.

Answers

Students' own answers

B
- Ask students to read the instructions and check that they understand what they have to do.
- Read the word pairs to the students and ask them to repeat them. Correct their pronunciation where necessary.
- Ask the students to work in pairs to discuss what the words in each pair mean.
- Go round the class monitoring students to make sure they are carrying out the task properly. Don't correct any mistakes at this point, but make a note of any problems in structure or pronunciation.
- Ask each pair to explain the difference between the words in the pairs until each pair has had a turn. Ask the others if they agree with what was said or if they have anything else to add.
- Write any structural mistakes made by students on the board without saying who made them, and ask them to correct them. Deal with any problems in pronunciation that came up.

Answers

- A *graphic artist* creates illustrations, pictures on a computer or digital pad. A *graffiti artist* uses spray paint to paint walls in urban areas.
- *Handicrafts* are cheap objects made by hand which people buy and sell. *Objects of art* (or *objet d'art*) are usually expensive pieces of art like sculptures and paintings created by established artists.
- A *street artist* is someone who creates works of art in the street. A *performance* (or *performing*) *artist* is someone who uses their body as an art form e.g. dancers, actors, mime artists, human statues.
- A *wall mural* is a large painting covering a wall for decorative purposes. A *sculpted wall* is one that has been made in an unusual way to resemble a work of art.

C
- Ask students to read the *Exam Close-up*.
- Ask them to quickly read the instructions in the *Exam Task* and elicit that students will have to do a number of things ranging from speculating, to evaluating and negotiating.
- Point out that in this task type, they must use appropriate structures during each stage.
- Ask students to read the instructions again and then ask them how many things they have to do here (*two*) and what they are (*talk about the kind of art each photo shows and decide which picture best portrays art in modern society*).
- As a class, elicit what kind of art is shown in each of the pictures and encourage students to think about which picture best portrays art in modern society.
- Ask students to do the task in pairs and to use the structures in *Useful Expressions* when evaluating and negotiating.
- Go round the class monitoring students to make sure they are carrying out the task properly. Don't correct any mistakes at this point, but make a note of any problems in structure or pronunciation.
- Ask each pair to tell the rest of the class which option(s) they chose and to say why. Ask the others if they agree with what was said or if they have anything else to add.
- Write any structural mistakes made by students on the board without saying who made them, and ask them to correct them. Deal with any problems in pronunciation that came up.

Answers

Students' own answers

Useful Expressions

- Read the *Useful Expressions* to the students and ask them to repeat them. Correct their pronunciation and intonation where necessary.
- Explain that these words and expressions can be used for evaluating and negotiating and that they should use some of these expressions when they do the *Exam Task*.

9 All That Jazz!

Ideas Focus

- Ask students to read the questions quickly and deal with any queries they may have.
- Ask students to work in pairs and to take it in turns to answer the questions.
- Go round the class monitoring students to make sure they are carrying out the task properly. Don't correct any mistakes at this point, but make a note of any problems in structure or pronunciation.
- Ask a student from each pair to answer one of the questions until each pair has had a turn. Ask other students if they agree or if they have anything else to add.
- Write any structural mistakes made by students on the board without saying who made them, and ask them to correct them. Deal with any problems in pronunciation that came up.

Answers

Students' own answers

Writing: a report

- Read the *Learning Focus* on recognising the purpose of a report to the students and explain anything they don't understand.
- Point out that normally reports are written following a specific request from someone wanting information about a place, services, etc. Elicit from students that in order to maintain a neutral and impersonal tone, they should use the first person singular as little as possible when presenting opinions and findings. Using the passive voice is a good way to achieve the correct tone and level of formality needed.
- Explain to students that reports are different to most kinds of writing as they are split into distinct sections. These sections don't have to flow into each other the way paragraphs in essays, stories and articles do. Explain that these sections may or may not include headings.

A

- Ask students to read the instructions and check that they understand what they have to do.
- Ask students to work in pairs to encourage discussion and ask them to write a list about what contributes towards making an outdoor music festival great in their notebooks.
- As a class, discuss the points raised by each pair and make a list on the board of suitable ideas.

Suggested answers

good line-up
good weather
good sound quality
good access to clean bathroom facilities
lots of parking spaces
good quality, cheap food and drinks

B

- Ask students to read the instructions and check that they understand what they have to do.
- Allow students time to read the short extract and deal with any queries students might have about unfamiliar words.
- Ask students to do the task individually, but check as a class.

Answers

1 the band he/she enjoyed the most
2 he/she praises the performance, mentions the lead singer/band, lists popular songs played
3 the audience loved the songs and reacted positively to them

C

- Ask students to read the instructions and check that they understand what they have to do.
- Ask students to read the writing task and explain anything they don't understand.
- Ask students to do the task individually, but check as a class.

Answers

1 peers (magazine readers)
2 semi-formal because the target reader is a peer
3 outline your favourite part of the festival; describe any problems; suggest improvements
4 no; you can make it all up

D

- Ask students to read the instructions and check that they understand what they have to do.
- Then ask students to read the example report and to underline any information that relates to all the parts of the question. Ask them to compare the parts they underlined with a partner.
- As a class, ask students if every point has been covered and to quote the parts in the report that deal with each part. Ask students to justify their answers.

Answers

Yes, all parts of the question have been covered.
1 outline your favourite part of the festival: *the highlight of the weekend was Rockfrog.*
2 describe any problems: *On the down side, parking was a problem.*
3 suggest improvements: *I would therefore suggest that parking points are added around the city during the next festival.*

E

- Ask students to read the instructions and check that they understand what they have to do.
- Ask students to look at the example report again and elicit that headings have not been used and that they are not necessary on this occasion.

- Ask students to read the example report again and to underline how the writer has indicated what will be discussed in each paragraph.
- Ask students to work in pairs to encourage discussion, but check as a class.

Answer

Headings are not necessary in this report; because the writer has used topic sentences to show what each paragraph will be about.

F

- Ask students how many things the task asks them to do (three – to choose one of the points they made about music festivals in A, to write a paragraph for a report about a real or made-up festival and to start it with a topic sentence).
- Ask students to choose one of the points they listed in A and to write their paragraph in their notebooks.
- Give students no more than ten minutes to write their paragraph and go round the class offering help where necessary.

Answers

Students' own answers

G

- Remind students that when they have finished a piece of writing they should always proofread it to check for spelling, grammatical and punctuation errors.
- Ask students to swap notebooks with a partner and give them a few minutes to read and underline any mistakes they find in their partner's paragraph. Explain that they don't have to correct them.
- Ask students to hand the notebooks back to their partner and to correct any mistakes that have been noted.
- As a class, ask several students to read out their paragraphs.

Answers

Students' own answers

H

- Ask the students to read the information in the *Exam Close-up* and point out that the writer of the example report did all the things on the list.
- Remind students that they can use the information here as a checklist when writing their own reports.
- Ask students to read the *Exam Task* and ask them to underline any key words and phrases in the task. Explain anything they don't understand.
- Ask students to answer the questions in C about this writing task so that they know what they have to do.
- As a class, ask students what they have to write their report on *(a music venue they have been to)* and how many things they have to include in their report *(three – outline the best thing about the venue, describe any problems they experienced and suggest improvements that they would like to see)*.

- Ask students to read the paragraph plan and ask them to make notes for each paragraph, if time allows.
- Set the *Exam Task* for homework.
- Encourage students to use the Writing Reference and checklist for reports on page 183.

Suggested answer

I was fortunate enough to attend a concert by The Skints on 15th May 2013. The concert was at a venue in Portsmouth called, 'The Wedgewood Rooms'. I have found the Wedgewood Rooms to be a brilliant venue for listening to live music or comedy.
By far the best thing about the venue was that it is quite small in size. Some people might think that is a bad thing, but I found it to be quite the opposite as it meant you could get very close to the band that was playing and really feel their energy. Also, there is no seating inside, so it was easy to move around. This means that if you suddenly found yourself standing behind a very tall person you can just move somewhere else without your experience being ruined.
On the downside, I had to queue for **20** minutes in order to buy refreshments and snacks. There should have been two places to buy drinks from yet only one was open. This resulted in me missing the first few minutes of the show while I was waiting to be served. An effective solution would be to employ more staff to work at the venue serving refreshments. That way, they could open the second bar which would provide another place for people to buy drinks and subsequently there would be smaller queues.

Useful Expressions

- Read the *Useful Expressions* to the students and ask them to repeat them. Correct their pronunciation and intonation if necessary.
- Ask them to circle any words and phrases from the list that are used in the example report *(On the down side …, I would therefore suggest …,)*.
- Elicit in which part of their report they can use each category of expressions. Tell them to use them when writing their report in H, but that they should not overuse them.

9 Eye Trick Town

General Note

Please see the information about the National Geographic videos on page 18 of this Teacher's Book.

Background Information

The phrase 'trompe l'oeil' is French and means to 'deceive the eye'. It is a style of painting that provides an illusion of photographic reality. Used for decorating houses, balconies, pools and walls, it is a technique which uses imagery to fool the eye to create an optical illusion.

Before you watch

A

- Explain to students that in this lesson they are going to watch a video about a special kind of art. Ask them to look at the globe and tell you in which part of the world this art is common for decorating buildings (*Italy*). Elicit what they know about Camogli, Italy and the architecture that they have there.
- Ask students to read the questions and answer any queries they may have.
- Tell students to answer the questions in pairs. Encourage them to draw on their own knowledge of art and architecture in their country.
- Go round the class monitoring students to make sure they are carrying out the task properly. Don't correct any mistakes at this stage, but make a note of any problems in structure and pronunciation.
- Ask each pair to answer one of the questions and repeat until each pair has had a turn.
- Write any structural mistakes that students made on the board without saying who made them, and ask them to correct them. Deal with any problems in pronunciation that came up.

Answers

Students' own answers

While you watch

B

- Explain to students that they are now going to watch the video and do a task based on what they hear.
- Ask students to read statements 1–6 and ask them what the documentary will be about (*an art form called 'trompe l'oeil'*).
- Explain anything in the statements that the students don't understand. Then ask them to think about which statements might be true and which ones might be false before they listen.
- Play the video all the way through without stopping and ask students to mark their answers. Ask students to compare their answers with a partner's and to justify any answers that are different. Play the video again so that they can check their answers.
- Ask students to do the task individually, but check as a class.

Answers

1 T (00:22)	4 T (01:54)
2 F (01:01)	5 F (03:16)
3 F (01:21)	6 T (03:33)

After you watch

C

- Explain to students that this is a summary of the information they heard on the video.
- Read the words in the yellow box to the students and ask them to repeat them. Ask them to write *N*, *V* or *Adj* beside each of the words depending on whether it is a noun, a verb or an adjective.
- Explain to students that they should read the whole summary before writing any answers first to work out what part of speech is missing.
- Tell students to re-read the text once they have finished to check their answers.
- Ask students to do the task individually, but check as a class.

Answers

1 look	6 façades
2 painted	7 methods
3 solid	8 apartments
4 bright	9 traditions
5 expensive	10 local

Ideas Focus

- Ask students to read the three questions and answer any queries they might have.
- Ask students to work in pairs and explain that they should both give their opinions on all three questions.
- Go round the class monitoring students to make sure they are carrying out the task properly. Don't correct any mistakes at this stage, but make a note of any problems in structure and pronunciation.
- Ask each pair to answer one of the questions and repeat until each pair has had a turn.
- Write about what kinds of architecture the students prefer and how they would change the look of the area they live in on the board.
- Write any structural mistakes that students made on the board without saying who made them, and ask them to correct them. Deal with any problems in structure or pronunciation that came up.

Answers

Students' own answers

10 Modern Living

Reading:	multiple-choice questions, finding your own method
Vocabulary:	work- and lifestyle-related vocabulary, word formation, phrasal verbs, collocations & expressions
Grammar:	passive voice, reporting with passive verbs, *seem* & *appear*, passive causative
Listening:	multiple-matching, focusing on attitude & opinion
Speaking:	talking about skills, qualities & qualifications, assessing strengths & weaknesses, comparing options
Writing:	article (2), understanding the aim of the article, composing an article, comparing & contrasting, providing information, offering advice, describing places

Unit opener

- Ask students to look at the title of the unit and ask them to explain what aspect of modern living is shown in the picture. Direct students' attention to the caption and ask them to look at the people in the picture. Ask them how they seem to feel about their architectural surroundings.
- Ask students why this type of architecture might be popular in modern times and how they think people in their country would react if something similar were built where they live.

Reading

A

- Ask students to cover up the instructions and to look at the pictures in A. Ask them what pictures 1–6 have in common *(they are all places of employment)*.
- Ask students to read the instructions and explain anything they don't understand.
- Ask students to work in pairs to discuss what the people who work in these places are called and the skills and qualities that are necessary to do the jobs.
- As a class, ask each pair to answer the questions for one of the photos. Repeat until each pair has had a turn and all the pictures have been discussed. Encourage students to justify their answers.

Suggested answers

1. archaeologist – patience, eye for detail, hard-working, dedication, respect for the past, ability to work in a team
2. pianist – musical talent, dedication, ability to work on own, be a good performer
3. artist – talent, creativity, eye for detail
4. deep sea diver/explorer – bravery, curiosity about ocean life, strong swimmer
5. photographer – eye for detail, creative
6. architect – good drawing skills, creative, knowledge of construction and materials

Extra Class Activity

If time allows, you could extend this activity by having a class discussion about what careers the students would like to pursue in the future. Ask students to talk about what skills and qualifications they would need in their chosen profession.

B

- Ask students to look at the picture to the left of the article and at the title of the article. Ask how they are related *(they are both connected to the ocean)*. Elicit what they think being an *Ocean Hero* might entail.
- Ask students to read the instructions for B and check that they understand what they have to do.
- Tell them to skim read the text to find the answer to the first question. Point out they will need to refer back to the jobs mentioned in A to complete the task.
- Remind students that they don't have to read the text in detail as they will have another opportunity to do that later. Ask students to do the task individually, but check answers as a class.
- Ask students at random round the class what job the writer actually does today and ask them to justify their answers with words and quotes from the text.

Answers

All of them: archaeologist, pianist, painter, photographer, deep sea explorer, architect.
She is now a marine archaeologist.

Word Focus

- Ask students to look at the words in red in the text and to re-read the sentences they are found in. Ask students to work in pairs to decide what each of the words means in the *Word Focus* box and to then find synonyms, if any, for each word.
- Ask students to compare their answers with another pair.

111

10 Modern Living

C

- Ask students to read the *Exam Close-up* and ask a student to explain what it says in his or her own words.
- Encourage students to try a different approach to dealing with multiple-choice tasks to see what approach works best for them.
- Explain that people have different ways of doing things and that it is important for them to find the approach which brings them, personally, the best results.
- Ask students to read the instructions in the *Exam Task* and items 1–7 with their options. Explain anything the students don't understand.
- Encourage students to guess the meaning of any unfamiliar words from the context before looking them up in their dictionaries. Explain any problem words and correct their pronunciation where necessary.
- Ask students to underline any key words in the items and options and to underline the parts in the text that refer to each of the items and options. Remind students that the information in the items follows the same order as the text.
- Ask students to read the text again and to underline information related to the questions while reading. Alternatively, allow students time to try out the approach suggested in the *Exam Close-up*.
- Ask students to do the task individually, but check as a class.
- Once the answers have been checked, ask students if they thought the new approach suggested in the *Exam Close-up* brought them better results than the usual approach that they have been using.

Answers

1b (… as I was growing up I was always chopping and changing what I wanted to be when I was older.)
2d (As a youngster, I was inspired by museum visits, finding arrowheads around my home and also the time I spent in and on the water. My grandfather and his love of boating also had an important role to play.)
3a (It's also the time for any questions or issues to be raised that weren't solved the previous day.)
4c (… everything needs to be tagged and protected by a series of conservation steps so that no harm comes to them.)
5a (A lot of patience is required for this part of the job as lab analysis can take months and months. Sometimes it seems to last forever!)
6c (Going on a boat is something they're always eager to do, …)
7d (I hope to make them aware of the fragile balance of ocean life. … helping others to appreciate the ocean and how our activities affect it.)

D

- Ask students to look at the words in the yellow box and to scan the text again to find and underline them. Ask them to say each of the words after you and elicit that they are all nouns or adjectives. Correct their pronunciation where necessary.
- Remind them that they should always try to work out the meaning of the word from its context and ask them to read the sentences in the text in which each word is contained.
- Ask students to read the instructions and check that they understand what they have to do. Encourage them to read all the sentences in D before writing any answers. Ask students to do the task individually, but check as a class.

Answers

1 formative
2 fragile
3 Field
4 day-care
5 marine
6 Rigorous

Ideas Focus

- Ask students to read the questions and answer any queries they might have.
- Ask students to work in pairs and explain that they should both give their opinions on both questions.
- Go round the class monitoring students to make sure they are carrying out the task properly. Don't correct any mistakes at this stage, but make a note of any problems in structure and pronunciation.
- Write any structural mistakes that students made on the board without saying who made them, and ask them to correct them. Deal with any problems in structure or pronunciation that came up.

Vocabulary

A

- Ask students to look at the picture to the right of the text in A and ask them to describe it. Ask them what the people are doing and how they might be feeling (*they all look very busy as they hurry through the city; they could be feeling stressed or tired*).
- Ask students to read the instructions and check that they understand what they have to do.
- Read the words and the opposites to the students and ask students to repeat them after you. Correct their pronunciation where necessary.
- Ask students to do the task individually, but check as a class.

Answers

1 c 2 d 3 e 4 b 5 f 6 a

B

- Ask students to read the instructions and check that they understand what they have to do.
- Explain to the students that they should use some of the words from A to complete the sentences.
- Encourage students to read all the sentences in B before filling in any answers.
- Ask students to do the task individually, but check as a class.

Answers

1. cosmopolitan
2. sedentary
3. hectic
4. solitary
5. reasonable
6. sociable

C

- Ask students to read the instructions and check that they understand what they have to do.
- Encourage students to read all three sentences before filling in any answers.
- Explain to students that the missing word in each set of sentences will be a fairly common one and that students should not spend time trying to find overly-difficult words.
- Tell students that the missing word in each set of sentences will be the same part of speech and that the word will have a different meaning in each sentence.
- Ask students to do the task individually, but check as a class.

Answers

1. safe
2. living
3. concerned
4. road

D

- Ask students to read the instructions and check that they understand what they have to do. Explain that they have to decide which order each of the words comes in each sentence.
- Read the words in the yellow boxes and ask students to repeat them after you. Correct their pronunciation where necessary.
- Encourage students to read the whole sentence before filling in any answers.
- Ask students to do the task individually, but check as a class.

Answers

1. juggle, balance
2. endure, struggle
3. excel, outdo
4. spoil, ruin

Teaching Tip

Point out to students that the pairs of words in D may be confusing as they are similar in some ways, but have slight differences in use. Stress the importance of looking at the meanings of the words in English, and writing example sentences to remember the correct context where they are used, instead of simply translating them into their own language.

E

- Ask students to read the title of the text and to look at the accompanying picture. Ask them how the picture might relate to the title (*the person in the picture appears to be addicted to his game that he is playing. He looks like he does not want to be disturbed*) – don't check their answer yet.
- Read the words in capital letters to the students and ask them to repeat them. Correct their pronunciation where necessary. Ask students which part of speech each word is (*verbs: interact, participate, obsess, recover; nouns: addict, society; adjectives: susceptible, irritable*) and which other parts of speech of these words they know.
- Ask students to read the text, without filling in any answers, to find out how the title relates to the picture (*as mentioned in previous column*).
- Ask students to read the instructions and check that they understand what they have to do. Ask them to work out what part of speech is missing from each gap before they write their answers.
- Remind students to re-read the text once they have finished to check their answers.
- Ask students to do the task individually, but check as a class.

Answers

1. addiction
2. susceptibility
3. Interaction
4. participants
5. obsessive
6. irritability
7. social/societal
8. recovery

F

- Read the phrasal verbs in the yellow box to the students and ask them to repeat them. Correct their pronunciation where necessary.
- Tell students that they have to consider the meaning of the verb and the particle together and not just focus on the verb.
- Ask students to read the instructions and check that they understand what they have to do.
- Ask them to read the sentences on their own to work out the meaning of the missing phrasal verb. Also encourage them to underline the subject of each sentence so that they write the verbs in the correct form.
- Ask students to do the task individually, but check as a class.
- Encourage students to copy the phrasal verbs and their meanings into their notebooks.

Answers

1. have pulled together
2. get by
3. wear ... down
4. come up against
5. do without
6. bounce back

G

- Read the expressions in the yellow box to the students and ask them to repeat them. Correct their pronunciation where necessary.
- Explain that they will use these expressions to replace the words and phrases in bold in the sentences.
- Encourage students to read all the sentences in G before writing their answers.
- Ask students to do the task individually, but check as a class.

113

10 Modern Living

> **Answers**
> 1 run yourself into the ground
> 2 keep your head above water
> 3 throw in the towel
> 4 hit rock bottom
> 5 burn the candle at both ends

Ideas Focus

- Ask students to read the questions and answer any queries they may have.
- Ask students to work in pairs and explain that they should both give their opinions on both questions.
- As a class, discuss the points raised by each pair and make a list of suitable ideas on the board.
- Start a class discussion about how our jobs, relationships and health have been affected by the points that have been listed on the board. Ask students to justify their answers and opinions.

> **Answers**
> Students' own answers

Extra Class Activity

After the students have finished their discussion of the topic, you could ask them to write an essay using their lists and any other ideas they might have come up with during the discussion. Direct students attention to page 176 of the Writing Reference *(in the Student's Book)* to help them write their essays.

Grammar

- Write the sentence below on the board and ask students if we know who did the action.
  - The promotion was given to him. *(We don't know who gave him the promotion, but we can assume it was his employer.)*
- Ask a student to come up to the board and underline the verb form in the sentence *(was given)* and elicit that the verb is in the passive voice. Elicit that the passive voice is used here as the action is more important than who did it.
- Ask students to write the sentence in the active voice *(Someone/His employer gave him a promotion.)* and elicit that the Past Simple tense is used because it talks about an action that occurred at a definite time in the past. Remind students that only verbs that have objects can be used in the passive voice.
- Ask students to look at the active sentence again and elicit that it has got two objects. Elicit from students how the sentence could be written in the passive voice in another way. *(He was given a promotion.)*
- Explain that when we want to change an active sentence with two objects into the passive, one becomes the subject of the sentence and the other one remains an object and elicit that we choose the object which we want to emphasise.

- Direct students' attention to the first sentence again and explain that if the personal object remains an object in the passive sentence, then we have to use a suitable preposition. Ask students what the preposition is in the sentence *(to)* and explain that other prepositions that are used in this way include *for, with,* etc.

A

- Ask students to read the instructions and check that they understand what they have to do.
- Ask students to read sentences 1–4 and to focus on the words in bold in each sentence.
- Elicit which passive forms are correct *(1: will be given; 2: will be given to, 4: is being reported to)*.
- Read the rules with the students, without circling any answers, and explain anything they don't understand. Explain to students that they should refer back to sentences a–d when choosing their answers and try to work out why the passive form is correct or incorrect each time.
- Ask students to do the task in pairs to encourage discussion, but check as a class.

> **Answer**
> 1, 2 and 4 are correct

B

- Read the rules with the students, without circling any answers, and explain anything they don't understand.
- Explain to students that they should refer back to sentences 1–4 when choosing their answers and try to work out why the passive form is correct or incorrect each time.
- Ask students to do the task in pairs to encourage discussion, but check as a class.

> **Answers**
> 1 two
> 2 one

- Write the sentences below on the board and ask students to identify the reporting verb in both *(think)*.
  - It is thought that living in a crowded city is stressful.
  - Living in a crowded city is thought to be stressful.
- Explain to students that both these sentences use the verb in the passive to report what someone has said.
- Underline *It is thought that* in the first sentence and ask students whether this is a personal or impersonal passive structure *(personal)*. Underline *Living in a crowded city is thought to be* in the second sentence and explain to students that this is an impersonal passive structure.

C

- Ask students to read the instructions and check that they understand what they have to do.
- Read the information about reporting with passive verbs to the students and explain anything that they don't understand.
- Ask students to do the task individually, but check as a class.
- Once the answers have been checked, ask students if the reporting passive verbs are transitive or intransitive.

Answers

1. It is known that
2. It has been agreed that
3. is expected to
4. There are thought to be

Extra Class Activity
If time allows, ask students to write the sentences in A and B in the active voice.

Now read the Grammar Reference on page 169 (10.1 to 10.3) with your students.

D

- Ask students to read the title and to then skim read the text to find out how the title relates to the picture *(the woman is getting an advantage over others by using modern technology; she is supporting her CV with a video).*
- Explain to students that they should think about which passive form is being used in each item and to refer back to the Grammar box if they need help when they are choosing their answers.
- Remind students to re-read the text once they have finished to check their answers.
- Ask students to do the task individually, but check as a class.

Answers

1. to be noticed
2. It is known
3. are shown
4. can be supported
5. will be brought
6. isn't needed
7. should be kept
8. being asked

E

- Ask students to read the instructions and check that they understand what they have to do. Point out that they may have to make other changes so that the new passive sentences make sense and to refer back to A when rewriting the sentences.
- Ask students to do the task individually, but check as a class.

Answers

1. It's a shame that the countryside is being littered every day.
2. The winner will not be announced until next month.
3. He's looking forward to being shown his new office.
4. There are believed to be two other serious offers.
5. He was presented with an award by the manager.
6. The park benches have been vandalised again.

F

- Read the information and the *Be careful!* about *seem* and *appear* to the students and explain anything they don't understand. Elicit when we tend to use *seem* (*to talk about impressions and emotions*) and when we tend to use *appear* (*to talk about more objective facts and impressions*).

- Read the instructions and check that they understand what they have to do.
- Ask students to read sentences a–i and grammar points 1–5 all the way through before trying to match them. Explain anything they don't understand.
- Ask students to do the task individually, but check as a class.

Answers

1 f,h 2 b,i 3 d,g 4 a,e 5 c

G

- Write the sentence below on the board.
  – Bob had a new house built in the city centre.
- Elicit from students whether Bob built the house or whether someone else built it for him *(someone else built it)*. Elicit from students what kind of form the sentence contains *(passive causative)*.
- Remind students that we use the passive causative to say that we have arranged for someone to do something for us, or instead of the passive when we want to refer to an unpleasant experience that happens to somebody.
- Elicit from students that the passive causative is formed with the correct form of *have* + object + past participle. Ask what word we use when we want to mention the agent *(by)*.
- Elicit that the passive causative can also be formed with the correct form of *get* + agent + full infinitive + object.
- Ask students to read the instructions and check that they understand what they have to do. Then ask students to read sentences 1–4 and to focus on the words in bold in each sentence. Elicit what tense of the passive causative form is used in each sentence.
- Ask students to read the uses of the passive causative form a–d all the way through before trying to match them with 1–4. Explain anything they don't understand.
- Ask students to do the task individually, but check as a class.

Answers

1 b 2 c 3 d 4 a

H

- Ask students to read the instructions and check that they understand what they have to do.
- Ask them to read the sentences and to focus on the words in bold in each sentence.
- Read the rule with the students, without circling any answers, and explain anything they don't understand. Tell students that they should refer back to the sentences if they need help when choosing their answer.
- Ask students to do the task in pairs to encourage discussion, but check as a class.

Answer

past participle

10 Modern Living

Extra Class Activity

If time allows, ask students to go back to the Reading text on pages **122** and **123** to see if they can find any examples of passive causative forms. (*Everything needs to be tagged and protected by a series of conservation steps, …, I have students and research assistants work through the thousands of samples gathered in the field.*) Ask them to identify the tense of each.

Now read the Grammar Reference on pages 169 & 170 with your students.

I

- Ask students to read the instructions and check that they understand what they have to do.
- Point out that they have to pay attention to when we use *seem* and when we use *appear* as well as to look carefully at what structure follows the verbs *seem* and *appear* in the sentences.
- Encourage students to look back at F and the *Be careful!* if they need help as they do the task.
- Ask students to do the task individually, but check as a class.

Answers

1. incorrect – appeared to be asleep
2. incorrect – It seems like
3. incorrect – It seems a pity
4. correct
5. incorrect – seem to have gone
6. correct

J

- Ask students to read the instructions and check that they understand what they have to do.
- Explain to students that they should think about which passive causative form is being used in each item and to refer back to the Grammar box if they need help when they are choosing their answers.
- Remind students to re-read the sentences once they have finished to check their answers.
- Ask students to do the task individually, but check as a class.

Answers

1. installed
2. delivered
3. had
4. broken
5. had
6. having

Listening

A

- Ask students to work in pairs to describe the pictures on page 128. One student should describe the picture in the top right-hand corner and the other should describe the one in the bottom left-hand corner of the page. Ask them to describe the situations and how the pictures are related (*both pictures seem to deal with different jobs*).
- Ask students to read the instructions and make sure they understand what they have to do.
- Read the sentences to the students and ask them to repeat them. Correct their pronunciation where necessary.
- Ask the students to work in pairs to complete the sentences.
- As a class, ask each pair to say how they completed one of the sentences.

Suggested answers

1. tiring / exhausting / demanding / stressful
2. independence / freedom / responsibility
3. play / film / TV show
4. promotion
5. town / city / urban area
6. motivation
7. painful / negative / distressing
8. opportunities

Teaching Tip

You can expand this task further by asking students to tell a partner about a situation or an experience where they have had to *slog it out* or where they have *had a door opened for them* and what the results were.

B

- Ask students to read the instructions for B and make sure they understand what they have to do.
- Ask students to also read the instructions for the *Exam Task* quickly too. Elicit who they will hear on the recording and what they will be talking about (*Speaker 1, talking about their lifestyle*). Read the questions to the students and explain anything they don't understand.
- Play the recording once all the way through and ask students to answer the questions. Ask students to compare their answers with a partner and to justify any answers they have that are different.
- Play the recording again to check their answers or to fill in any missing answers.
- Check answers as a class and ask students to justify their answers.

Answers

1. to become a chef
2. no
3. It was too stressful and restricting.
4. sell food from a catering van at festivals in Britain
5. yes
6. He enjoys seeing people's surprise at the quality of food he offers so cheaply.

C

- Ask students to read the *Exam Close-up*.
- Remind students of any differences in the answers they might have had in B. Explain to students that the A–H items do not come in the same order found on the recording.
- Point out that they should ask themselves questions like the ones in B for each speaker between the first and second listening.
- Ask students to read the instructions and check they understand what they have to do.
- Explain that they will hear five people talking in five different situations, but that they will all be talking about their lifestyles.
- Explain that in this type of listening task, the topic is always given and that they should read it carefully so they will be able to predict, to a degree, what might be said by each speaker.
- Elicit that they have to do two things here: *decide which reason best reflects why each person chose his or her current lifestyle* and *to match the speakers to the main advantage each mentions about his or her lifestyle*.
- Ask students to read A–H in both tasks and to underline any key words. Answer any questions they might have about them.
- Then ask students to work with a partner to discuss which of the reasons in Task 1 are positive and which are negative *(A–E are negative, F and H are positive)*. Encourage them to look back at the sentences in A for ideas.
- Remind students that they won't need to use three of items A–H in each of the tasks.
- Play the recording and ask students to mark their answers. Then ask students to discuss their answers with a partner and to justify any answers they have that are different.

D

- Play the recording again and ask students to check their answers and to fill in any missing answers.
- Check the answers as a class and ask students to justify their answers.

Answers

Task 1
1E 2H 3A 4G 5B

Task 2
6C 7E 8F 9H 10A

Speaking

A

- Ask students to read the three questions and answer any queries they may have about them.
- Ask students to work in pairs and to take it in turns to ask and answer the questions about themselves.
- Go round the class monitoring students to make sure they are carrying out the task properly. Don't correct any mistakes at this point, but make a note of any problems in structure or pronunciation.
- Ask each pair to ask and answer one question and repeat until each student has had a turn.

- Write any structural mistakes made by students on the board without saying who made them, and ask them to correct them. Deal with any problems in pronunciation that came up.

Answers

Students' own answers

B

- Ask students to read the instructions and the list of skills, qualities and qualifications an ideal English teacher would have in B. Answer any questions they might have about them. Ask students to think about what they personally think is important for being an ideal English teacher and to rank the skills, qualities and qualifications in the order that they consider to be important.
- Ask students to work in pairs to compare and discuss their answers.
- Go round the class monitoring students to make sure they are carrying out the task properly. Don't correct any mistakes at this point, but make a note of any problems in structure or pronunciation.
- Write numbers 1–6 as headings on the board and ask students which skills, qualities and qualifications they chose as the most important. Call out each of the skills, qualities and qualifications in turn and ask students from each pair to report how each one was ranked. Write their answers on the board under the headings with the number of students who chose this as the most important. Encourage students to discuss the results.
- Write any structural mistakes made by students on the board without saying who made them, and ask them to correct them. Deal with any problems in pronunciation that came up.

Answers

Students' own answers

C

- Ask students to read the *Exam Close-up*.
- Ask students to quickly read the instructions for the *Exam Task* and elicit that they will be working with prompt cards and that, in pairs, they have to do two things here: tell each other about the candidates *(present options to a partner)* and decide together which candidate would be most suitable for the post *(weigh up the merits and weaknesses of each candidate)*.
- Stress that when they are presenting their options and listening to their partner's options, they should try and think which points are most relevant to the task and why.

D

- Ask students to read the instructions again and check that they understand what they have to do.
- Ask students to work in pairs and to decide who will be Student A and who will be Student B. Ask them to spend a few minutes looking at their prompt cards *(Student A: Prompt cards A and B; Student B: Prompt cards C and D)* to compare and contrast the merits and weaknesses of their candidates and explain anything that they don't understand.

117

10 Modern Living

- Remind students that this is a decision-making task and that each student is expected to speak about and discuss their options with a partner before coming to a mutual decision about which candidate would be most suitable for the postition.
- Ask Student A to begin presenting their options (A and B) and for Student B to listen very carefully and to agree or disagree with what their partner is saying. They should also justify why they agree or disagree in a polite, logical manner. Explain that they should try to think which points are most relevant to the task and why. Then ask Student B to talk about their options (C and D) and Student A listens very carefully and agrees or disagrees with what their partner is saying. They should also justify why they agree or disagree in a polite, logical manner. Once both presentations have been made, encourage students to reach a decision on which candidate would be most suitable for the postition.
- Go round the class monitoring students to make sure they are carrying out the task properly. Don't correct any mistakes at this point, but make a note of any problems in structure or pronunciation.
- Ask one pair of students to carry out the task in front of the class and ask the other students if they have anything to add.
- Write any structural mistakes made by students on the board without saying who made them, and ask them to correct them. Deal with any problems in pronunciation that came up.

Answers
Students' own answers

Useful Expressions
- Read the *Useful Expressions* to the students and ask them to repeat them. Correct their pronunciation and intonation where necessary.
- Explain that these words and expressions can be used when comparing options and that they should use some of these expressions when they do D.

Teaching Tip
Remind students that they should try and reach a decision together, but it is more important to have a meaningful discussion about all the candidates in a natural sounding way than it is to agree with each other on everything. Remind them that if they can't agree, one student can choose one candidate and the other student can choose another candidate.

Ideas Focus
- Ask students to read the questions quickly and deal with any queries they may have.
- Ask students to work in pairs and to take it in turns to answer the questions.
- Go round the class monitoring students to make sure they are carrying out the task properly. Don't correct any mistakes at this point, but make a note of any problems in structure or pronunciation.
- Ask a student from each pair to answer one of the questions until each pair has had a turn. Ask other students if they agree or if they have anything else to add.

- Write any structural mistakes made by students on the board without saying who made them, and ask them to correct them. Deal with any problems in pronunciation that came up.

Answers
Students' own answers

Writing: an article (2)

- Elicit from students what an article is and remind them where they usually appear (*in magazines or newspapers*). Ask them in which previous unit they wrote an article (*Unit 8*) and ask them what the topic of their article was and what title they gave it.
- Explain to students that in this lesson they are going to deal with writing articles again, but with a different focus.
- Read the *Learning Focus* on understanding the aim of an article to the students and explain anything they don't understand.
- Ask students what the main purpose of their article in Unit 8 was (*to interest and engage the reader while expressing their view on a given topic*) and elicit what other aims an article can have (*to advise, suggest, inform, compare and contrast, describe, give an opinion or present a balanced argument*).

A
- Ask students to read the instructions and check that they understand what they have to do.
- Ask students to read the task extracts 1–4 and aims a–d all the way through before trying to match them. Explain anything they don't understand.
- Ask students to do the task individually, but check as a class.

Answers
1 b **2** c **3** d **4** a

B
- Ask students to read the instructions for B and also to look at the task extracts in A again. Ask students to think about which task they would personally have the most to say about and why. Then ask students to work in pairs to compare and discuss their answers.
- Write numbers 1–4 as headings on the board and ask students which task they chose. Call out each of the tasks in turn and ask students from each pair to report which task was chosen. Write their answers on the board under the headings with the number of students who chose each task. Count up the numbers to see which task was most popular. Encourage students to discuss the results.

Answers
Students' own answers

C

- Ask students to read the instructions and check that they understand what they have to do.
- Ask students to read the writing task and explain anything they don't understand.
- Ask students to do the task individually, but check as a class.

Answers

1. no; a wide age group
2. to give your opinion on how life has improved and worsened in the last 50 years and to say what you think the future holds
3. an introduction, a paragraph on an improvement, a paragraph on changes for the worse, a paragraph about the future, a conclusion – 5 paragraphs in all
4. Students' own answers

D

- Ask students to read the instructions and check that they understand what they have to do.
- Ask students to read the example article and to underline information that relates to the writer's opinion. Then ask them to compare the parts they underlined with a partner.
- As a class, ask students if they agree with the writer's opinion. Ask students to justify their answers.

Answers

Students' own answers

E

- Ask students how many things the task asks them to do (*two – read the example article again and summarise each paragraph in one sentence*).
- Ask students to do the task individually, but check as a class.

F

- Ask students to read the instructions and check that they understand what they have to do.
- Ask students to look at the example task they chose in A and write a summary of it in their notebooks.
- Give students no more than five minutes to write their summaries and go round the class offering help where necessary.
- Ask students at random round the class to read their summaries out. You could hang all the summaries on the wall and ask students to read each other's work.

Answers

Students' own answers

G

- Ask the students to read the *Exam Close-up* and point out that the writer of the example article did all the things on the list.
- Remind students that they can use the information here as a checklist when writing their own articles in the *Exam Task*.

- Ask students to read the *Exam Task* and ask them to underline any key words and phrases in the task. Explain anything they don't understand.
- Ask students to answer the questions in C about this writing task so that they know what to do.
- As a class, ask students which of the four writing tasks they will choose and why.
- Ask students to read the paragraph plan and ask them to make notes for each paragraph, if time allows. Ask students how many paragraphs their article will contain (*five*).
- Set the *Exam Task* for homework.
- Encourage students to use the Writing Reference and checklist for articles on page 182.

Suggested answer

LONDON LIFE

When English writer, Samuel Johnson said to his friend, 'when a man is tired of London, he is tired of life; for there is in London all that life can afford,' he was exactly right. London is one of the world's most vibrant and exciting capital cities and here's why…

The ideal time to go to London is probably during the spring and autumn months when the weather is likely to be bright with blue skies and mild in temperature. I wouldn't recommend visiting in the summer months as, although London is always busy, it is literally swarming with tourists during July and August.

Be prepared for a very busy trip! There is so much to see and do in London you won't know where to start. It will take you quite a while to see all the sights, such as Big Ben, Parliament, Buckingham Palace and London Bridge before you even start on the multitude of galleries, museums and of course, shops!

London is a great place to visit because there is something for everyone to do. In contrast to some other capital cities, no matter what age you are you will not be disappointed. If you want to take it easy you can stroll along the banks of the River Thames. Culture vultures can visit the Tate Modern museum or the National Portrait gallery and, well, London is a shopaholics' heaven to say the least.

In conclusion, if you want a busy exciting break, London leaves other capital cities in the shade.

Useful Expressions

- Read the *Useful Expressions* to the students and ask them to repeat them. Correct their pronunciation and intonation if necessary.
- Elicit in which part of their article they can use each category of expressions and tell them to use them when writing their article in the *Exam Task*.

Video 10 Zoo Dentists

General Note

Please see the information about the National Geographic videos on page 18 of this Teacher's Book.

Background Information

People have been performing dental procedures on animals for centuries. Sadly, as there were no anaesthetics and little was known about the physical and mental make-up of many animals, treatment was often painful, traumatic and ineffective. Progress in this field of dentistry was very slow, but in **1762** the first veterinary dental school was opened in France and it brought about a huge increase in knowledge in regards to animal dentistry. The most important changes in animal dentistry have occurred over the past two decades. Nowadays, animal dentistry is regarded as a specialty by the American Veterinary Medical Association.

Before you watch

A

- Explain to students that in this lesson they are going to watch a video about animal dentistry. Ask them to look at the globe to see a place where animal dentistry is practised *(San Francisco)*. Elicit what they know about San Francisco and ask them if they would like to go there.
- Ask students to read the questions and answer any queries they may have about them.
- Ask students to answer the questions in pairs. Encourage them to draw on their own knowledge of animals in the wild and animals in captivity.
- Go round the class monitoring students to make sure they are carrying out the task properly. Don't correct any mistakes at this stage, but make a note of any problems in structure and pronunciation.
- Ask each pair to answer one of the questions and repeat until each pair has had a turn.
- Deal with any problems in pronunciation that came up.

Answers

Students' own answers

While you watch

B

- Explain to students that they are now going to watch the video and do a task based on what they hear.
- Ask students to read sentences 1–6 and explain anything they don't understand.
- Ask them to think about which words may be correct before watching.
- Play the video all the way through without stopping and ask students to circle their answers. Ask students to compare their answers with a partner's and to justify any answers they have that are different. Play the video again so that they can check their answers.
- Ask students to do the task individually, but check as a class.

Answers

1 work	(00:43)	4 toothache	(04:39)
2 captivity	(02:04)	5 worse	(06:23)
3 six	(03:54)	6 healthy	(07:19)

After you watch

C

- Explain to students that this is a summary of the information they heard on the video.
- Read the words in the yellow box to the students and ask them to repeat them. Ask them to write *N*, *V* or *Adj* beside each of the words depending on whether it is a noun, a verb or an adjective.
- Explain to students that they should read the whole summary before writing any answers first to work out what part of speech is missing.
- Tell students to re-read the text once they have finished to check their answers.
- Ask students to do the task individually, but check as a class.

Answers

1 jaws	6 tusks
2 longer	7 anaesthetised
3 wild	8 unfortunate
4 chew	9 filling
5 diseased	10 responsibility

Ideas Focus

- Ask students to read the three questions and answer any queries they might have.
- Ask students to work in pairs and explain that they should both give their opinions on all three questions.
- Go round the class monitoring students to make sure they are carrying out the task properly. Don't correct any mistakes at this stage, but make a note of any problems in structure and pronunciation.
- Ask each pair to answer one of the questions and repeat until each pair has had a turn.
- Write what responsibilities pet owners have towards their pets and what responsibilities we have in general towards the animal kingdom on the board.
- Deal with any problems in structure or pronunciation that came up.

Answers

Students' own answers

120

Review 5

Units 9 & 10

Objectives
- To revise vocabulary and grammar from Units 9 and 10
- To practise exam-type tasks

Revision
- Explain to students that Review 5 revises the material they saw in Units 9 and 10.
- Remind students that they can ask you for help with the exercises or look back at the units if they need help with an answer. Stress that the review is not a test.
- Decide how you will carry out the review. You could ask students to do one task at a time and then correct it immediately, or ask students to do all the tasks and correct them together at the end. If you do all the tasks together, let students know every now and again how much time they have got left to finish.
- Ask students not to leave any answers blank and to try to find any answers they don't know in the units.
- When checking students' answers to the review tasks, make a note of any problem areas in vocabulary and grammar that they still have. Try to do extra work on these areas so that your students will progress well.

Vocabulary Revision
- Play a word association game with the vocabulary from Units 9 and 10. Say one word related to music or work and lifestyle and ask each student in turn to say another word which they associate with the previous word, for example, *top-selling – singles*; *hectic – city*.
- Write the expressions below on the board and ask students to write sentences of their own using them.
  - change one's tune
  - face the music
  - sell something for a song
  - blow one's own trumpet
  - make a song and dance about something
- Ask students to explain the difference between the following pairs of words: *lyrics/verses*, *played/set*, *choices/tastes*, *beats/pulses*, *copies/pieces*.
- Write the verbs *bounce*, *come up*, *do*, *get*, *pull* and *wear* in one column and the particles *down*, *together*, *back*, *against*, *by* and *without* in another column on the board and ask them to match them up to form the phrasal verbs that they learnt in Unit 10. Then ask them what each phrasal verb means and to write a sentence using them.
- Write these words on the board and ask students what part of speech they are: *profession (n)*, *energy (n)*, *compare (v)*, *exhibit (n, v)*, *except (prep, v)*, *price (n, v)*, *solitude (n)*, *province (n)*, *relax (v)* and *equal (v, adj)*. Ask students to write down any other parts of speech of these words that they know.

Grammar Revision
- Write these sentences on the board and ask students to complete them with one word. Then revise the various forms of comparison of adjectives and adverbs that students learnt in Unit 9.
  - Pam is a _____ talented musician than Lily. *(more/less)*
  - What's _____ best way to get tickets for Glastonbury? *(the)*
  - Is this album _____ good as that one? *(as)*
  - The _____ I listen to jazz, the more I like it. *(more)*
- Write the sentence below on the board and ask students to find and correct the mistake. Then revise the qualifiers that students learnt in Unit 9.
  - The band is sort of late; we've been waiting for them to start playing for over two hours! *(sort of; the correct word is 'rather' or 'very')*
- Write the sentences below on the board and ask students to complete each sentence using *too, enough, so* or *such*.
  - There's no such thing as having _____ much money. *(too)*
  - I've got _____ little time to myself these days that I'm going mad! *(so)*
  - His guitar is very old, but he hasn't got _____ money to buy a new one. *(enough)*
  - It was _____ a rainy day that we decided to stay in and watch TV. *(such)*
- Write the sentences below on the board and ask students to rewrite them in the passive. Then revise all the passive forms that the students learnt in Unit 10.
  - Everyone knows that city living is expensive. *(It is known that city living is expensive.)*
  - They expect that the air pollution will get worse. *(Air pollution is expected to get worse.)*
  - They will give her a new position. *(She will be given a new position./A new position will be given to her.)*
  - The homeowner is reporting the break-in. *(The break-in is being reported by the homeowner.)*
- Write these sentences on the board and ask students to complete them with *seem* or *appear* in the correct form. Then revise the grammar points about *seem* and *appear* that the students learnt in Unit 10.
  - Billy _____ a bit down today. I think it's because he didn't go to the concert. *(seems)*
  - The group _____ to have disbanded. *(appears)*
- Ask students how we form the passive causative using the verbs *have* and *get* and ask them to write sentences of their own using these structures. Then ask students around the class to say what they want done using the verbs *need/prefer* + object + past participle.

A
- Ask students to read the instructions and check that they understand what they have to do.
- Ask students to read the title and to tell you what they think it might mean.

121

10 Modern Living

- Ask students to skim read the text, without filling in any answers, to find out what *Mods vs Rockers* means in the context of the text *(they are two kinds of musical subcultures that differ greatly)*.
- Encourage students to pay particular attention to the words immediately before and after each gap to work out what part of speech is missing. However, remind them that they have to take into consideration the general context of the sentence so that they understand what structure is being used.
- Remind students to re-read the text once they have finished to check their answers.

Answers

1. such
2. who
3. preferred/liked
4. by
5. more
6. most
7. perform/play
8. were
9. too
10. taken
11. deal
12. like
13. particularly
14. than
15. as/when

B

- Ask students to read the instructions and check that they understand what they have to do.
- Ask students to read the title of the text and ask them what it might mean. Ask them to skim read the text, without filling in any answers, to find out what cities the text describes *(London and New York)*.
- Ask students if they would like to live in a big city like these and why or why not.
- Read the words to the right of the text to the students and ask them to repeat them. Correct their pronunciation where necessary.
- Ask students to read back through the text and to decide which part of speech is missing from each gap, and to complete the gaps using the correct form of the words given.
- Remind students to re-read the text once they have finished to check their answers.

Answers

16. professionals
17. energetic
18. incomparable
19. exhibitions
20. exceptional
21. pricey
22. solitary
23. provincial
24. relaxed/relaxing
25. unequalled

C

- Ask students to read the instructions and check that they understand what they have to do.
- Encourage students to read all three sentences before filling in any answers.
- Explain to students that the missing word in each set of sentences will be a fairly common one and that students should not spend time trying to find overly-difficult words.
- Tell students that the missing word in each set of sentences will be the same part of speech and that the word will have a different meaning in each sentence.
- Remind students to re-read the completed sentences once they have finished to check their answers.

Answers

26. single
27. set
28. shade
29. high
30. ear

D

- Ask students to read the instructions and check that they understand what they have to do.
- Ask students to read both sentences in each item and to underline the information in the first sentence that is missing from the second sentence. Then ask them to look at the word given to decide how the missing information could be inserted into sentence two using this word. Remind students that they will have to use a different structure in order to keep the meaning the same.
- Remind students that they mustn't change the word given in bold in any way.
- Encourage students to re-read the completed sentences once they have finished to check their answers.

Answers

31. such a controversial title that
32. not so/as popular a genre
33. didn't/did not have enough time to
34. sold so few paintings
35. it has been agreed that
36. is having her piano tuned
37. appear to have left

11 Sports Crazy!

Reading:	multiple-choice questions, dealing with different text types
Vocabulary:	sport-related vocabulary, phrasal verbs, prepositions, collocations & expressions
Grammar:	reported speech, reporting verbs, reported questions
Listening:	multiple-choice questions, focusing on adverbs & time expressions
Speaking:	talking about sport, discussing questions, opening questions, developing answers to personal questions
Writing:	informal letter, following letter writing conventions, responding appropriately, acknowledging a letter, using suitable openings & endings, giving opinions & advice, recommending

Unit opener

- Ask students to look at the title of the unit and to guess what it means (being obsessed with sport).
- Ask them which other words they know that can mean sports crazy in this context (athletics/sports fan, fitness/sports fanatic).
- Ask students to look at the picture and to read the caption. Ask students to tell the rest of the class one positive and one negative thing about doing the kind of sport shown in the picture.
- Ask students to look at the picture again and ask them what is happening. Ask them to guess how the person in the picture might be feeling and why.
- Ask them how the picture corresponds to the theme of the unit (somebody might have to be a bit crazy to participate in the sport shown in the picture) and whether they would like to do the sport shown.

Reading

A

- Ask students to read the instructions and check that they understand what they have to do.
- Read the words in the yellow box to students and ask them to repeat them. Correct their pronunciation where necessary.
- Ask students to do the task individually, but check answers as a class.
- Once answers have been checked, ask students to read the two questions and answer any queries they may have about them.
- Ask students to work in pairs and to take it in turns to ask and answer the questions about themselves.
- Go round the class monitoring students to make sure they are carrying out the task properly. Don't correct any mistakes at this point, but make a note of any problems in structure or pronunciation.
- Ask each pair to ask and answer one question and repeat until each student has had a turn.
- Write any structural mistakes made by students on the board without saying who made them, and ask them to correct them. Deal with any problems in pronunciation that came up.

Answers

1 skydiving
2 swimming with sharks
3 wheel gymnastics
4 spinning

Students' own answers

Extra Class Activity

If time allows, ask students to work in pairs to write down the names of as many sports as they can in English in three minutes. The team who writes down the most sports is the winner.

B

- Ask students to look at the titles of the three texts and elicit how they are related (they all have to do with extreme sport). Ask them if they have ever done an extreme sport, and if they have, what kind of extreme sport it was.
- Ask students to read the instructions for B and check that they understand what they have to do.
- Ask them to skim read the texts to find relevant information regarding the question. Explain that they don't have to read the texts in detail as they will have another opportunity to do that later.
- Ask students to do the task individually, but check answer as a class.

Answers

- Text 1 tries to persuade readers to take part in a risky activity.
- Text 2 gives instructions as to how to minimise risks while using specific sports equipment.
- Text 3 explains why some people take risks while others play it safe.

11 Sports Crazy!

Word Focus

- Ask students to look at the words in red in the text and to re-read the sentences they are found in.
- Ask students to work in pairs to decide what each of the words means in the *Word Focus* box and to then find synonyms, if any, for each word.
- Ask students to compare their answers with another pair. Explain anything they don't understand.

C

- Ask students to read the *Exam Close-up* and ask a student to explain what it says in his or her own words. Explain that in multiple-choice tasks they should always consider the visual layout of the texts for clues as to what kind of texts they might be.
- Remind students to skim read the texts first to get a general idea of what kind of texts they are before marking any answers.
- Remind students to always read the questions carefully and underline any key words.
- Elicit from students what the purpose of each text in B is (*1st text: persuade; 2nd text: advise and warn; 3rd text: report and inform*).
- Ask students to read the instructions and items 1–6 and their options. Explain anything the students don't understand.
- Ask students to underline any key words in the items and the options, and to underline the parts in the texts that refer to each of the items. Point out that the information in the items follows the same order as the texts.
- Encourage students to think about the purpose of each text as they do the task.
- Ask students to do the task individually, but check as a class.

Answers

1 c (Connery was the first person to jump … in his specially-designed suit. … Now you too can don a wingsuit.)
2 a (…skydive from a plane or helicopter without a parachute and land safely. 'Impossible', I hear you cry? Not if you're wearing a wingsuit!)
3 b (Nothing specific to underline as the whole text is relevant to answering the question.)
4 b (Maintenance work must be carried out to … on a regular basis.)
5 d (This study will examine what drives some people to embrace extreme risks, while others are extremely safety-conscious.)
6 c (They recognise the risk involved and do whatever they can to minimise it.)

D

- Ask students to read the instructions and check that they understand what they have to do.
- Point out that they have to replace the words and phrases in bold in the sentences with others from the texts with the same meaning.
- Encourage students to read all the sentences in D before scanning the texts for synonymous words and phrases.
- Ask students to do the task individually, but check as a class.

Answers

1 Do you have what it takes
2 given the go-ahead
3 borne in mind
4 holds us back
5 strong craving

Ideas Focus

- Explain to students that they are going to answer some questions about extreme sports and risk-taking. Ask students to read the questions and explain anything they don't understand.
- Ask students to answer the questions in pairs and encourage them to draw on their own personal experience as much as possible.
- Go round the class monitoring students to ensure they are carrying out the task properly. Don't correct any mistakes at this point, but make a note of any problems in structure or pronunciation.
- Ask students at random round the class to answer each of the questions and encourage the other students to give their opinions.
- Write any structural mistakes made by students on the board without saying who made them and ask them to correct them. Deal with any problems in pronunciation that came up.

Answers

Students' own answers

Vocabulary

A

- Ask students to read the instructions and check that they understand what they have to do.
- Ask them to skim read the text, without circling any answers and elicit what the text is about (*sports announcers/commentators*).
- Read the words in options 1–10 and ask students to repeat them after you. Correct their pronunciation where necessary. Explain anything they don't understand.
- Tell students that they should consider all four options before circling their answers.
- Remind students to re-read the text once they have finished to check their answers.
- Ask students to do the task individually, but check as a class.

Answers

1a 2a 3c 4a 5c 6c 7a 8d 9a 10b

B

- Ask students to read the instructions and check that they understand what they have to do.
- Ask students how many things the task asks them to do (two – circle the correct words and match the commentaries 1–6 to the sports).
- Ask students to read the commentaries without circling any words at this stage. Explain anything they don't understand.
- Read the words in red to students and ask them to repeat them. Correct their pronunciation where necessary. Point out that this part of the task tests words that are often confused, so the correct answers will depend on how naturally each option fits in with the context of the sentence.
- Ask students to do the task individually, but check as a class.
- Read out the words in the yellow box and ask students to repeat them after you. Correct their pronunciation where necessary.
- Encourage students to read all the commentaries in B again before matching them to the sports.
- Ask students to work in pairs to encourage discussion, but check as a class.

Answers

1 serves, set; tennis
2 hole, club; golf
3 shoots, buzzer; basketball
4 holders, baton; relay race
5 lane, lap; swimming
6 referee, diving; football

C

- Ask students to read the instructions and check that they understand what they have to do.
- Read sets of words 1–8 to the students and ask them to repeat them after you. Correct their pronunciation where necessary.
- Ask students to work in pairs to encourage discussion, but check the answers as a class. Ask students to explain why one of the words is the odd one out in each item.

Answers

1 conquer (*The others are synonyms meaning to go up against others to fight for athletic supremacy, but 'conquer' means to defeat others.*)
2 leap (*The others are verbs which describe running fast, but 'leap' means to 'jump' in the air.*)
3 row (*The others are words related to things you can do with a ball, but 'row' is something you do on a boat using oars to propel it through the water.*)
4 hinder (*The others are all ways to say you beat your opponent easily, but 'hinder' means to get in the way of, or prevent something from happening.*)
5 aspire (*The others are to do with improving the quality of a skill, but 'aspire' means to desire or hope for something.*)
6 command (*The others are ways of saying you put a lot of effort into achieving a particular goal, but 'command' means to order or tell someone to do something.*)
7 obstruct (*The others describe ways of being prohibited from doing something, but 'obstruct' means to make something more difficult than it has to be.*)
8 revive (*The others are ways of supporting someone taking part in an event, but 'revive' means to be brought back to life or consciousness.*)

D

- Ask students to read the instructions and check that they understand what they have to do.
- Read sentences 1–5 and then a–e and ask students to underline the phrasal verbs. Explain anything they don't understand.
- Ask students to do the task individually, but check as a class.
- Point out that they will be better able to remember phrasal verbs if they record them in their notebooks and include their definitions as well as a sentence demonstrating their use.

Answers

1d 2e 3a 4c 5b

E

- Ask students to look at the picture to the right of the text in E and ask them to describe what they see and where the picture might have been taken (*athletes starting a race, at an athletics meeting somewhere*). Ask them if they have ever been in a situation like this one, and if they have, ask them what the outcome was.
- Read the prepositions in the yellow box to the students and explain that they will use these to complete the text. Point out that they should use each preposition only once, except for *on* (which they will use three times).

11 Sports Crazy!

- Ask students to read the text carefully and to pay attention to the words before or after the gap and try to think of a preposition which follows or precedes the words without filling in any answers at this stage.
- Ask students to do the task individually, but check as a class.

Answers

1 of	5 for
2 in	6 on
3 off	7 on
4 to	8 on

F

- Ask students to read the instructions and check that they understand what they have to do.
- Read the words in the yellow box to students and ask them to repeat them. Correct their pronunciation where necessary.
- Ask students to read the sentences without writing any answers at this stage and explain that each one contains an expression. Remind students that in English there are lots of colourful expressions and that some of these expressions deal with sport.
- Ask students to work in pairs to encourage discussion, but check as a class.
- Once the answers have been checked, ask students to answer the two questions in pairs.
- Go round the class monitoring students to ensure they are carrying out the task properly. Don't correct any mistakes at this point, but make a note of any problems in structure or pronunciation.
- Ask students at random to answer each of the questions and encourage the other students to give their opinions.
- Write any structural mistakes made by students on the board without saying who made them and ask them to correct them. Deal with any problems in pronunciation that came up.
- Point out that they will be better able to remember expressions if they record them in their notebooks and include their definitions as well as a sentence demonstrating their use.

Answers

1. court; it is your responsibility to make the next move; tennis
2. gate; to be the first to do something that others are also trying to do; horse racing
3. corner; to have someone's support or help; boxing
4. ball; make a mistake, be unreliable; American football, rugby, basketball
5. hurdle; go wrong or fail at the first stage; hurdling
6. bull's-eye; be exactly right about something; archery, shooting, darts

Ideas Focus

- Ask students to read the instructions and check that they understand what they have to do.
- Ask students to read the quotes about sport.
- Ask students to get into pairs and to discuss whether they agree with the quotes and if so, why.
- Go round the class monitoring students to ensure they are carrying out the task properly. Don't correct any mistakes at this point, but make a note of any problems in structure or pronunciation.
- Ask students at random to discuss one of the quotes and encourage the other students to give their opinions as well.
- Write any structural mistakes made by students on the board without saying who made them, and ask them to correct them. Deal with any problems in pronunciation that came up.

Answers

Students' own answers

Grammar

- Write the sentences below on the board and ask students what the people would have actually said.
  - He said that tennis camp was very helpful. (*'Tennis camp is very helpful.'*)
  - She said that the coach had been too hard on me. (*'The coach has been/was too hard on you.'*)
  - They said charging a fee to enter the race might be a good idea. (*'Charging a fee to enter the race may/might be a good idea.'*)
  - She said that she would help me train for the marathon. (*'I'll help you train for the marathon.'*)
- Revise the changes that are made when changing direct speech to reported speech (*tenses move back in time after a past tense reporting verb; some modal verbs change in reported speech and others don't; the Past Perfect stays the same; words referring to people, places and time change in reported speech according to the new situation*).

A

- Ask students to read the instructions and check that they understand what they have to do.
- Read out the first rule to students and explain anything they don't understand. Read out the direct speech sentence and then ask them to read the reported speech sentence to themselves.
- Explain to students that they should think about what the rule says before circling any answers. Remind students to re-read the sentences once they have finished to check their answers.
- Repeat for rules 2–6. Check answers as a class.

Answers

1 scored	5 said to Jim, told me about
2 those, hers	
3 wouldn't, had to	6 told, asked
4 would, should	

Now read the Grammar Reference on pages 170 & 171 (11.1 & 11.2) with your students.

B

- Ask students to read the instructions and check that they understand what they have to do. Ask students to read the two sentences in item 1. Then ask them to underline the part in the first sentence that is missing from the second sentence. Explain to students that in order to complete the second sentence they will have to make a structural change(s) involving changing direct speech into reported speech.
- Ask students to complete the first item and correct it before they move on to the rest of the task.
- Ask students to do the task individually, but check as a class.

Answers

1. was arriving in their city the following/next day
2. their team would fly to Barcelona that night
3. had been training in the rain the day before/the previous day
4. would celebrate its 100-year anniversary the following/next weekend
5. was going to buy a tennis racquet that week
6. not to be late for practice that day

C

- Ask students to read the instructions and check that they understand what they have to do.
- Ask a student to read out a quote and explain anything they don't understand until all the quotes have been read.
- Point out that they have to make changes to the direct quotes so that the new reported quotes make sense.
- Encourage students to refer back to A if they need help when rewriting the quotes.
- Ask students to do the task individually, but check as a class.

Suggested answers

1. Emil Zatopek said that an athlete couldn't run with money in his pockets. He had to run with hope in his heart and dreams in his head.
2. Babe Ruth explained that you might have the greatest bunch of individual stars in the world, but if they didn't play together as a team, the club wouldn't be worth a dime.
3. Ayrton Senna told a journalist that when you were fitted in a racing car and you raced to win, second or third place was not enough.
4. Alberto Tomba remarked that he really lacked the words to compliment himself that day.

D

- Read the information about reporting verbs to the students and elicit what the three most common reporting verbs are *(say, tell and ask)*.
- Ask students to look back at the second Reading text on extreme sports on pages 136 and 137 to find an example of a reporting verb *(claim)* and elicit what structure it is followed by *(that)*.
- Ask students to read the instructions and check that they understand what they have to do.

- Explain that they must use the words in brackets in the correct form in the reported sentences.
- Ask students to read the two sentences in item 1. Then ask them to underline the part in the first sentence that is missing from the second sentence.
- Explain to students that in order to complete the second sentence they will have to make a structural change involving changing direct speech into reported speech.
- Ask students to complete the first item and correct it before they move on to the rest of the task.
- Ask students to do the task individually, but check as a class.

Answers

1. apologised for missing
2. offered to help
3. warned me/us not to surf
4. encouraged me to become

E

- Ask students to read the instructions and check that they understand what they have to do.
- Read out the first rule to students and explain anything they don't understand. Read out the direct speech sentence and then ask them to read the reported speech sentence to themselves.
- Explain to students that they should think about what the rule says before writing any answers. Remind students to re-read the sentence once they have finished to check their answers.
- Repeat for rules 2 and 3. Check answers as a class.

Answers

1. if/whether the player had renewed
2. when I was leaving
3. why I didn't like

Now read the Grammar Focus on page 171 (11.3 & 11.4) with your students.

F

- Ask students to read the instructions and check that they understand what they have to do.
- Ask a student to read out a paragraph and explain anything they don't understand until all three paragraphs have been read.
- Point out that they have to make changes to the underlined text in the paragraphs so that the new reported text makes sense.
- Encourage students to refer back to D and E if they need help when rewriting the underlined text.
- Ask students to do the task individually, but check as a class.

Answers

1. what he attributed his team's success to; he attributed it to himself
2. if he had visited the Parthenon; he couldn't really remember the names of the clubs they had gone/been to
3. what his game was like; it was like Pythagoras' Theorem. Not too many people knew the answer to it

11 Sports Crazy!

Teaching Tip

Remind students to refer to the Grammar Focus pages to see which grammar rule matches their answers and to refer back to it if they make a mistake to see why their answers were incorrect. Remind them to ask you if they have any difficulty understanding a grammar rule so that you can go over any points that they need help with before you move on

Listening

A

- Ask students to read the instructions and check that they understand what they have to do.
- Read the words in the yellow box to students and ask them to repeat them. Correct their pronunciation where necessary.
- Ask students to read all the sentences in A before writing any answers. Explain to students that in English there are lots of expressions and that these sentences contain expressions so they should look at the words before and after the gaps to help them choose their answers.
- Ask students to work in pairs to encourage discussion, but check as a class.

Answers

1. bargain
2. kick
3. fence
4. stray
5. wriggle
6. heart
7. hands

B

- Ask students to read the instructions and make sure they understand what they have to do.
- Allow students time to read the questions and options quickly and to underline the adverbs of frequency, adverbs of degree and time expressions.
- Ask them to compare what they have underlined with a partner. Check what they have underlined as a class.
- Explain that students will hear a woman talking. Ask them to look back at the questions and options and ask students around the class to guess what she might be talking about (being a successful cyclist).
- Play the recording all the way through and ask students to circle their answers. Then ask students to discuss their answers with a partner.
- Play the recording again and ask students to check their answers and to fill in any missing answers.
- Check the answers as a class.

Answers

1. a only recently
   b always
   c sometimes
2. a regularly
   b only
   c constantly

1b 2c

C

- Ask students to read the instructions and make sure they understand what they have to do.
- Play the recording from B again and ask students to check why the options, other than the options they chose in B, are incorrect.
- Ask students to get into pairs and to discuss why the other options were incorrect. Ask students to justify their answers using what they underlined in the questions and options in B and expressions they heard on the recording.
- Check answers as a class and ask students to justify their answers.

Suggested answers

1. Option a is wrong because the woman says, 'For as long as I can remember, I've been interested in cycling,' which shows she has liked cycling for many years not just recently.
   Option c is wrong because the woman says, 'I've never once thought about what I would do with myself if I didn't cycle. There's no question of me not getting on my bike every day.' which shows she has no intention of giving up cycling.
2. Option a is wrong because the woman talks about being lazy during her spare time but then goes on to say, 'But that doesn't happen very often…,' which means she obviously doesn't regularly have time off to relax.'
   Option b is wrong because the woman says, 'I can be a bit of a couch potato when I want…,' which means she is probably watching TV and not always thinking about cycling.

D

- Ask students to read the Exam Close-up.
- Remind students of any differences in the answers they might have had in B and explain that this task shows how important it is to pay attention to the adverbs of frequency and degree and time expressions in the questions and options before they listen to the recording in this type of listening task.
- Stress that sometimes the main idea in an option may be correct, but that the adverbs of frequency and degree and time expressions are incorrect, meaning the whole option is actually a wrong answer.
- Ask students to read the instructions and check they understand what they have to do.
- Explain that they will hear three different segments and that there are two questions for each segment.
- Give students time to read 1–6 and to underline the adverbs of frequency, adverbs of degree and the time expressions in the questions and options.
- Ask students to compare what they have underlined with a partner and to justify their answers.
- Play the recording once all the way through and ask students to circle their answers. Then ask students to discuss their answers with a partner and to justify any answers they have that are different.
- Check the answers as a class and ask students to justify their answers.

Answers

1a 2c 3c 4b 5b 6c

Speaking

A

- Ask students to read the three questions and answer any queries they may have about them.
- Ask students to work in pairs and to take it in turns to ask and answer the questions.
- Go round the class monitoring students to make sure they are carrying out the task properly. Don't correct any mistakes at this point, but make a note of any problems in structure or pronunciation.
- Write any structural mistakes made by students on the board without saying who made them, and ask them to correct them. Deal with any problems in pronunciation that came up.

Answers

Students' own answers

B

- Ask students to read the instructions and check that they understand what they have to do. Make sure that each pair has a watch to use between them.
- Ask students to read the six topics and answer any queries they have about them.
- Go round the class monitoring students to make sure they are carrying out the task properly. Don't correct any mistakes at this point, but make a note of any problems in structure or pronunciation.
- As a class, ask one student from each pair to tell the rest of the class what he or she said about a topic making sure all six topics are covered. Ask the others if they agree or if they have anything else to add.
- Write any structural mistakes made by students on the board without saying who made them, and ask them to correct them. Deal with any problems in pronunciation that came up.

Answers

Students' own answers

C

- Ask students to read the *Exam Close-up*.
- Ask students to read the first questions for each student in the *Exam Task*. Get them to apply what they have just read in the *Exam Close-up* to show they have understood what they need to do when answering these types of questions.

Answers

Students' own answers

Useful Expressions

- Read the *Useful Expressions* to the students and ask them to repeat them. Correct their pronunciation and intonation where necessary.
- Explain to students that all these expressions can be used to develop answers to personal questions in the long turn part of the speaking task.
- Point out to students that they should use some of these expressions when they do the *Exam Task*.

D

- Ask students to read the instructions again and check that they understand what they have to do.
- Ask students to work in pairs and to decide who will be Student A and who will be Student B. Ask them to spend a few minutes looking at each of their questions.
- Ask students to read through the rubric and the *Exam Task*. In pairs, students should take turns answering each set of questions.
- Go round the class monitoring students to make sure they are carrying out the task properly. Don't correct any mistakes at this point, but make a note of any problems in structure or pronunciation.
- Ask a student from each pair to answer one of the questions until each pair has had a turn. Ask the other students if they agree or if they have anything else to add.
- Write any structural mistakes made by students on the board without saying who made them, and ask them to correct them. Deal with any problems in pronunciation that came up.

Answers

Students' own answers

Ideas Focus

- Ask students to read the questions quickly and deal with any queries they may have.
- Ask students to work in pairs and to take it in turns to answer the questions.
- Go round the class monitoring students to make sure they are carrying out the task properly. Don't correct any mistakes at this point, but make a note of any problems in structure or pronunciation.
- Ask a student from each pair to answer one of the questions until each pair has had a turn. Ask other students if they agree or if they have anything else to add.
- Write any structural mistakes made by students on the board without saying who made them, and ask them to correct them. Deal with any problems in pronunciation that came up.

Answers

Students' own answers

11 Sports Crazy!

Writing: an informal letter

- Explain to students that in this lesson they are going to deal with writing letters.
- Ask students to read the *Learning Focus* on following letter writing conventions and explain anything they don't understand. Ask them how many things they will be expected to do in a letter task *(two)* and elicit what they are *(respond appropriately to the situation presented in the question and address every point or query raised in the input material)*.
- Elicit from students what types of things they might have to do in a letter task *(provide or request information, express an opinion, persuade someone to do something, give advice, etc.)*.
- Remind students that they must always follow the conventions of letter writing which means they must include an appropriate beginning and ending, and they must use clear paragraphing.

A

- Ask students to read the instructions and check that they understand what they have to do.
- Ask students to work in pairs to come up with as many ways of beginning and ending a letter as they can.
- Go round the class monitoring students to make sure they are carrying out the task properly.
- Ask each pair to read out their lists; one student could read out the beginnings and the other could read out the endings. Write all the appropriate beginnings and endings on the board.
- When all the pairs have had the chance to talk about their lists, start a short discussion as a class about who the students would be addressing with each of the beginnings and endings that are on the board.

Suggested answers

Beginnings: Hi!, Dear Mary, Dear Mr Smith, To whom it may concern
Endings: Bye for now, Take care, Yours sincerely, Yours faithfully, Best wishes, Kind regards

Teaching Tip

Encourage students to write the best beginnings and endings in their notebooks and to make a note for each about when it would be appropriate to use them i.e. with a friend, an employer, etc.

B

- Ask students to read the instructions and check that they understand what they have to do.
- Ask students to read the writing task and explain anything they don't understand.
- Ask students to do the task individually, but check as a class.

Answers

1 Lisa Jones, you met her in her professional capacity as the manager of a sports complex, semi-formal but friendly register.
2 Dear Lisa/Dear Ms Jones; Best wishes/Yours sincerely (*though somewhat formal*)
3 express an opinion on certain aspects (*what you liked and disliked*), explain (*why you liked/didn't like something*), recommend improvements
4 three main paragraphs: 1) what you liked, 2) what was disappointing, 3) suggestions for improvement

C

- Ask students to read the instructions and check that they understand what they have to do.
- Ask students to read the example letter and underline information that relates to the style in the writing task. Then ask them to compare the parts they underlined with a partner.
- As a class, ask students how they would describe the style of the letter and to quote the parts in the letter that justify their answers. Then discuss what features give the letter a friendly tone. Ask students to justify their answers.

Answers

semi-formal and friendly style
features which give it a friendly tone:
'Thanks' instead of 'Thank you'
contractions (*weren't, don't think, they're, we're all looking forward*)
offering reasons (*I suppose the fact ... played a role in this*)
'Best wishes' rather than 'Yours sincerely'

D

- Ask students to read the instructions and check that they understand what they have to do.
- Ask students how many things the task asks them to do (*two – look at the example again and answer the questions*).
- Ask students to read the example letter again and to find information that relates to the questions in the task. Then ask them to compare the parts they have found with a partner and justify any things they have underlined that are different.
- Ask students to work in pairs to encourage discussion, but check as a class.

Answers

1 Dear Ms Jones; Best wishes,
2 Yes, the writer has done everything required
3 Students should underline the following:
– It was our favourite activity
– staff were extremely helpful, knew what they were doing, patient, made us feel safe
– changing rooms were cramped,
– the place seemed quite full, having to wait to do some activities
4 yes, she would know what to do and, as such, has been fully informed

E

- Ask students to read the instructions and check that they understand what they have to do.
- Ask students to look at the example letter again, choose either the positive or negative comments made by the students and write a paragraph in their notebooks.
- Give students no more than five minutes to write their paragraph and go round the class offering help where necessary.
- Ask some students to read out their paragraph to the rest of the class. You could hang all paragraphs on the wall and ask students to read each other's work.

Answers

Students' own answers

F

- Ask the students to read the *Exam Close-up* and point out that the writer of the example letter did all the things on the list.
- Remind students that they can use the information here as a checklist when writing their own letters.
- Ask students to read the *Exam Task* and ask them to underline any key words and phrases in the task. Explain anything they don't understand.
- Ask students to answer the questions in B about this writing task so that they know what they have to do.
- As a class, ask students who they are writing to *(their friend, Emily)* and what style they will use *(a friendly, informal style)*.
- Ask students to read the paragraph plan and to make notes for each paragraph if time allows. Ask students how they will begin and end their letters.
- Set the *Exam Task* for homework.
- Encourage students to use the Writing Reference and checklist for letters on page 184.

Suggested answer

Hi Emily,
Thanks for your letter. I'm happy to give you some advice on how to get fit and healthy.
I'm really pleased with the facilities on offer at *Sports Now* and in my opinion it's by far the best sports club in town. It has great facilities, it's always really clean and the staff are really friendly. No other place can match it. You can do many different team sports there like football, basketball and volleyball along with individual sports such as swimming, tennis and golf. You mentioned wanting to take up either volleyball or swimming in your letter. If I were you I'd take up volleyball because it would get you fit in no time. It's a fun and fast-paced game that involves lots of running, jumping and squatting.
You also asked if there were any other things you could do to help you get fit. Have you considered going for long walks? This is a lovely way to get gentle exercise and breathe in lots of fresh air at the same time, which will make you feel great. How about we meet and go for a long walk together? We can keep fit and catch up at the same time.
I hope my advice is useful to you. Let me know how you get on and let me know if you would like to meet up for a walk.
Love,
Jessie

Useful Expressions

- Read the *Useful Expressions* to the students and ask them to repeat them. Correct their pronunciation and intonation if necessary.
- Elicit in which part of their letter they can use each category of expressions and tell them to use them when writing their letter for the *Exam Task*.

11 Flying Pumpkins

General Note

Please see the information about the National Geographic videos on page 18 of this Teacher's Book.

Background Information

Pumpkin throwing is a sport or competition which involves throwing a pumpkin as far as possible using some sort of mechanical device. The devices used in the sport range from simple slingshots to elaborate cannons, but no explosives are allowed. Pumpkin-throwing competitions are common in the autumn in many places across the US. The World Championship, 'Punkin Chunkin' which is held in the state of Delaware, is believed to be the biggest and oldest of these yearly competitions.

Before you watch

A

- Explain to students that in this lesson they are going to watch a video about a special competition. Ask them to look at the globe and tell you in which part of the world the competition is held. Elicit what they know about Delaware, USA and the competitions that people take part in there.
- Read words 1–4 to the students and ask them to repeat them. Then ask students to read meanings a–d and explain anything they don't understand.
- Ask students to do the task individually, but check as a class.

Answers

1b 2c 3d 4a

While you watch

B

- Explain to students that they are now going to watch the video and do a task based on what they hear.
- Ask students to read statements 1–6 and ask them what the documentary will be about (a pumpkin throwing competition).
- Explain anything in the statements that the students don't understand. Then ask them to think about which statements might be true and which might be false before they listen.
- Play the video all the way through without stopping and ask students to mark their answers. Ask students to compare their answers with a partner's and to justify any answers they have that are different. Play the video again so that they can check their answers.
- Ask students to do the task individually, but check as a class.

Answers

1 F (00:17)   4 T (02:09)
2 F (00:55)   5 T (02:26)
3 T (01:09)   6 F (02:44)

After you watch

C

- Explain to students that this is a summary of the information they heard on the video.
- Read the words in the yellow box to the students and ask them to repeat them. Ask them to write N, V, Adj, Adv or Prep beside each of the words depending on whether it is a noun, a verb, an adjective, an adverb or a preposition.
- Explain to students that they should read the whole summary before writing any answers first to work out what part of speech is missing.
- Tell students to re-read the text once they have finished to check their answers.
- Ask students to do the task individually, but check as a class.

Answers

1 weigh   6 teams
2 aim   7 machines
3 common   8 Unfortunately
4 started   9 break
5 feet   10 Despite

Ideas Focus

- Ask students to read the instructions and make sure they understand what they have to do. Then ask them to read the three questions and answer any queries they might have.
- Ask students to work in pairs and explain that they should both give their opinions on all three questions.
- Go round the class monitoring students to make sure they are carrying out the task properly. Don't correct any mistakes at this stage, but make a note of any problems in structure and pronunciation.
- Ask each pair to answer one of the questions and repeat until each pair has had a turn.
- Write about whether they think children should be encouraged to take part in competitive sport and how important it is to be competitive in other areas of life on the board.
- Deal with any problems in structure or pronunciation that came up.

Answers

Students' own answers

12 Fast Forward

Reading:	missing paragraphs, checking for coherence & cohesion
Vocabulary:	words related to space, science, technological advances and the future, word formation, prepositions, sentence transformation
Grammar:	clauses of reason, clauses of purpose & result, clauses of contrast, *neither ... nor, either ... or*
Listening:	sentence completion, spelling & numbers
Speaking:	talking about life in the future, follow-up questions, interacting with your partner, supporting opinions with examples
Writing:	essay (2), using formal expressions in moderation, writing an effective essay, introducing, talking about the future, predicting

Unit opener

- Ask students to look at the title of the unit and to guess what it might mean *(moving quickly into the future)*.
- Ask students to look at the picture and read the caption. Then ask them to say how the picture relates to the unit *(the picture is of the gardens at the Eden Project in Cornwall, England. It is a place which preserves seeds and plants for the future)*.
- Give students a minute to write down as many space related-words and words related to technological advances in English as they can. Then write the headings *space-related words* and *technological advances* on the board and ask students to call out the words they have written down. They should also tell you which column the words should go in. Elicit the words *moon* and *satellite* if the students don't mention them.
- If students seem interested, give them more information about the Eden Project using the Background Information box below.

Background Information

The Eden Project is a multiple greenhouse complex in Cornwall, England which is open to visitors. It has a massive collection of plants from all over the world maintained inside several temperature-controlled biomes. There is a tropical biome which contains banana trees and bamboo amongst other things. There is also a mediterranean biome where you'll find olive and grape vines. The Eden Project first opened to visitors in May 2000 and has since hosted concerts and various cultural events.

Reading

A

- Ask students to look at the picture to the left of the article and to describe it.
- Ask students to read the title of the text and elicit how it relates to the picture *(the picture shows the moon, and the article discusses the moon)*.
- Ask students to read the instructions for A and check that they understand what they have to do.
- Ask students to discuss statements 1–6 in pairs to encourage discussion, but check answers as a class.
- Find out which information surprised them the most and why.

Answer
All the statements are true.

B

- Explain to students that they are going to work in pairs to complete the table.
- Ask students to read the instructions and check that they understand what they have to do.
- Ask students to take it in turns to ask and answer questions about the statements in the table and ask them to tick the appropriate boxes.
- Go round the class monitoring students to make sure they are carrying out the task properly. Don't correct any mistakes at this point, but make a note of any problems in structure or pronunciation.
- Ask each pair to talk about one of the statements and repeat until they have all had a turn.
- Write any structural mistakes made by students on the board without saying who made them, and ask them to correct them. Deal with any problems in pronunciation that came up.

Answers
Students' own answers

C

- Ask students to read the instructions for C and check that they understand what they have to do.
- Tell them to read headings 1–4 and then to skim read the text to find the one that fits the text best. Explain that they should only concentrate on information that deals with choosing the best heading and that they don't have to read the text in detail as they will have an opportunity to do that later.
- Ask students to do the task individually, but discuss as a class. Ask students to justify why they chose the heading that they did and ask the other students if they agree or have anything else to add.

133

12 Fast Forward

Answer

3 – because the text discusses the possible exploitation of the moon's natural resources as well as other possible lunar business projects.

Word Focus

- Ask students to look at the words in red in the text and to re-read the sentences they are found in. Ask students to work in pairs to decide what each of the words means in the *Word Focus* box and to then find synonyms, if any, for each word.
- Ask students to compare their answers with another pair. Explain anything they don't understand.

D

- Ask students to read the *Exam Close-up* and ask a student to explain what it says in his or her own words.
- Explain that missing paragraph tasks test understanding of overall structure and development of the text. Ask students why they should pay attention to contrasting links and phrases (*the topic of each paragraph follows on from the paragraph before it and any change of topic is signalled by a contrasting link or phrase*). Ask students for examples of contrasting links and phrases (*however, on the other hand, though, while, whereas, etc.*) and explain that these contrasting links and phrases offer valuable clues for finding the correct missing paragraph.
- Explain to students that it's a good idea to get into the habit of checking why the paragraph they haven't used doesn't fit anywhere in the text.
- Ask students to read the instructions and check that they understand what they have to do.
- Elicit that this is a missing paragraph task and that six paragraphs have been removed from the text and that students must choose from seven paragraphs (*there is one extra paragraph which they do not need to use*) the one which fits each of the six gaps in the text.
- Ask students to read paragraphs A–G and to underline any clues which might help them understand what information they can follow on from or any contrasting links and phrases.
- Ask students to read the text again and to decide where each paragraph goes. Tell them to pay attention to the paragraphs before and after each gap.
- When they have finished tell them to re-read the text to make sure the paragraphs they have chosen make sense in the gaps and to check that the paragraph they haven't used doesn't fit anywhere.
- Ask students to do the task individually, but check as a class.

Answers

1 F 2 A 3 D 4 B 5 G 6 E

E

- Ask students to read the instructions and check that they understand what they have to do.
- Ask students to look at the words in the yellow box and ask them to say each of the words after you. Correct their pronunciation where necessary.
- Tell students that the words in italics in sentences 1–5 are expressions and the missing words will complete the expressions. Encourage students to read all the sentences in E once before writing any answers.
- Ask students to skim read the text again to find and underline the words. Remind them that they should always try to work out the meaning of the word from its context and ask them to read the sentences in the text in which each word is contained.
- Ask students to do the task individually, but check as a class.

Answers

1 pockets   4 cash
2 guns   5 killing
3 secret

Ideas Focus

- Explain to students that they are going to answer some questions about space. Ask students to read the questions and explain anything they don't understand.
- Ask students to answer the questions in pairs and encourage them to draw on personal experience as much as possible.
- Go round the class monitoring students to ensure they are carrying out the task properly. Don't correct any mistakes at this point, but make a note of any problems in structure or pronunciation.
- Ask students at random round the class to answer each of the questions and encourage the other students to give their opinions.
- Write any structural mistakes made by students on the board without saying who made them, and ask them to correct them. Deal with any problems in pronunciation that came up.

Answers

Students' own answers

Vocabulary

A

- Ask students to read the instructions and check that they understand what they have to do. Ask them to read the sentences without circling any words at this stage. Explain anything they don't understand.
- Read the words in red to students and ask them to repeat them. Correct their pronunciation where necessary.
- Point out that the task tests words that are often confused so the correct answers will depend on how naturally each option fits in with the context of the sentence.
- Ask students to do the task individually, but check as a class.

Answers

1 shape	5 speculate
2 holds	6 educated
3 outcome	7 coming
4 hunch	8 omen

B

- Read the nouns in the yellow box to the students and ask them to repeat them. Correct their pronunciation where necessary.
- Ask students to read the instructions and check that they understand what they have to do.
- Ask them to read all the sentences for meaning and underline the words that come before the gaps. Explain that the missing word in each case can form a compound noun with the underlined words.
- Remind students to re-read the sentences once they have finished to check their answers.
- Ask students to do the task individually, but check as a class.
- Encourage students to copy the compound nouns and their meanings into their notebooks.

Answers

1 breakthroughs	4 engineering
2 intelligence	5 telecommunications
3 agencies	6 recognition

C

- Ask students to read the instructions and check that they understand what they have to do.
- Read the words in the yellow box to students and ask them to say them after you. Correct their pronunciation where necessary.
- Ask students to read all the sentences first to work out the meaning of the missing word.
- Remind students to re-read the sentences once they have finished to check their answers.
- Ask students to do the task individually, but check as a class.

Answers

1 eternity	2 infinity	3 posterity

D

- Ask students to read the instructions and check that they understand what they have to do.
- Read sets of words 1–6 to the students and ask them to repeat them after you. Correct their pronunciation where necessary.
- Ask students to work in pairs to encourage discussion, but check the answers as a class. Ask students to explain why one of the words is the odd one out in each item.

Answers

1 intended (*The others mean unaffected by time or change, but 'intended' means something planned or in the future.*)
2 preceding (*The others mean to do something that hasn't been done before perhaps by developing new methods, but 'preceding' means something that happened or came before.*)
3 critical (*The others refer to the fact that something dangerous or intimidating may be about to happen, but to be 'critical' means to make negative judgments.*)
4 rational (*The others are ways of expressing that something is going to happen, but 'rational' means to use logic or reason when thinking about a problem.*)
5 unaware (*The others are ways of expressing that you didn't know or are not able to predict that something is about to happen, but 'unaware' means that you are not conscious of something that is happening.*)
6 disposable (*The others are ways of expressing that you will not be able to avoid doing something, but 'disposable' means something that is designed to be thrown away after use.*)

E

- Ask students to read the title of the text and to look at the accompanying picture. Ask them how the picture might relate to the title (*it might be a picture of Shanghai*) – don't check their answer yet.
- Read the words in capital letters to the students and ask them to repeat them. Correct their pronunciation where necessary.
- Ask students which part of speech each word is (*verbs: boom, construct, complete, accelerate, imagine; nouns: boom, future, magnet, commerce*) and which other parts of speech of these words they know.
- Ask students to read the text, without filling in any answers, to find out how the title relates to the picture (*as above*).
- Ask students to read the instructions and check that they understand what they have to do. Ask students to work out what part of speech is missing from each gap before they write their answers.
- Remind students to re-read the text once they have finished to check their answers.
- Ask students to do the task individually, but check as a class.

Answers

1 booming	5 magnetic
2 futuristic	6 commercially
3 construction	7 acceleration
4 completion	8 unimaginable

12 Fast Forward

F

- Ask students to read the instructions and check that they understand what they have to do. Ask them to also read the title of the text and to look at the accompanying picture. Ask students how the picture might relate to the title *(perhaps people are taller now than in the past)* – don't check their answer yet.
- Read the words in red to students and ask them to repeat them. Correct their pronunciation where necessary. Point out that the task tests prepositions so the correct answers will depend on what comes before or after the gaps.
- Ask students to read the text, without filling in any answers, to find out how the title relates to the picture *(as above)*.
- Remind students to re-read the text once they have finished to check their answers.
- Ask students to do the task individually, but check as a class.

Answers
1 by
2 of
3 in
4 in
5 to
6 about

G

- Ask students to read the *Exam Close-up* and check that they understand what they have to do.
- Ask students to read both sentences in each item and to underline the information in the first sentence that is missing from the second sentence. Then ask them to look at the word given to decide how the missing information could be inserted into sentence two using this word. Remind students that they will have to use a different structure in order to keep the meaning the same.
- Remind students that they mustn't change the word given in bold in any way.
- Encourage students to re-read the completed sentences once they have finished to check their answers.

Answers
1 was refused a job
2 will be able to travel
3 Despite knowing nothing
4 don't find it easy
5 It was such a far-fetched

Grammar

- Write the sentences below on the board.
  - Scientists are looking for a planet similar to Earth **in order to** find a place we could possibly move to one day.
  - Scientists are looking for a planet similar to Earth **because** we might have to move one day.
  - The chances of ever finding a planet similar to Earth are slim. **Nevertheless**, scientists are still looking.
  - The scientists thought they had found a planet similar to Earth; they were **so excited that** they stood up and cheered!

- Ask students what the words in bold all have in common *(they introduce clauses)*. Elicit from students which sentence contains a clause of reason *(2nd sentence)*, which sentence contains a clause of purpose *(1st sentence)*, which sentence contains a clause of result *(4th sentence)* and which sentence contains a clause of contrast *(3rd sentence)*.
- Explain that in this part of the lesson, they are going to revise clauses of reason, clauses of purpose & result, and clauses of contrast.

A

- Read the information about clauses of reason to the students and elicit one or two common words or phrases that introduce them *(because, because of, since, etc.)*.
- Ask students to read the instructions and check that they understand what they have to do.
- Ask students to read the sentences and the questions and explain anything they don't understand about clauses of reason.
- Ask students to focus on the words in bold in each sentence as they do the task.
- Ask students to do the task individually, but check as a class.

Answers
1 as, since, seeing that/as
2 owing to, due to, for, with
3 as, because, so, since, seeing that/as
4 because of, owing to, due to, for, with
5 with
6 so

B

- Ask students to read the instructions and check that they understand what they have to do.
- Ask students to read the sentences and explain anything they don't understand about clauses of purpose and result.
- Ask students to focus on the words in bold in each sentence as they decide which structures introduce a purpose and which are used to show a result.
- Ask students to do the task in pairs to encourage discussion, but check as a class.

Answers
purpose: *for, in order/so as* + full infinitive, full infinitive, *for* + *-ing*
result: *so* + adjective/adverb + *(that)*, *such* + *a(n)* + adjective + singular noun + *(that)*, *too* + adjective + full infinitive, *(not)* + adjective + *enough* + full infinitive

C

- Read the information about clauses of contrast to the students and elicit one or two common words or phrases that introduce them *(However, Whereas, etc.)*.
- Ask students to read the instructions and check that they understand what they have to do.

- Ask students to read sentences 1–4 all the way through before trying to match them to expressions a–d and explain anything they don't understand.
- Ask students to do the task individually, but check as a class.

Answers

1 d 2 b 3 c 4 a

Now read the Grammar Reference on pages 171 & 172 (12.1 to 12.3) with your students.

D

- Ask students to read the title and then to skim read the text to find out how the title relates to the picture. *(The text is about how people constantly strive to do better and better. This relates to the picture because the man /astronaut has probably worked very hard to get to where he was at the moment the picture was taken.)*
- Explain to students that they should think about which type of clause is being used in each item and to refer back to the Grammar box if they need help when choosing their answers.
- Remind students to re-read the text once they have finished to check their answers.
- Ask students to do the task individually, but check as a class.

Answers

1 So as
2 With
3 Whereas
4 so important that
5 to watch
6 In order to

Extra Class Activity

If time allows, ask students to go back to the Reading text on pages 148 and 149 and underline all the clauses. Ask them to identify the clauses as clauses of reason, clauses of purpose & result, or clauses of contrast.

- Write the sentences below on the board.
  - I will either watch a film about Mars or a film about Saturn this evening.
  - Neither the film about Mars nor the film about Saturn were very interesting.
- Ask students which sentence uses a construction to offer a choice between two possibilities *(1st sentence)*.
- Ask students which construction in the two sentences could be replaced by *neither of (neither ... nor)* and ask students what form of the verb *be* follows the construction *(singular)*. Explain that subjects connected by *neither ... nor* take either a plural or singular verb conjunction depending on the subject closer to the conjugated verb.
- Ask students to look back at the Reading text on the moon on pages 148 and 149 to find an example of one of the constructions contained in the sentences on the board and ask them what it refers to *(neither ... nor / space exploration projects will be neither affordable nor sustainable)*.
- Explain that in this lesson they are going to revise the use of the constructions *neither ... nor* and *either ... or*.

E

- Ask students to read the instructions and check that they understand what they have to do. Ask students to read the sentences all the way through before circling any answers.
- Ask students to do the task individually, but check as a class.

Answers

1 *wants* because 'Buzz', which is closer to the verb, is singular
2 *watch* because 'my sisters', which is closer to the verb, is plural

F

- Ask students to read the instructions and check that they understand what they have to do.
- Ask a student to read out the sentence. As a class, elicit answers to the two questions.
- Read out the *Be Careful!* to students and explain anything they don't understand about the *neither ... nor* construction.

Answers

it is inverted; no, he didn't – *nor* means it is negative

G

- Read the information about the *Either ... or* construction to the students and explain anything they don't understand.
- Ask students to read the instructions and check that they understand what they have to do. Explain that only one of the two sentences is correct.
- Ask students to do the task individually, but check as a class.
- Read out the *Be Careful!* to students and explain anything they don't understand about the *Either ... or* construction.

Answers

Sentence 1 is correct because 'Mars' is singular and it is the subject closest to the verb.

Now read the Grammar Reference on page 172 (12.4 & 12.5) with your students.

H

- Ask students to read the instructions and check that they understand what they have to do.
- Ask students to read the first sentence and elicit what form of the verb *be* is needed *(plural)* to complete the gap and why *(it is closer to the word 'friends')*. Ask students to fill in the answer before moving on.
- Explain that they should analyse sentences 2–6 in this way to help them decide which verb forms should be used in each gap.
- Ask students to do the task individually, but check as a class.

12 Fast Forward

Answers

1 are
2 wants
3 support
4 is
5 has
6 is/was able

I

- Ask students to read the instructions and check that they understand what they have to do.
- Encourage students to read the whole sentence before writing any answers to look for any clues to the right answer.
- Encourage students to look back at E, F and G if they need any help while doing the task.
- Remind students to re-read the sentences once they have finished to check their answers.
- Ask students to do the task individually, but check as a class.

Answers

1 either of
2 Either
3 neither of
4 either of
5 Neither

J

- Ask students to read the instructions and check that they understand what they have to do. Explain that they mustn't change the word in bold in any way in the second sentence.
- Ask students to read the two sentences in item 1. Then ask them to underline the part in the first sentence that is missing from the second sentence.
- Explain to students that in order to complete the second sentence they will have to make a structural change.
- Ask students to complete the first item and correct it before they move on to do the rest of the task.
- Ask students to do the task individually, but check as a class.

Answers

1 Either you enter the competition or
2 neither admitted nor denied
3 neither Chloe nor Courtney is
4 nor did he start

Listening

A

- Ask students to read the instructions and check that they understand what they have to do.
- Ask students to read the sentences and think about the syntax, synonyms and vocabulary that they contain.
- Ask students to do the task in pairs to encourage discussion, but check as a class.

Answers

1 The answer repeats information from the rest of the sentence as a *cheap* car is one that doesn't *break the bank*.
2 There is repetition as *middle of* and *mid* mean the same thing.
3 The word *omissions* doesn't make sense in the context so it can't be the right answer.
4 There's a grammatical error as an adjective is needed here, not just an adverb and *electrically* is an adverb.
5 The verb *are* needs to be followed by a plural noun, but here we have a singular (*Japan*).

B

- Ask students to read the instructions and make sure they understand what they have to do.
- Ask students to read the sentences in A again and to think about what the answers might be before they listen.
- Play the recording once all the way through and ask students to write their answers on the lines in A. Ask students to compare their answers with a partner and to justify any answers they have that are different.
- Play the recording again so they can check their answers or fill in any missing answers.
- Check answers as a class and ask students to justify their answers.

Answers

1 sustainable car
2 19th century
3 emissions
4 electrically powered
5 Japan and America

C

- Ask students to read the *Exam Close-up*.
- Remind them of any differences in any answers they might have had in B and explain that this task shows how important it is to re-read the sentences at the end of the task to make sure that their answers make sense in the context of the sentences.
- Explain to students that if answers contain numbers, they can write these either as figures, as words or a figure plus a word.
- Stress to students that their answers should be spelled correctly.
- Ask students to read the instructions and check they understand what they have to do.
- Explain that they will hear someone talking about a project on an alternative form of fuel.
- Explain that in this type of listening task, the situation is always given and that they should read it carefully so they will be able to predict, to a degree, what might be said on the recording.
- Give students time to read questions 1–8 and to underline any key words in the situation and the sentences. Answer any questions they might have about them.

- Play the recording once all the way through and ask students to complete any sentences they can. Then ask them to discuss their answers with a partner and to justify any answers they have that are different.

D
- Play the recording again and ask students to check their answers and to fill in any missing answers.
- Encourage students to re-read the sentences at the end of the task to make sure that their answers make sense in the context of the sentences.
- Check the answers as a class and ask students to justify their answers.

Answers

1 over 24,000 km
2 vegetable oil
3 to demonstrate
4 refuelling
5 harmful emissions
6 production (process)
7 divide
8 hectic

Extra Class Activity

If time allows, ask students to look at the picture at the bottom of the page and discuss what it depicts in pairs. Then as a class, discuss whether the picture is an effective way to depict alternative energy cars.

Speaking

A
- Ask students to read the instructions and check that they understand what they have to do.
- Ask students to read the five statements and answer any queries they have about them.
- Point out to students that in this task they have to tick how far they agree with each statement (*completely agree, partly agree* or *completely disagree*).
- Give students time to tick their answers and then ask them to discuss their views on each statement in pairs.
- Go round the class monitoring students to make sure they are carrying out the task properly. Don't correct any mistakes at this point, but make a note of any problems in structure or pronunciation.
- As a class, ask each pair to discuss their views on one statement until everyone has had a turn. Ask the others if they agree or if they have anything else to add.
- Write any structural mistakes made by students on the board without saying who made them, and ask them to correct them. Deal with any problems in pronunciation.

Answers

Students' own answers

B
- Ask students to read the instructions and ask them how many things they have to do here (*two*) and what they are (*talk together about what aspect of life in the future each photo shows and decide which picture best portrays how our lives will probably change*).
- Remind students that in discussion and decision-making tasks like this, they should try to give examples to support their answers, but their examples shouldn't be too personal in nature.

- As a class, elicit what aspect of life in the future is shown in each of the pictures and encourage students to think about which picture best portrays how our lives will change.
- Ask students to do the task in pairs and to use the vocabulary in *Useful Expressions* to support their opinions with examples and to talk about the future.
- Go round the class monitoring students to make sure they are carrying out the task properly. Don't correct any mistakes at this point, but make a note of any problems in structure or pronunciation.
- Ask each pair to tell the rest of the class which option(*s*) they chose and to say why.
- Write any structural mistakes made by students on the board without saying who made them, and ask them to correct them. Deal with any problems in pronunciation that came up.

Answers

Students' own answers

C
- Ask students to read the *Exam Close-up*.
- Ask students to quickly read the instructions for the *Exam Task* and elicit that students should try to support their answers with examples.
- Point out to students that in this type of speaking task their examples shouldn't be too personal in nature.

Useful Expressions

- Read the *Useful Expressions* to the students and ask them to repeat them. Correct their pronunciation and intonation where necessary.
- Ask students for examples of expressions that they can use to support opinions with examples (*... is a classic example of how ...* or, *If we take into consideration ..., it's clear that life in the future ...*) and also ones which they can use to talk about the future (*In years to come, ...* or, *In the future, ...*).
- Point out to students that they should use some of these expressions when they do the *Exam Task*.

Ideas Focus

- Ask students to read the questions quickly and deal with any queries they may have.
- Ask students to work in pairs and take it in turns to answer the questions.
- Go round the class monitoring students to make sure they are carrying out the task properly. Don't correct any mistakes at this point, but make a note of any problems in structure or pronunciation.
- Ask a student from each pair to answer one of the questions until they have all had a turn. Ask the other students if they agree or if they have anything else to add.
- Write any structural mistakes made by students on the board without saying who made them, and ask them to correct them. Deal with any problems in pronunciation that came up.

Answers

Students' own answers

139

12 Fast Forward

Writing: an essay (2)

- Elicit from students what an essay is and remind them what the main purpose of an essay is (*to present an argument and give reasons for it*). Ask them in which previous unit they wrote an essay (*Unit 2*) and what the topic of their essay was. Finally ask them what register they used in their essay.
- Explain to students that in this lesson they are going to deal with writing essays again, but with a different focus.
- Read the *Learning Focus* on using formal expressions in moderation to the students and explain anything they don't understand.
- Ask students how many paragraphs their essay in Unit 2 contained (*four*) and elicit what types of structures beside sequencers can be used to add a formal tone to an essay (*passive voice, inversion and participle clauses*).

A

- Ask students to read the instructions and check that they understand what they have to do.
- Point out to students that they should bear in mind the structures and formal set expressions in the paragraph when making their decisions.
- Ask students to read the paragraph and explain anything they don't understand.
- Ask students to work in pairs to encourage discussion, but check as a class.

Answers

Yes, it does; there are too many set expressions - Firstly, In my opinion, Furthermore, Moreover, Therefore, I strongly disagree, that is to say.

B

- Ask students to read the instructions and check that they understand what they have to do.
- In pairs, ask students to rewrite the paragraph in their notebooks.
- Once they have finished rewriting the paragraph, ask students at random to read their paragraph out loud. Ask the rest of the class for their opinion on the paragraphs or if they have anything to add. You could hang all the paragraphs on the wall and ask students to read each other's work.

Suggested answer

It is my belief that life in the future will be less than ideal. The problems will be so great that we will be unable to overcome them. Furthermore, we won't have the means to deal with them because we will all be living primitive lives. Neither will we have a memory of an earlier, better time. I therefore disagree with the view that life will be better in the future. Instead, it is more likely to be worse.

C

- Ask students to read the instructions and check that they understand what they have to do.
- Ask students to read the writing task and explain anything they don't understand.
- Ask students to do the task individually, but check as a class.

Answers

1. possible changes in the future for people and society
2. no, just need to present your view
3. with examples; with reference to the past and the present

D

- Ask students to read the instructions and check that they understand what they have to do.
- Ask students to read the example essay and to underline any information that relates to the writer's attitude about the future. Then ask them to compare the parts they underlined with a partner.
- As a class, ask students if the writer is optimistic or pessimistic about the future and discuss why. Ask students to justify their answers and to quote the parts of the essay that deal with the writer's attitude towards the future and why he/she has that attitude.

Answers

optimistic
Students' own answers

E

- Explain to students that they are going to look back at the example essay to analyse and comment on what set expressions and structures are used, and how it is organised.
- Ask students to read the questions and explain anything they don't understand.
- Ask students to work in pairs to encourage discussion, but check as a class.

Answers

1. yes, just one – On the contrary, no – it flows well
2. food shortages and poor health have been dealt with, Were that not true, Driven by technology, Admittedly, in order to replace
3. at the end of the introduction (*On the contrary, I believe that in the future people will be better off and more satisfied …*)
4. its purpose is to support the writer's view that the future will be better

F

- Ask students to read the instructions and check that they understand what they have to do.
- Remind students that they should imagine they are writing an essay about what changes they foresee in the future regarding people and society. Explain that they have to write a paragraph giving and supporting their view.
- Give students no more than five minutes to write their paragraph and go round the class offering help where necessary.
- Ask some students to read their paragraphs out loud. You could hang all the paragraphs on the wall and ask students to read each other's work.

Answers

Students' own answers

G

- Ask students to read the instructions and check that they understand what they have to do.
- Remind them that when they have finished a piece of writing they should always proofread it to check for spelling, grammatical and punctuation errors.
- Ask students to swap notebooks with a partner and give them a few minutes to read and count how many different structures have been used and to decide if their partner's paragraph needs a bigger range of language or not. Explain that they don't have to correct their partner's paragraph.
- Ask students to hand the paragraph back and to correct anything their partner has noted.
- As a class, ask several students to read out their paragraph.

Answers

Students' own answers

H

- Ask the students to read the *Exam Close-up* and point out that the writer of the example essay did all the things on the list.
- Remind students that they can use the information here as a checklist when writing their own essays.
- Ask students to read the *Exam Task* and ask them to underline any key words and phrases in the task. Explain anything they don't understand.
- Ask students to answer the questions in C about this writing task so that they know what to do.
- As a class, ask students to answer the two questions (*What problems do you think your generation will face in the future?*; *Do you think your generation will be able to overcome them?*) and encourage a small discussion.
- Ask students to read the paragraph plan and ask them to make notes for each paragraph, if time allows. Ask students what kind of language they will need to use for their essay (*formal and impersonal*).
- Set the *Exam Task* for homework.
- Encourage students to use the Writing Reference and checklist for essays on page 176.

Suggested answers

You may often hear people asking themselves, 'What does the future hold?' They might say it after they have been talking about something negative, in a despairing sense. Although it can be used in an optimistic sense as well. In my opinion, my generation will face plenty of big problems in the future, but given time and a positive attitude hopefully they can be overcome, or at least improved upon.

In the years to come, we will probably come across a variety of problems in the world, but some of the more serious ones might include increasing pollution and nuclear waste, overpopulation, food shortages and also extreme poverty and lack of access to clean water and sanitation.

It is plain to see that there are many problems and more often than not they seem to be getting worse. This is despite politicians and lobby groups all over the world talking about ways to overcome them. For example, if we look at overpopulation, it is evident that in the past few decades there have been many attempts to control it with family planning advice and education yet the problem has got increasingly worse.

I think that in the not too distant future the general state of the world will have deteriorated. There are so many ongoing problems that there is little hope of them all being fixed or improved on any time soon. The only thing we can all do is adopt a positive attitude and try to work together to try to improve the quality of life for ourselves and future generations.

Useful Expressions

- Read the *Useful Expressions* to the students and ask them to repeat them. Correct their pronunciation and intonation if necessary.
- Elicit in which part of their essay they can use each category of expressions and tell them to use them when writing their essay for the *Exam Task*.

 12 Space Walk

General Note

Please see the information about the National Geographic videos on page 18 of this Teacher's Book.

Background Information

Officially, a space walk involves an astronaut who has fully or partially left a spacecraft. The first spacewalk is attributed to the Russian Aleksei Leonov, who walked in space for a period of 12 minutes on March 18, 1965. One of the more recent space walks was taken by Sunita Williams, an Indian American astronaut who, as of November 2012, has made seven space walks totalling an amazing 50 hours and 40 minutes.

Before you watch

A

- Explain to students that in this lesson they are going to watch a video about walking in space. Elicit what they know about any past space walks.
- Ask students to read the instructions and the three questions and explain anything they don't understand.
- Ask students to answer the questions in pairs. Encourage them to draw on their own knowledge of space and astronauts.
- Go round the class monitoring students to make sure they are carrying out the task properly. Don't correct any mistakes at this stage, but make a note of any problems in structure and pronunciation.
- As a class, ask students at random to answer each of the questions and ask the others if they agree or if they have anything to add.
- Write any structural mistakes that students made on the board without saying who made them, and ask them to correct them. Deal with any problems in pronunciation that came up.

Answers

Students' own answers

While you watch

B

- Explain to students that they are now going to watch a video and do a task based on the information in it.
- Ask students to read sentences 1–6 and explain anything they don't understand. Then ask them to think about which words may be correct before watching.
- Play the video all the way through without stopping and ask students to circle their answers. Ask students to compare their answers with a partner's and to justify any answers they have that are different. Play the video again so that they can check their answers.
- Ask students to do the task individually, but check as a class.

Answers

1 survive	(00:41)	4 construction	(02:11)
2 boiling	(01:02)	5 successful	(02:40)
3 perform	(01:55)	6 forward	(03:06)

After you watch

C

- Explain to students that this is a summary of the information they heard on the video.
- Read the words in the yellow box to the students and ask them to repeat them. Ask them to write N or Adj beside each of the words depending on whether it is a noun or an adjective.
- Explain to students that they should read the whole summary before writing any answers first to work out what part of speech is missing.
- Tell students to re-read the text once they have finished to check their answers.
- Ask students to do the task individually, but check as a class.

Answers

1 hostile	6 steps
2 radiation	7 missions
3 Spaceships	8 solar
4 tough	9 gravity
5 temperatures	10 weightless

Ideas Focus

- Ask students to read the instructions and make sure they understand what they have to do. Then ask them to read the three questions and answer any queries they might have.
- Ask students to work in pairs and explain that they should both give their opinions on all three questions.
- Go round the class monitoring students to make sure they are carrying out the task properly. Don't correct any mistakes at this stage, but make a note of any problems in structure and pronunciation.
- Ask each pair to answer one of the questions and repeat until each pair has had a turn.
- Write the reasons why space programmes are important and what researchers will discover about space in the future on the board.
- Deal with any problems in structure or pronunciation that came up.

Answers

Students' own answers

Review 6

Units 11 & 12

Objectives
- To revise vocabulary and grammar from Units 11 and 12
- To practise exam-type tasks

Revision
- Explain to students that Review 6 revises the material they saw in Units 11 and 12.
- Remind students that they can ask you for help with the exercises or look back at the units if they need help with an answer. Stress that the review is not a test.
- Decide how you will carry out the review. You could ask students to do one task at a time and then correct it immediately, or ask students to do all the tasks and correct them together at the end. If you do all the tasks together, let students know every now and again how much time they have got left to finish.
- Ask students not to leave any answers blank and to try to find any answers they don't know in the units.
- When checking students' answers to the review tasks, make a note of any problem areas in vocabulary and grammar that they still have. Try to do extra work on these areas so that your students will progress well.

Vocabulary Revision
- Ask students to explain the difference between the following pairs of words: *round/set, hole/spot, club/bat, shoots/tosses, buzzer/whistle, baton/cylinder, lane/row, referee/umpire*.
- Elicit from students the phrasal verbs they learnt in Unit 11 which are related to sports (*catch up with, pull out of, drop back to, knock out, warm up*) and ask them to write sentences of their own using these phrasal verbs.
- Write the words below on the board and ask students to fill in the missing prepositions.
  been a source _____ , be _____ great shape, get _____ to a good start, come _____ a sudden halt, work _____ , fight _____ , lean _____ , _____ one's own
  (*of, in, off, to, for, on, on, on*)
- Write the words *eternity, infinity* and *posterity* on the board and ask students to write sentences of their own using these words. Encourage students to write sentences that clarify the difference in meaning between each of these words.
- Write the following on the board and ask students to fill in the missing letters to make words related to space, science and technological advances.
  a _ _ _ _ _ , b _ _ _ _ _ _ _ _ _ _ _ _ , e _ _ _ _ _ _ _ _ _ _ ,
  i _ _ _ _ _ _ _ _ _ _ _ ,
  r _ _ _ _ _ _ _ _ _ _ , t _ _ _ _ _ _ _ _ _ _ _ _ _ _ _ _
  (*agency, breakthrough, engineering, intelligence, recognition, telecommunications*)

Grammar Revision
- Write these sentences on the board and ask students to rewrite them in reported speech. Then revise the changes that take place when we change direct speech into indirect speech that students learnt in Unit 11.
  - 'OK. I'll show you how to improve your serve,' Larry said. (*Larry said he would show me how to improve my serve.*)
  - 'This is the worst football match I've ever been to,' Pam said. (*Pam said that that was the worst football match she had ever been to.*)
  - 'You can't go swimming until you've cleaned your room,' Dad told us. (*Dad told us that we couldn't go swimming until we had cleaned our room.*)
  - 'Get moving or you're off the team!' the coach said to Patrick. (*The coach told Patrick to get moving or he was off the team.*)
  - 'Has she ever broken a world record?' he said to me. (*He asked me if/whether she had ever broken a world record.*)
- Ask the students to rewrite the first four reported sentences using the reporting verbs *insist, complain, warn* and *agree*.
  - (*Larry agreed to show me how to improve my serve.*)
  - (*Pam complained that that was the worst football match she had ever been to.*)
  - (*Dad insisted on us cleaning our room before we went swimming.*)
  - (*The coach warned Patrick to get moving or he was off the team.*)
- Write the sentences below on the board and ask students to identify words and phrases that introduce a clause of reason (*because*), a clause of purpose (*in order to*), a clause of result (*so disappointed that*) and a clause of contrast (*Nevertheless*). Revise similar words and phrases that students learnt in Unit 12.
  - The rocket was sent into space in order to take pictures.
  - The rocket was sent into space because scientists wanted some pictures.
  - The chances of the rocket taking pictures are slim. Nevertheless, scientists sent it into space.
  - The scientists didn't receive any pictures from the rocket; they were so disappointed that they gave up the project.
- Write the structures '*neither ... nor*' and '*either ... or*' on the board and ask students to write sentences of their own using the two structures, Revise other similar structures that students learnt in Unit 12.

A

- Ask students to read the instructions and check that they understand what they have to do.
- Ask students to read the title of the text and ask them what they think the text will be about. Then ask them to skim read the text, without circling any answers, to find out what *best of the best* means in the context of the text (*our obsession with success*).
- Point out to students that they should read all four options for each item before deciding which word best fits the gap. Remind them to pay attention to the whole sentence each gap is in as the general context will help them understand what word is missing.
- Remind students to re-read the text once they have finished to check their answers.

Answers

1 B	5 A	9 B
2 A	6 D	10 D
3 D	7 C	11 C
4 D	8 A	12 B

B

- Ask students to read the instructions and check that they understand what they have to do.
- Ask students what they know about the history of robots and if they think robots can do things as well as humans.
- Ask students to skim read the text, without filling in any answers, to find out what has been happening lately in robotics (*the development of artificial intelligence*).
- Encourage students to pay particular attention to the words immediately before and after each gap to work out what part of speech is missing. However, remind them that they have to take into consideration the general context of the sentence so that they understand what structure is being used.
- Remind students to re-read the text once they have finished to check their answers.

Answers

13 told	19 Despite
14 either	20 for
15 its	21 because/as
16 nor	22 be
17 to	23 Like
18 if	24 With

C

- Ask students to read the instructions and check that they understand what they have to do.
- Encourage students to read all three sentences before filling in any answers.
- Explain to students that the missing word in each set of sentences will be a fairly common one and that students should not spend time trying to find overly-difficult words.
- Tell students that the missing word in each set of sentences will be the same part of speech and that the word will have a different meaning in each sentence.
- Remind students to re-read the completed sentences once they have finished to check their answers.

Answers

25 bring	28 next
26 time	29 hit
27 future	

D

- Ask students to read the instructions and check that they understand what they have to do.
- Ask students to read both sentences in each item and to underline the information in the first sentence that is missing from the second sentence. Then ask them to look at the word given to decide how the missing information could be inserted into the second sentence using this word. Remind students that they will have to use a different structure in order to keep the meaning the same.
- Remind students that they mustn't change the word given in bold in any way.
- Encourage students to re-read the completed sentences once they have finished to check their answers.

Answers

30 told him that he needed
31 in spite of losing
32 Lionel nor his friends are
33 if/whether she had broken his
34 either of us could win
35 success was due to/because of
36 asked me to take him

Recording Script Student's Book C1

Unit 1 Scaling the Heights

TRACK 1.1

N: Listening, Unit 1, Page 12, B

M: I've just finished reading Luke Sanderson's latest book in his *Human Successes Trilogy*, called *The Rise of the Maya*. His previous two books were fascinating to read, but this one just wasn't up to scratch. His whole narrative style seems to have changed.

W: Really? I couldn't put that book down! But then again the Mayan civilisation has always mesmerised me. Isn't it just amazing how they achieved such great things like building huge pyramids without the help of modern technology?

M: Don't get me wrong, I'm a big fan of the Mayans, too. I just thought their story could have been presented in a more appealing way.

W: That wasn't a problem I had. But then I haven't read the first two books, so I can't really compare this work with his previous works.

TRACK 1.2

N: Listening, Unit 1, Page 12, E

ExN: You will hear two different extracts. For questions 1 – 4, choose the answer (a, b or c) which fits best according to what you hear.

ExN: Extract 1

ExN: You hear two people on an arts programme talking about a famous artist.

W: I'm not saying that she isn't a very capable artist, it's just there's been an awful lot of hype around much of her work. Her latest show at the Turner Contemporary is a classic example. Everyone's raving about it being her best exhibition to date, but I couldn't help feeling there was something missing.

M: I couldn't agree more. I turned up expecting to see first-class works of art. But she seems to have only produced second-rate sketches and signs that most school kids are capable of producing.

W: That's a bit harsh, but I do think she could have created much more impressive works if she had put her mind to it. She hasn't really fulfilled her potential, has she?

M: Not in the slightest. In a sense, that's typical of famous artists. After a few good shows with excellent reviews, their standards tend to drop.

ExN: Extract 2

ExN: You hear part of a radio interview with a woman who has just completed a marathon.

INT: So, Joyce, how did you feel on reaching the finishing line?

W: Well, there was a whole host of feelings going on inside me: relief that it was over, sheer joy that I had done a full marathon at long last, exhaustion, but something I hadn't expected to experience was a sense of deep sorrow that I couldn't see the finishing line itself and all the people cheering me on. I've been blind since birth, so I've learnt to cope over the years with not having a visual image of my surroundings. It's just something I've come to terms with. But for some reason, I felt a real need to see on that occasion.

INT: This is not the first marathon you've taken part in, is it?

W: No, I've been running in half marathons for around ten years now, but it's the first time I've attempted a full marathon. I was also running for the first time with my new dog, Shane, following the demise of Rex, a dog I'd had for over 15 years. Even as I grew more experienced and confident as a runner, I had never attempted a full marathon with Rex. I didn't think he could handle it.

Unit 2 Like Comment Share

TRACK 2.1

N: Listening, Unit 2, Page 24, B

I don't know how I survived without my iPad! I mean, what a great invention. I use it for all sorts of things, but I've been addicted to a National Geographic app over the past two months that even lets you keep in touch with a team of climbers on an expedition on Mount Everest! It's awesome! To think that climbers like Mallory and Hillary spent their time on mountains completely cut off from the rest of the world, and now mere mortals like me can tune in every day to talk to real climbers. Cool, eh? Through videos broadcast on YouTube, users of the app can chat with team members and find out how they're feeling, what difficulties they're facing and what the next leg in the expedition involves. You can even talk to Conrad Anker, the team leader. What an honour – he was the person who discovered Mallory's remains on an expedition back in 1999.

TRACK 2.2

N: Listening, Unit 2, Page 24, D

ExN: You will hear someone talking about his views on an aspect of technology. For questions 1 – 7, complete the sentences with a word or short phrase.

Some people say that technology in itself isn't a bad thing, but it's the way people use it that can lead to dangers. I'm inclined to agree with these people. For example, when mobile phones first came on the scene, we didn't use them nearly so often as we do today. I remember when I got my first mobile way back in 1997, not everyone possessed one, so I couldn't use it to keep in touch with all my friends and acquaintances. Now, prices have dropped considerably which has led us all to over-use our mobile phones. So in a sense, it's really service providers who prompt us to use these devices to the extent that they might be harmful to our health.

But what really worries me, is that as mobile phones, computers, tracking systems and the like have developed, our privacy seems to be invaded to a greater extent. Already we've got real-time satellites collecting images of us in our own backyards from up above, and now it seems that mobile phones will include GPS systems. This means that others will be able to track you down whenever your mobile is in use. Surely this will make stalking people child's play?

As far as I know, there are no laws in place yet to cover people's privacy in relation to their location, as these technologies haven't been around long enough for legal aspects to be hashed out.

Don't get me wrong, even I understand that GPS systems in phones can have huge benefits, especially for parents. Being able to locate their offspring in real time by tracking their location on maps on their phone screens must give them a sense of safety. But what happened to good old-fashioned trust? There are even services which allow parents to 'geofence' their children by sending an alert to the parents' mobiles whenever their children go beyond their boundaries.

Before you know it, you'll have employers using similar services to keep an eye on their employees. To my mind, these services are just too intrusive. Unless, of course, they come with sophisticated mechanisms allowing users to remain in control by being able to select who can access their personal information.

Unit 3 Just for the Health of It

TRACK 3.1

N: Listening, Unit 3, Page 38, B

M: But when we think of common, deadly diseases and serious medical conditions that affect us these days, we tend to think of things like HIV-Aids, cancer, heart disease and so on.

W: That's right, but there are so many other common illnesses out there which can be potentially life-threatening that most people don't really think about. Take skin cancer, for example. Although we're all perfectly aware of the dangers of the sun, we still expose ourselves to its harmful rays. Although skin cancer is treatable by removing problematic cells or with chemotherapy, if it isn't treated in time it can move to other parts of the body and be fatal.

M: Another classic example of a condition which could be wiped out with preventative measures is tooth decay. It's unbelievable how common this is today. It makes me so angry when I see young children sucking on lollipops. It's as if their parents aren't aware of the damage being done to their teeth and gums due to the build-up of acid in their little mouths. What I'd love to do is take a photo of their child smiling then replace their teeth with teeth blackened due to decay to show them what lollipops can do.

W: That sounds like a bit of an exaggeration to me. Surely there are more serious things for us to worry about?

M: What like cholera or the plague?

W: No laughing matter now that you mention them. They're both more common today than people think. Did you know that cholera infects 3 to 5 million people a year due to poor sanitation and 120,000 of these people die? And it's particularly dangerous because there are no symptoms to begin with. Of course, both cholera and the plague are treatable with antibiotics if detected in time.

M: It's enough to make you lose sleep!

W: Try not to let it; we all need to get enough sleep every night. Sleep deprivation is another serious condition affecting people today. And it can have major consequences like causing car accidents when people fall asleep at the wheel.

TRACK 3.2

N: Listening, Unit 3, Page 38, D

ExN: You will hear a radio interview about the Black Death. For questions 1 – 6, choose the best answer, a, b, c or d which fits best according to what you hear.

INT: Welcome to tonight's edition of *Health: Yesterday, Today and Tomorrow*. Tonight's guest is epidemiologist Sue Banks, who's here to discuss the Black Death. Now, the Black Death appeared in Europe during medieval times and has been the deadliest plague so far – it killed 30 to 50 million people in the 1340s. Tonight, Sue will present startling new evidence about this plague.

SUE: That's right. We carried out new research on bacteria from the skeletons of Black Death victims. A close examination of samples from 46 teeth and 53 bones has brought to light some very interesting findings!

INT: One finding in particular is rather startling. Can you tell listeners about it?

SUE: Well, I don't want to set alarm bells ringing, but it appears that the Black Death epidemic is the cause of the plague that infects humans today. The plague, which is spread by fleas carried on rodents, now strikes around 3,000 people annually, mainly in the US, Madagascar, China, India and South America.

INT: So does this mean we're on the brink of another epidemic?

SUE: Thankfully, no! 3,000 victims may sound a lot, but not in comparison to the Black Death which killed almost half of Europe's population! The study is interesting because it shows that, genetically speaking, the plague has changed very little in nearly 700 years.

INT: Does this mean that the plague is still deadly for modern sufferers?

SUE: Due to modern treatments, such as antibiotics, 85% of modern victims survive the plague. Medical knowledge and improved hygiene conditions have also resulted in people being less susceptible to the disease. These are probably the main reasons why the disease remains in check and no longer devastates whole populations.

INT: So, what are the symptoms of the modern plague?

SUE: They're fairly similar to the medieval plague, really. Just recently a man in his 50s came to hospital several days after he developed a very high fever. The lymph nodes in his armpits and at the top of his legs were swollen and he had extreme abdominal pain and bleeding. These are the symptoms of the Black Death.

INT: Wow! How did he manage to contract the disease?

SUE: He told doctors at the hospital that he was bitten on the hand while trying to remove a mouse from the jaws of a stray cat. <u>But we can't know whether he contracted the disease from the cat or the mouse.</u>

INT: Poor guy...

Unit 4 Lights, Camera, Action!

TRACK 4.1

N: Listening, Unit 4, Page 50, A

N: Speaker 1

I'm so glad I've landed a decent part at last! Quite honestly, I was beginning to think I'd never make the big time, <u>so 'phew' is the only thing I can say really</u>!

N: Speaker 2

<u>It's always the same. It comes down to who you know rather than what you know</u>! Obviously, the girl who got the part can't act to save herself. But she was the only one at the audition who was the director's niece.

N: Speaker 3

<u>I wish I had been more thorough editing that film.</u> As a matter of fact, it makes me cringe every time I see the silly mistakes and inconsistencies between scenes.

N: Speaker 4

<u>Considering the obstacles we came up against</u> during rehearsals, I'd say we pulled it off quite nicely. <u>I'm pleased as punch</u> that major disasters were avoided on stage by the cast.

TRACK 4.2

N: Listening, Unit 4, Page 50, C

ExN: You will hear five people talking about their roles in film and cinema. Complete both tasks as you listen.

ExN: Task 1: For questions 1 – 5, choose from the list A – H the person who is speaking.

Task 2: For questions 6 – 10, choose from the list A – H what each person is expressing.

ExN: Speaker 1

I suppose it was by chance really that I ended up in this field. Actually, I had always imagined myself to be an adventurer or an explorer, and if it hadn't been for years of experience of doing extreme sports, I don't think I'd ever have got into this line of work. <u>I can't believe how successful I've been so far.</u> The idea came while canyoning in the States – the conditions were perfect, the team were on form, and <u>I had this urge to get their jaw-dropping stunts on film. Since then I've invested in state-of-the-art camera equipment and never go on a trip without my laptop so that I can get all the action on film.</u>

ExN: Speaker 2

When I was younger, my parents were always going on about how I was born for the stage. In school plays, I was always chosen to play a leading role. I was super-confident, a capable singer and dancer, above all, and I relished being in the limelight. Although I've been to drama school and done a few adverts and stuff, the big parts always seem to go to someone more experienced. <u>Still, how are you supposed to get experience if nobody will give you a break? Every day, I dream that an agent or film director will come in for a bite to eat and recognise that a potential star is serving them!</u>

ExN: Speaker 3

My friends are under the assumption that my job is dead exciting because I get to rub shoulders with the stars. But to be honest, I have very little contact with them as they use the back-door entrance <u>while I'm always out front</u>. It's really only at after-show parties that I get to see anyone famous and then normally I'm too shy to approach them. It's more the general public I enjoy working with. Don't get me wrong, <u>it can get a bit monotonous sitting in such a confined space all evening and it's definitely one of the less glitzy theatre jobs, but I wouldn't swap it for the world.</u>

ExN: Speaker 4

I'm a real people-person so there's nothing I love more than making contacts and pulling strings for others. In a sense, being so outgoing has helped me build up an impressive network of clients and industry contacts. What gives me a real sense of satisfaction is going to a premiere and seeing one of the actors I represent on the big screen. 'That's my girl!', I say to myself. Admittedly, I can get really smug when I've helped someone to land a big part – especially when it's obviously the start of a brilliant acting career.

ExN: Speaker 5

When the director shouts 'It's a wrap!' a film is far from complete. For me, although I'm usually on-set throughout to get a feel for what the director's aiming at, that's when the hard work begins. It takes weeks, and sometimes months, to go through all the filmed material frame by frame and to glue the whole thing together to produce a coherent end product. I guess the hardest part is when I don't see eye-to-eye with a director or if the director tries to do my job for me. Sometimes they can have real issues letting me do my bit. It's as if they're afraid I'll destroy their vision of the whole project.

Unit 5 Eat Up!

TRACK 5.1

N: Listening, Unit 5, Page 64, A

N: A

M: How about grilled cuttlefish and a green salad for lunch?

W: Seafood again? We had octopus for dinner last night.

M: But the cuttlefish will go off if we don't eat it today.

N: B

W: Wow! I see you've been sticking to your low-carb diet! You're in better shape than ever.

M: The best thing is that it's been so easy to stick to.

W: Has it? I certainly don't have your willpower!

TRACK 5.2

N: Listening, Unit 5, Page 64, E

ExN: **You will hear eight short conversations. For questions 1 – 8, choose the best answer, (a, b or c) that is true according to what you hear.**

ExN: 1

M: I'm famished, but lunch won't be for another hour.

W: It's a bit late now to complain. You should have had a big breakfast this morning like me.

M: You know I'm not much of an eater in the morning.

ExN: 2

M: How long have you been head chef at Harry's?

W: It's been almost six years now. My first appointment after leaving college was as a sous chef in a department store canteen.

ExN: 3

W: Do you know how many calories are in that sesame bar you're eating?

M: I'd be more worried about how much fat is in your chocolate milk drink if I were you. At least sesame seeds are nutritious!

ExN: 4

W: That new fish restaurant has had great reviews. Fancy going there tonight for a change instead of our usual curry?

M: Why not? A lighter meal would be better in this heat.

ExN: 5

M: Excuse me, can you tell me where the chickpeas are?

W: If we have any, they'll be three aisles down in the rice and pulses section.

M: Why do they keep moving things around?

ExN: 6

M: It's 7.30. You're an hour late! Dinner's gone cold now!

W: I left a message with Mark to tell you I'd be home later tonight. Didn't he tell you?

M: You did, did you? Well, I haven't seen Mark since this morning.

ExN:	7		M:	Another singer that's had a species named after him is Elvis Presley. The species *Preseucoila imallshookupis* – commemorating the King's 1957 hit *All shook up* – is a kind of wasp.
M:	I'd like to book a table for six between 8 and 8.30.			
W:	I'm sorry, but you've got the wrong number. You've called Maggie's hairdressing salon.		W:	Seriously? The biologist who gave it its name must have had a sense of humour!
M:	Oh, it was the oyster bar next door I was after.		M:	Then there's the lichen, a plant that looks like moss that was called *Caloplaca obamae* in 2007 after Barack Obama.
ExN:	8			
W:	Would Janie prefer fish fillets to roast chicken?		ExN:	Extract 2
M:	Neither. We've been vegetarian for years now.		ExN:	You will hear part of an interview about the discovery of unusual skeletons.
W:	Have you? She couldn't get enough meat when she was younger!		M:	Now if you were under the impression that Dr Frankenstein began with Mary Shelley's novel, you'd better think again. Scientists have just made an amazing discovery that makes us re-examine what we know about man-made people! Dr Kelly Winterman, can you tell us a bit more about the discovery.

Unit 6 Living Planet

TRACK 6.1

N: Listening, Unit 6, Page 76, C

ExN: You will hear two different extracts. For questions 1 – 4, choose the best answer (a, b or c). There are two questions for each extract.

ExN: Extract 1

ExN: You will hear two people talking about species named after famous people.

M: I've always been a huge Marley fan. I love the laid-back feeling of reggae music.

W: Mm, it brings to mind summer and lazing around on sandy beaches. So it's no surprise that Marley's name was given to a species of sea creature.

M: That's news to me! What kind of sea creature?

W: Well, its scientific name is *Gnathia marleyi* and it's a small parasite that lives off the blood of fish. It's a crustacean that hides among coral in Caribbean waters waiting for fish to pass so that they can attack them and infest them. But the really bizarre thing about these crustaceans is that they only eat in the juvenile stage of their lives. Once they reach adulthood, they stop eating altogether, so they make sure they get enough fuel inside them while they're young to last them for the rest of their lives.

W: Well the story began a decade ago when two 3,000-year-old mummies were found in a prehistoric village on the Scottish island of South Uist. Following years of DNA experiments and isotopic dating, scientists have concluded that the bodies were actually made up of various body parts from six different people.

M: Were they even related in any way?

W: Not only did they have no biological relation, but one of the mummies – a male – is composed of body parts of people who died hundreds of years apart. The female mummy, on the other hand, is composed of body parts that all date back to roughly the same period.

M: My next question has got to be why did members of the prehistoric community 'build' mummies in this way?

W: That part of the puzzle still remains shrouded in mystery. Some say it was for practical reasons, for example, if a body part fell off and got lost, they would just replace it with another spare one. Others claim it was done to create a symbolic ancestor that possessed the traits of people from multiple lineages.

Unit 7 Eureka!

TRACK 7.1

N: Listening, Unit 7, Page 90, B

No sooner had we moved into our house than we had the solar panels installed on our roof. It's not that we were all that interested in converting to sustainable technology by using a clean energy form. It just seemed like a good way to help pay for part of the mortgage. The company that sold them to us promised they'd pay for themselves eventually due to the savings we'd see on our energy bills. They also told us that we could even make a profit by selling electricity generated on our house to the national grid. But I think they greatly overestimated the kilowatt-hours of electricity we'd be able to produce. And then there's the maintenance. Only once they were fitted did that even cross our minds. It's Murphy's Law really; as soon as the guarantee runs out something's sure to go wrong. We've had to have repairs done twice this year already and my husband keeps going on about how we'd be able to harness more energy if we had bought more modern panels. But that's technology for you – you can never keep up with it.

TRACK 7.2

N: Listening, Unit 7, Page 70, C

ExN: You will hear a presentation about a new way to generate electricity. For questions 1 – 8, complete the sentences.

W: And now it's Mark's turn to present his report on an innovative way to create electricity. Mark, would you like to begin?

M: Sure. My report is about a revolutionary new floor tile developed by Laurence Kemball-Cook as part of his degree course in industrial design and technology at Loughborough University. These tiles, designed to be used in places where pedestrians pass through in large numbers, can harness the kinetic energy generated from the footsteps of passers-by. One construction project that has adopted these new tiles is the Westfield Stratford City Mall in east London – Europe's largest urban mall to date. It's estimated that 40 million pedestrians a year will use the outdoor walkway to the mall that sports 20 of Kemball-Cook's bright green rubber tiles. This means that their footsteps will generate hundreds of kilowatt-hours of electricity, which can be used to supply energy for half of the outdoor lighting at the mall. Not only will a clean energy form be used, but huge savings will be made on the mall's overall energy bill.

It is hoped that the tiles, which measure 45 by 60 cms, can be installed in other places such as train and bus stations, airports and schools. The hustle and bustle of pedestrians in these locations can be turned to good use by providing electricity for low-power applications such as lighting, signs and digital adverts.

One of the first projects to adopt these tiles was the Simon Langton Grammar School for Boys near Canterbury. Since 2010, its 1,100 students have been helping to keep their school corridor lit by walking across the four tiles installed in the school's hallway. The head teacher at the school, Matthew Baxter, is highly satisfied with the tiles. He claims that despite heavy-duty use by the 'boisterous boys' at the school, the tiles remain in excellent condition. An added bonus is that they have encouraged the students to think about sustainable technology.

As for how the tiles work, for the moment Kemball-Cook refuses to divulge this information. All we know is that it is a hybrid technology, which he claims to be 200 times more efficient at generating energy than any similar product. While it may be more efficient, one obstacle that he has come up against is the high production cost of these tiles. Although the price of the tiles dropped 70% in 2011, they must become cheaper still to make them a viable and competitive product on the market.

Kemball-Cook not only hopes to reduce the price in the future, but also to expand the range of uses that the tiles can be put to. At the moment, they can only be used to produce low-power applications, but he's confident that his company will soon be able to take the design a stage further so that they can handle greater power demands, such as powering entire music festivals!

Unit 8 Money Mad

TRACK 8.1

N: Listening, Unit 8, Page 102, B

1 Do you know what the interest rate is today?
2 Where did you train to be an accountant?
3 How much money did you put aside this month?
4 Who does this credit card belong to?
5 Why did you apply for a loan?
6 When does the contract run out?

TRACK 8.2

N: Listening, Unit 8, Page 102, C

ExN: You will hear 14 questions. From the three answer choices given, choose the one (a, b or c) which best answers the questions.

ExN: 1

Did you manage to persuade your boss to give you a pay rise in the end?

ExN: 2

Why don't you apply for a credit card if you are having cash flow problems?

ExN: 3

Do you know why this supermarket is so much more expensive than last month?

ExN: 4

Can you lend me 100 euros until payday?

ExN: 5

What kind of salary would you expect if we hired you?

ExN: 6

I've been waiting at the bank for ages. What took you so long?

ExN: 7

Do you have any idea what the company share prices are today?

ExN: 8

Do you know anyone who can help me with my tax forms?

ExN: 9

Are you keeping up-to-date with your loan repayments?

ExN: 10

I really wish they would pay us. Why have they been so late in depositing the money?

ExN: 11

How much money did you spend at the mall?

ExN: 12

Why don't we target this product at the teenage market?

ExN: 13

Do you realise how much of a loss the company has made this quarter?

ExN: 14

I want to change £6000 into dollars. Have you seen today's exchange rate?

Unit 9 All That Jazz!

TRACK 9.1

N: Listening, Unit 9, Page 116, B

W: Listen to this! In 2010, an art-lover bought 5 paintings at a garage sale in the US for $5. Pretty cheap, huh?

M: I suppose so, but garage sales aren't exactly well-known for high-quality goods, you know.

W: Not normally, but this guy's luck was most certainly in. He decided to reframe one of the pictures and what do you think he found behind it?

M: Oh, I don't know: a ten dollar bill?

W: He found another sketch which was the work of none other than the founder of pop art: Andy Warhol! He could make millions if he sold that sketch.

M: Lucky him! One of my favourite funny art stories

is about Pablo Picasso. I'm not entirely convinced it's true, mind you, but it would be great if it was. Pablo had asked a carpenter to make a chest of drawers for him and did a quick sketch of the kind of thing he had in mind. He showed it to the carpenter and asked him how much it would cost. The cunning carpenter replied 'Sign it,' making sure he could make a killing on the sketch.

TRACK 9.2

N: Listening, Unit 9, Page 116, E

ExN: You will hear two people talking about lost works of art. For questions 1 – 6, choose the best answer (a, b, c or d).

M: What is it about lost art and garages? First it was Picasso works, now it's Klimt.

W: Oh yes, I remember the Picasso findings from a few years back – 2010 if I'm not mistaken. Around 270 undocumented works of art by Picasso were unveiled by his former electrician in France, who had stored them in his garage for around 40 years. There was a huge controversy at the time because he claimed that the artist had given him the works as a gift, but Picasso's son Claude suspected that they had actually been stolen. He claimed that Picasso always signed and dated his gifts. I wonder where these works are now.

M: Well, the collection was immediately seized by authorities and they're currently being held in a vault in Nanterre, which is just outside Paris. The works are thought to be worth around £50 million, so they're being kept under lock and key by France's Central Office for the Fight Against Traffic in Cultural Goods until a full investigation is carried out.

W: So what's the Klimt story?

M: Well, there was a fresco that used to adorn the ceiling in the studio of art nouveau artist Gustav Klimt. He shared the studio with his brother Ernst between 1883 and 1892. But, the fresco went missing after a lift was installed in the building in the 1980s. The fresco, which is called Trumpeting Putto, shows Cupid playing a trumpet and has been widely sought after in art circles since the 1960s.

W: Where was the painting eventually found?

M: The story goes that it turned up in a garage in northern Austria. The man who found it had only recently become aware of its significance because Klimt had been in the news rather a lot due to his 150th birthday celebrations.

W: That's a bit of a coincidence, isn't it? I'm sure that's bound to push up the value of the painting no end.

M: Well, first of all they've got to establish its authenticity.

W: What, do you mean it might not be an original?

M: Some art experts are disputing the fact that the fresco was done by Gustav on the grounds that it isn't a signed piece nor is it a particularly good work of art.

W: So who do they think did it then? Is it just something the finder rustled up in his spare time?

M: No, nothing like that. There's no doubt that the fresco is the one that adorned Klimt's studio. What is in dispute is whether it was painted by Gustav or Ernst, who was also an artist, though much less talented and celebrated. It's also said to bear similarities to other frescoes Ernst created. Some say that at best, the painting was a joint effort by the two brothers.

Unit 10 Modern Living

TRACK 10.1

N: Listening, Unit 10, Page 128, B

My greatest ambition in life was to become a chef. I'd always fancied myself as a bit of a Jamie Oliver, working in top restaurants rustling up delicious meals for customers. After a few years slogging it out in various establishments, it dawned on me I just wasn't cut out for the heat of top-class kitchens. It was just too stressful, not to mention restricting. So, I invested in a catering van with money I'd saved over the years and now I do the rounds of Britain's music and performing arts festivals. That way I don't feel penned in to the one place. What makes it all worthwhile for me is the look on people's faces when they see the gourmet menu I serve up. They come up to the van expecting the usual van nosh – hamburgers, hot dogs and stuff – but are pleasantly surprised that they can get a decent meal at a reasonable price.

TRACK 10.2

N: Listening, Unit 10, Page 128, C

ExN: You will hear five people talking about their lifestyles. Complete both tasks as you listen.

ExN: Task 1: For questions 1 – 5, choose from the list A – H the reason which best reflects why each person chose his or her current lifestyle.

Task 2: For questions 6 – 10, choose from the list A – H the main advantage of the lifestyle mentioned by each speaker.

ExN: Speaker 1

My greatest ambition in life was to become a chef. I'd always fancied myself as a bit of a Jamie Oliver, working in top restaurants rustling up delicious meals for customers. After a few years slogging it out in various establishments, it dawned on me I just wasn't cut out for the heat of top-class kitchens. It was just too stressful, not to mention restricting. So, I invested in a catering van with money I'd saved over the years and now I do the rounds of Britain's music and performing arts festivals. That way I don't feel penned in to the one place. What makes it all worthwhile for me is the look on people's faces when they see the gourmet menu I serve up. They come up to the van expecting the usual van nosh – hamburgers, hot dogs and stuff – but are pleasantly surprised that they can get a decent meal at a reasonable price.

ExN: Speaker 2

My childhood was very traumatic. Both my parents died from illnesses when I was very young. I was then taken to an orphanage where I spent the worst years of my life. While I was there, I saw a picture of a ballet dancer. It seemed like the most beautiful thing in the world to me. I hid the picture in my clothes for years and even took it with me to America when I was adopted. My new mother said I could become a dancer if I worked hard. I did, and now I'm landing parts I'd never imagined possible. That has been a dream come true for me. I'll never be able to thank my adopted parents enough for the opportunity they've given me.

ExN: Speaker 3

Having done an apprenticeship in plumbing as soon as I left school at 16, I had bags of experience. I've never considered climbing the career ladder as I've always been a hands-on person. When an opening for a shift supervisor came up in the company I work for, my boss said, 'Why don't you apply for it?'. It was more money and everything but, to be honest, I'd rather just be one of the lads and get on with the job than tell the others what to do. We have a good laugh messing about together and I wouldn't change that for the world. That's what would happen if I was suddenly above them – it would change our whole relationship. Do you know what I mean?

ExN: Speaker 4

It's hard going now what with the recession and everything, that's why I'm so relieved we took the decision to downscale before we were forced to anyway. We'd been saying for a few years that we'd love to buy a farm in the Highlands and become subsistence farmers. Everyone thought it was just a pipe dream but we've made it work for us. Gone are our stressful jobs in the city. We've swapped them for the peace and tranquillity of the agricultural lifestyle. Don't get me wrong, it's demanding work physically and the hours can be just as long, but at least we get to see the fruits of our labour immediately and don't have to get involved in soul-destroying office politics.

ExN: Speaker 5

It was years of unemployment that made us finally emigrate to Australia. There was no hope back home and luckily Lindsay had family out here who agreed to sponsor us. Even though I had been out of the job market for a long, long time, it was relatively easy for me to get a post as an architect in one of the big firms here.

Career-wise the move has been the right one. It's opened up all sorts of doors for me and I can at last put all those years of training to good use.

Unit 11 Sports Crazy!

TRACK 11.1

N: Listening, Unit 11, Page 142, B

For as long as I can remember, I've been interested in cycling. But it's only been in the past ten years that I've got into track cycling. People sometimes ask me if I ever get frustrated cycling round in circles in a track, but it's my whole life. I've never once thought about what I would do with myself if I didn't cycle. There's no question of me not getting on my bike every day. I guess it's my passion. I always train hard as I want good results, but in my spare time, I'm usually very lazy. I can be a bit of a couch potato when I want. But that doesn't happen very often.

TRACK 11.2

ExN: Listening, Unit 11, Page 142, D

N: You will hear three short segments from a radio program. After each talk, you will hear some questions. From the three answer choices given (a, b or c), you should choose the one that best answers the question according to the information you heard.

ExN: Segment 1

INT: Dan, this is your third Tough Mudder race. What exactly is it all about? Is it just running in muddy conditions?

M: Not in the slightest – in fact, mud is the least of your worries. It's more of an obstacle course over a distance of ten to twelve miles. As you run, you come across a number of challenges such as swimming across ice baths, swinging across buttered monkey bars and running through a field of live wires. The event was the brainchild of a British Special Forces agent who wanted an alternative to ordinary, dull marathons. And I can assure you, in Tough Mudder, there's never a dull moment.

INT: From what I gather, it's not all serious stuff, is it?

M: That's right. Having fun is much more important than winning. In fact, contestants would rather help each other out than fire on towards the finishing line. So there's a real sense of, 'we're all in this together'. Also, contestants often wear ridiculously funny costumes. After the race they even get Mohawk haircuts.

ExN: Segment 2

INT: Gemma, you're only fifteen-years-old, but you've been competing nationally as a gymnast for five years now. How did you get started?

G: Actually, it's four years now. My first national competition was when I was eleven. Before that I had only competed locally. But to answer your question, my aunt was a gymnast and I remember admiring photos of her in action as well as her collection of medals and trophies when I was very young. I would think to myself, 'That'll be me one day.' Luckily my parents agreed to sign me up for classes at my local gym, but I found them a bit boring. They just weren't challenging enough, so my aunt agreed to be my personal coach.

INT: What's it like having a family member as a coach?

G: It has its ups and downs, I suppose. It's really important for a competing gymnast to trust her coach, so I know I'm in good hands. My aunt has got my best interests at heart and knows just how far I can go. If I'm not ready to compete in an event, she won't let me. She'll put me on a realistic training programme that fits in with the rest of my life.

INT: Do you ever worry that she doesn't push you hard enough?

G: Not at all! She's not a soft touch! If anything, I'm the one that takes advantage of our relationship and try to wriggle my way out of the odd training session. But she never lets me stray from the path.

ExN: Segment 3

INT: Sport today is ridden with many ills: doping of athletes and hooliganism are just two of the most prominent. Jack Farley is a reformed football hooligan. Jack what made you get out?

M: It was after a big European match in Milan. Me and the rest of the gang caused a bit of a stir-up in the stand. Nothing too serious: throwing chairs and bottles, that kind of thing. We knew the real action would take place later outside the stadium. What we hadn't bargained for was that the Milan gang would have us trapped in the streets. And we were outnumbered by about 4 to 1. To cut a long story short, in the mayhem me and my best mate Sean landed in hospital with severe injuries. That was a wake-up call for me.

INT: But what has this kind of violence got to do with sport?

M: Oh, I don't know. It's a tribal thing I suppose. It's about showing you're superior to the enemy.

Once the adrenalin gets going, there's nothing that can stop you. Before Milan, I used to thrive on that feeling. Now I get more of a kick out of trying to convince those still in the game to seek help. It's funny 'cause I'm even helping those who used to be on the other side of the fence. I know I can never make up for all the damage I've done, but I guess I've come to realise that the differences I used to think were between us are false. We're actually more alike than we think.

Unit 12 Fast Forward

TRACK 12.1

N: Listening, Unit 12, Page 154, B

Cars of the future won't just be about futuristic designs. One of the greatest challenges facing car manufacturers these days, is how to produce a sustainable car that won't break the bank. In a sense, the way forward seems to be to look to the past. The history of the electric car dates back to the mid-19th century. By the 1930s, though, production of electric cars was discontinued in favour of petrol burning engines. Concerns about toxic emissions from cars and a need to find an alternative to fossil fuels have raised interest in electrically-powered vehicles once again. In 2012, production and sales of electric and hybrid cars shot up as green consumers decided it was time to switch to a clean energy form to power their cars. With Japan and America currently the biggest consumers of these cars, it is predicted that the future of the car industry is electric.

TRACK 12.2

N: Listening, Unit 12, Page 154, C

ExN: **You will hear someone talking about a project on an alternative form of fuel. For questions 1 – 8, complete the sentences with a word or short phrase.**

For decades now we've been warned that fossil fuels are running out and that alternative forms of generating energy must be found. A recent project that caught my attention is being put to the test by students from Middlebury College in Vermont. They call themselves the Project BioBus team and plan to travel over 24,000 km in their veggie-fuelled Biobus. Their aim is to prove that using biodiesel – a fuel derived from vegetable oil – could be the way forward.

Their bus, which is powered solely by biodiesel, is like an ordinary school bus, apart from the fact that it has been painted with eye-catching scenes of cornfields. The team take the bus to schools, colleges and other institutions to demonstrate that biodiesel can be used in bus fleets which usually burn diesel, without any modifications needed to the buses.

So where does biodiesel come from? During their trip, the team make frequent stops at fast food restaurants for refuelling. They take used vegetable oil from deep-fat fryers and combine it with two other substances: lye and methanol. According to the team, this makes it a 'safe, renewable, clean burning, domestically-produced fuel'. But the advantages don't stop there. Schools that jump on the bandwagon and convert to biodiesel won't have to make any major changes to the way they operate, but will drastically cut the harmful emissions that come from their buses and will be less dependent on increasingly expensive oil.

Biodiesel is so easy to produce that the team are able to demonstrate the production process to students in school science labs. So, not only are they made aware of the alternative energy form, but they get a practical chemistry lesson too. The team members claim that this is a part of their work that school students love. And if they can win over the next generation, then it's more likely that this alternative form of fuel will be widely used in the future.

While on the road, the team members divide up their duties to ensure that everything runs smoothly. Their tasks range from driving the bus, locating fuel stops, giving interviews and presentations at schools and colleges, researching and answering questions posted on their website and making the necessary preparations for future exhibitions that they will attend. This hectic schedule means that they're often up before dawn and don't stop until after midnight. But that's a small price to pay if they can convince institutions to follow their example and switch to biodiesel.

WORKBOOK C1 KEY

Unit 1

Reading
A
Student's own answer

B
1C 2D 3A 4B 5C 6D 7C 8A 9B
10C 11D 12B

Vocabulary
A
1b 2a 3c 4a 5c 6b

B
1 discrimination
2 accomplishments
3 persistence
4 failure
5 achievements
6 understanding
7 realisation
8 adaptability

C
1 positive
2 conceited
3 defeated
4 modest
5 impetuous
6 upbeat
7 apprehensive
8 headstrong
9 triumphant
10 generations

D
1 get ahead
2 come up against
3 fallen through
4 hang on
5 blown away
6 knuckle down
7 pull off
8 break through

E
1 light
2 places
3 up
4 mile
5 hitch
6 get
7 do
8 plate

Grammar
A
1 has been painting
2 freezes
3 've just finished
4 's always forgetting
5 drives
6 Have you been waiting
7 'm revising
8 've never disagreed

B
1 He's just left
2 We've been camping
3 I've just heard
4 Susan hasn't received
5 We're really looking forward
6 How are you getting on
7 Jenny never hands
8 Anthony is always complaining

C
1 had decided
2 fell
3 set up
4 had been
5 hadn't been sleeping
6 was shaking
7 were
8 stampeded
9 explained
10 found

D
1c 2b 3c 4c 5b 6a 7c 8a

E
1c 2h 3b 4e 5g 6f 7a 8d

Listening
A
Student's own answer

C
1b 2c 3a 4b

Writing
A
1F 2T 3T 4F

B
1 To whom it may concern,
2 Yours faithfully,

C
Student's own answer

Unit 2

Reading
A
Student's own answer

B
1c 2a 3b 4d

Vocabulary
A
1 choice
2 contact
3 personal
4 views
5 legitimate
6 updated
7 identity
8 click

B
1 criticism
2 defence
3 reaction
4 accessible
5 bothering
6 provocation
7 excitement
8 shocking

C
1 remark
2 observed
3 offended
4 criticism
5 avoided
6 relates
7 value
8 resist

D
1 aback
2 to
3 for
4 at
5 out
6 in
7 up
8 down

E
1c 2b 3c 4a 5c 6b 7a 8c

Grammar
A
1 Shall I bring
2 will be revising
3 will have finished

158

4 will have been writing
5 will manage/is going to manage
6 am going to look
7 fly
8 will enjoy

B
1 will have peaked
2 will become
3 will sound
4 will continue
5 are going to expect
6 won't be able to follow
7 will be moving
8 will have realised

C
1 Shall I carry
2 will have been married
3 I'll go
4 we arrive
5 we're driving
6 will have been working
7 I'm not going to/I won't help you anymore!
8 I'll be sunbathing

D
1b 2f 3d 4a 5e 6c

E
1 will have been living
2 will be late
3 will still be tidying up
4 are meeting
5 soon as you've finished your homework
6 were going to meet up
7 they were starting their journey
8 he would apply to medical school

Listening
A
Student's own answer

C
1 paper books
2 sound
3 declining
4 outweigh
5 hooked
6 French
7 upgrading
8 at the beach

Writing
A
Tick 1, 2, 4, 5, 7, 8

B
1 Secondly
2 Thirdly
3 As a result
4 However
5 though
6 Nevertheless

C
Student's own answer

Review 1

Vocabulary
A
1c 2b 3a 4d 5c 6b 7a 8d 9c 10c
11a 12d 13b 14c 15a 16d 17a
18b 19b 20d

Grammar
B
1c 2a 3c 4d 5c 6d 7b 8c 9c 10b
11a 12c 13d 14a 15c 16c 17d
18b 19c 20a

Use of English
C
1d 2a 3b 4d 5d 6a 7d 8a 9b
10b 11a 12c

D
1 off
2 ahead
3 without
4 through
5 against
6 warning
7 all
8 by
9 in
10 did
11 occasion
12 on
13 there
14 break
15 away

E
1 access
2 confidence
3 guess
4 horse
5 construction

F
1 took my words out of context
2 say it to your face/tell you to your face
3 aren't up to scratch
4 got a lot on my plate
5 get the green light
6 was taken aback by
7 work around the clock
8 not to get back at

Unit 3

Reading
A
Student's own answer

B
1D 2F 3B 4E 5C

Vocabulary
A
1 mixed
2 oblivious
3 muscular
4 forgetful
5 nutritious
6 beneficial
7 bony
8 treatment

B
1 relieved
2 psychological
3 emotional
4 anorexic
5 intravenous
6 dehydrated
7 physical
8 undernourished
9 monitored
10 recovered

C
1b 2a 3c 4b 5a 6c 7a 8b

D
1 running
2 coughing
3 bodily
4 failing
5 internal
6 terminal
7 chemical
8 splitting

E
1c 2f 3e 4a 5d 6b

Grammar

A
1. herself
2. Those
3. nothing
4. each other
5. Anyone
6. one another's
7. these, those
8. all

B
1. something
2. herself
3. Everyone
4. Some
5. Others
6. yourself
7. Nothing
8. someone

C
1. never
2. with her aunt and uncle
3. tomorrow
4. in three weeks
5. to get rid of my headache
6. incredibly

D
1. absolutely
2. wide
3. hard
4. uncomfortably
5. highly
6. Unfortunately
7. Strangely
8. late

E
1. desperately
2. late
3. high
4. carefully
5. utterly
6. highly
7. fast
8. lately

Listening

A
Student's own answer

C
1c 2d 3b 4d 5a 6c

Writing

A
1F 2T 3T 4F

B
1. Comfortable clothes
2. A great night's sleep
3. Essential stuff
4. Health and safety

C
Student's own answer

Unit 4

Reading

A
Student's own answer

B
1b 2c 3b 4b 5a 6d

Vocabulary

A
1. groundbreaking
2. heart-rending
3. agent
4. film editor
5. producer
6. lines
7. usher
8. stage

B
Student's own answer

C
1d 2c 3d 4a 5b 6c

D
1c 2b 3a 4b 5a 6b 7c 8c

E
1. performance
2. Animated
3. lead
4. role
5. rehearsals
6. portrayal
7. fright
8. ovation

F
1e 2c 3g 4a 5f 6h 7b 8d

Grammar

A
1. not giving
2. to buy
3. Acting
4. hurry
5. to go
6. watching
7. to bring
8. to let

B
1. seeing
2. watching
3. going
4. to see
5. do
6. to play
7. being
8. losing

C
1a 2c 3b 4c 5c 6b 7a 8a

D
1. in fact
2. As a matter of fact
3. evidently
4. apparently
5. obviously
6. quite honestly
7. Anyway

E
1c 2f 3b 4a 5d 6e

Listening

A
Student's own answer

C
1e 2g 3a 4d 5c 6e 7h 8c 9b 10a

Writing

A
1. people interested in the theatre/plays and shows
2. a theatre production
3. No, they aren't theatre.
4. No, you need to choose something you liked and would recommend.

B
1b 2f 3e 4c 5a 6d

C
Student's own answer

Review 2

Vocabulary

A
1c 2a 3d 4c 5b 6a 7c 8c 9d 10b
11b 12a 13c 14d 15c 16c 17b
18a 19d 20d

B
1b 2c 3d 4a 5b 6c 7d 8b 9a
10d 11c 12d 13b 14a 15c 16b
17c 18d 19d 20b

Use of English

C
1c 2d 3a 4d 5d 6b 7b 8c 9a
10b 11c 12a

D
1. bodily
2. imbalance
3. dehydrated
4. thirsty
5. internal
6. undernourished
7. fright
8. heartstrings
9. disorders
10. headaches

E
1. mixed
2. talk
3. lead
4. notice
5. play

F
1. an actor by profession
2. putting on an act
3. remained/was still in character
4. overcame all (the) obstacles
5. had a change of heart
6. at the top of his lungs
7. always/constantly at each other's throats
8. bite my head off

Unit 5

Reading

A
Student's own answer

B
1a 2b 3a 4b

Vocabulary

A
1. appetite
2. fizzy
3. culinary
4. cuisine
5. famished
6. pile
7. simmer
8. shed

B
1E 2C 3E 4T 5T 6C 7T 8C

C
1. banquet
2. helping
3. ravenous
4. mouldy
5. scrumptious
6. starved
7. salty
8. sip

D
1c 2b 3b 4a 5c 6b 7a 8b

Grammar

A
1. dined out
2. passed out
3. gulp down your juice/gulp your juice down
4. has come down with (the) flu
5. the sale fell through
6. will get ahead in her career
7. picked at his dinner
8. tucked in

B
1. fight it off
2. polish them off
3. keep up with her
4. warm it up
5. came up with it
6. get away with it

C
1. have
2. shall
3. would
4. is
5. would
6. is
7. did
8. could

D
1. she would
2. do you
3. that is
4. she should
5. would you
6. do you
7. they aren't
8. I do

E
1. I'm going to stick to a low-carb diet from now on, **I am.**
2. correct
3. Max hasn't got any time to cook at the moment, **he hasn't.**
4. I don't suppose I could use your espresso machine, **could I?**
5. correct
6. correct
7. correct
8. I'm sure I brought the biscuits home with me, **I am.**

Listening

A
Student's own answer

C
1c 2b 3b 4c 5b 6a 7b 8c

Writing

A
1. the college principal
2. formal or semi-formal
3. four
4. one of the menus

B
Suggested answers
Introduction: The purpose of this proposal is to recommend a menu for the Leaver's Dinner.
Conclusion: I can't recommend the Mediterranean choice highly enough. Although widespread and popular, it will still seem special, festive and memorable.

C
Student's own answer

Unit 6

Reading

A
Student's own answer

B
1B 2F 3D 4E 5A

Vocabulary

A
1b 2f 3d 4a 5c 6e

B
1. endure extreme weather conditions
2. trigger a landslide
3. absorb oxygen
4. emit carbon dioxide
5. spew ash and magma
6. harness energy

C
1. must
2. blistering
3. on
4. down
5. surroundings
6. to
7. who
8. but

D
1 unreliable
2 sufficient
3 migration
4 surrounding
5 elements
6 insistence
7 alternative
8 indifferent

E
1 down
2 up
3 up
4 up
5 down
6 over

Grammar
A
1 needn't
2 couldn't
3 would
4 should
5 must (should)
6 Can/Could
7 mustn't/can't
8 might/may/could

B
1 May I leave now
2 needn't lock your doors here
3 can't be at home
4 could take the train
5 is bound to be late
6 don't have to buy tickets in advance
7 should read this publication
8 must be somewhere in

C
1 must have finished
2 may have left/might have left
3 needn't have worried
4 could have given/would have given
5 can't have tidied
6 shouldn't have gone/ought not to have gone

D
1 must have become
2 would have thrown
3 must have starved
4 would have spewed
5 could have survived
6 might have been
7 wouldn't have been able
8 may have spread

E
1b 2e 3c 4a 5d

Listening
A
Student's own answer

C
1b 2a 3c 4b

Writing
A
1F 2T 3F 4T

B
1 aims
2 thrive
3 include
4 disposing
5 to saving
6 to improve

C
Student's own answer

Review 3

Vocabulary
A
1c 2a 3d 4b 5b 6c 7d 8a 9c 10c 11d 12b 13b 14c 15a 16d 17c 18a 19d 20b

Grammar
B
1c 2d 3a 4d 5c 6a 7b 8c 9a 10c 11b 12d 13a 14b 15c 16b 17d 18a 19c 20b

Use of English
C
1c 2b 3c 4d 5a 6b 7b 8d 9d 10a 11b 12a

D
1 would
2 have
3 up
4 clear
5 down
6 against
7 on
8 would
9 into
10 but
11 life
12 bound/likely/able
13 by
14 of
15 it

E
1 whip
2 feed
3 skim
4 spill
5 chain

F
1 must have been bucketing down for
2 might not have known
3 mustn't interfere with
4 a complete/total waste of time
5 could have polished off all (of)
6 no use crying over spilt milk
7 put up with him
8 must wake up and smell the

Unit 7

Reading
A
Student's own answer

B
1E 2G 3B 4A 5D 6E 7C 8F 9G 10D

Vocabulary
A
1b 2c 3b 4a 5b 6c 7b 8a

B
1 automation
2 purity
3 assembly
4 corrosion
5 displacement
6 computerised
7 replacement
8 assumptions

C
1 material
2 process
3 substance
4 properties
5 hardness
6 artificial
7 gemstone
8 industry

D
1 home page
2 recycle bin
3 search engines
4 double click
5 hard drive
6 laser printer
7 memory stick
8 control panel

E
1f 2c 3e 4a 5d 6b

Grammar
A
1 hadn't got
2 won't pass
3 could help
4 would still be
5 would have got
6 had never invented
7 would be
8 mix

B
1 if
2 unless
3 as long as
4 provided
5 won't
6 Supposing
7 otherwise
8 would
9 If
10 could

C
1e 2a 3h 4c 5g 6b 7f 8d

D
1 Hannah wasn't always late
2 he had revised for the test
3 I were a musician/I could be a musician
4 he were/was going on holiday with his friends
5 you would do the washing-up

E
1 Not only is this book extremely long, but it's also very boring
2 Nowhere will you find a more patient teacher.
3 Rarely were we allowed to do experiments when we were children.
4 Not until I was thirty was I able to afford a car.
5 No sooner had they got to the beach than they ran into the sea.
6 Under no circumstances are you to lift this by yourself as it's much too heavy.

Listening
A
Student's own answer

C
1 mobile phones
2 financial
3 transparency
4 cheaper
5 reality
6 reunite
7 weather
8 genuine

Writing
A
1 the editor and other journalists working for the college science magazine
2 a medical researcher
3 No, they can be from any century.
4 formal language

B
2, 4, 1, 3

C
Student's own answer

Unit 8

Reading
A
Student's own answer

B
1c 2d 3a 4c 5d 6b

Vocabulary
A
1 dollars
2 cash
3 money
4 pounds
5 bank teller
6 forgeries
7 counterfeit
8 currency

B
1 fraudulent
2 broke
3 withdraw
4 laundering
5 economical
6 poverty
7 recession
8 rating

C
1d 2a 3f 4e 5b 6c

D
1 on
2 in
3 back
4 out
5 out
6 down

Grammar
A
1d 2h 3f 4c 5a 6j 7i 8g 9b 10e

B
1b 2c 3c 4a 5b 6a 7b 8a

C
1a 2f 3e 4b 5d 6c

D
1 going out
2 Having saved
3 Being
4 Having inherited
5 ordered
6 Having survived

E
1 What
2 All
3 thing
4 reason
5 where
6 when

Listening
A
Student's own answer

C
1a 2b 3b 4a 5c 6c 7a 8b 9a 10c
11b 12c 13a 14b

Writing
A
1 college students primarily
2 semi-formal
3 the pros and cons of online auctions

B
1st main paragraph: what you like about online auction websites
2nd main paragraph: what you dislike about online auction websites
3rd main paragraph: the effect of online auction websites on conventional shops

C
Student's own answer

Review 4

Vocabulary

A
1b 2c 3d 4a 5a 6c 7b 8b 9c
10d 11a 12d 13c 14b 15b 16a
17d 18c 19d 20b

Grammar

B
1c 2b 3a 4d 5a 6c 7c 8a 9c 10b
11d 12d 13c 14a 15d 16c 17b
18d 19c 20a

Use of English

C
1 for
2 who
3 no
4 than
5 had
6 would/might
7 Having
8 on
9 which
10 Being
11 then
12 worth
13 when
14 edge
15 out

D
1 billionaires
2 prosperous
3 trader
4 leading
5 economic
6 loss
7 downgrade
8 financial
9 statement
10 savings

E
1 effective
2 wires
3 money
4 chip
5 panel

F
1 light years ahead of
2 it isn't rocket science
3 who throws money around
4 reason (that/why) he's wealthy is
5 1883 is the year (that)
6 at cost price
7 push the panic button
8 hadn't tried to reinvent

Unit 9

Reading

A
Student's own answer

B
1C 2D 3A 4D 5B 6F 7A 8E 9B
10E 11F 12C

Vocabulary

A
1b 2c 3a 4c 5b 6c 7c 8a

B
1 movement
2 controversy
3 portrait
4 commissions
5 landscapes
6 oil
7 canvas
8 subjects

C
1 reproductions
2 exhibition
3 culmination
4 performance
5 opening
6 backing

D
1 mainstream
2 tour
3 display
4 debut
5 contract
6 vocalist
7 heart
8 management

E
1e 2c 3g 4a 5h 6f 7b 8d

Grammar

A
1 I don't think Lady Gaga is a **more** talented singer than Katy Perry, do you?
2 correct
3 correct
4 Mary felt she wasn't **as** gifted a musician as her sister.
5 Those paintings aren't as impressive **as** you'd imagine.
6 correct
7 They're not **such** expensive tickets as I'd thought they'd be.
8 correct

B
1 much worse than
2 a bit shorter than
3 considerably fewer than
4 a great deal less popular than
5 a lot less interesting than
6 far more bands than

C
1 the most important
2 the largest
3 (the) best known
4 as vibrant
5 longer
6 bigger
7 more sprawling
8 the most entertaining
9 the most visited
10 best loved

D
1 serious enough
2 too tired
3 quietly enough
4 talented enough
5 too lazy
6 too late
7 enough paintings
8 too famous

E
1 such, positive
2 such, flop
3 so long
4 So complex
5 so easy
6 Such, determination

Listening

A
Student's own answer

C
1b 2c 3c 4a 5d 6b

Writing

A
1F 2F 3T 4F

B
1 privileged
2 Artistically
3 simplicity
4 improvement
5 attention

C
Student's own answer

Unit 10

Reading

A
Student's own answer

B
1c 2c 3a 4a 5d 6c

Vocabulary

A
1. cosmopolitan
2. sedentary
3. formative
4. rigorous
5. provincial
6. pricey
7. solitary
8. hectic

B
1. struggling
2. juggling
3. enduring
4. balancing
5. concerned
6. spoiling
7. excelled
8. outdone

C
1. metropolitan
2. Obsessive
3. active
4. irritable
5. susceptible
6. addictive
7. unsophisticated
8. sociable

D
1c 2e 3b 4g 5a 6h 7f 8d

E
1. hit rock bottom
2. came up against
3. safe and sound
4. burn the candle at both ends
5. ruined your chances
6. wear down
7. throwing in the towel
8. do without

Grammar

A
1. are you being overlooked
2. aren't you being promoted
3. you haven't been chosen
4. not being noticed
5. dealing with
6. to be seen
7. to deliver
8. is recognised
9. are identified
10. wasn't built

B
1. was given to the most deserving person
2. is known that there aren't any more opportunities for growth this year
3. are expected to be made
4. I got for the meeting have been eaten
5. was decided that our groups would be merged
6. schools are expected to close early

C
1. appears to have lost
2. seems to be getting
3. appear to have left
4. seems (to be)
5. appears to be improving/ appears to have improved
6. seems to have disappeared

D
1. painted
2. decorated
3. stuck
4. dyed
5. removed
6. broken
7. cleaned
8. ruined

E
1. appears to have been/can be resolved
2. seem to have adapted/that they are
3. doesn't seem to have listened to/seem as if she's followed
4. seem to have really meant it/ seem as if/like you're very keen
5. seem to have forgotten that you promised/your promise/to be reading it
6. appears to have done/seems that every dish in the house has been used

Listening

A
Student's own answer

C
1E 2H 3B 4D 5F 6D 7F 8A 9H 10C

Writing

A
1F 2F 3T 4F 5T

B
Student's own answers

C
Student's own answer

Review 5

Vocabulary

A
1b 2d 3c 4c 5a 6b 7c 8c 9b 10a
11c 12b 13d 14d 15c 16a 17c
18b 19d 20a

Grammar

B
1b 2a 3c 4a 5d 6b 7c 8b 9d
10c 11a 12c 13b 14d 15b 16a
17c 18b 19c 20d

Use of English

C
1d 2a 3b 4a 5d 6b 7d 8b 9c
10a 11a 12b

D
1. without
2. down
3. the
4. bottom
5. say
6. against
7. ground
8. if/though
9. back
10. as
11. such
12. by
13. changing
14. throw
15. above

E
1. opening
2. chart
3. spoilt
4. field
5. stroke

F
1. would be music to my ears
2. aren't enough places to sit
3. need the stage curtains to be
4. long as to put people
5. the more expensive the tickets will
6. having her paintings put on
7. were so few participants (that)
8. was so confusing a project (that)

Unit 11

Reading

A
Student's own answer

B
1b 2c 3d 4a 5a 6c

Vocabulary

A
1. hindrance
2. coverage
3. dazzling
4. Conducting
5. holder
6. dedication

B
1. cheered
2. applause
3. relay
4. lap
5. baton
6. obstructed
7. disqualified
8. ban

C
1. off
2. for
3. up
4. back
5. out
6. up
7. out
8. on

D
1a 2b 3c 4a 5b 6b 7b 8c

Grammar

A
1c 2f 3a 4e 5b 6d

B
1. forget to bring your trainers tomorrow
2. 'll train for an hour every day until you're
3. I join the basketball team next term
4. we put away the equipment now
5. 'll meet you at the pool at eight tonight
6. bring me your

C
1. offered to help me put up
2. advised me to warm up before I started
3. decided not to get the green sweatshirt
4. promised to be there at 10.30
5. complained that Stella always arrived too late
6. apologised for missing
7. encouraged me to join
8. warned me not to overdo the stretches

D
1. if/whether I had brought my
2. why he wasn't playing football
3. when Rob was going on
4. Sarah how she was getting
5. if his son's team had won
6. Vincent if/whether he knew where the team was staying
7. his mother where his tennis racket was
8. Rose wanted to know why Tina didn't like

Listening

A
Student's own answer

C
1c 2b 3b 4a 5c 6b

Writing

A
1. Simon Perez
2. tell him the principal has asked you to reply
3. two: one about facilities in the college and another about facilities in town
4. semi-formal as Simon is a young student, but you don't know him

B
1. regarding
2. delighted
3. instructor
4. Additionally
5. available
6. charge
7. satisfactory
8. forward

C
Student's own answer

Unit 12

Reading

A
Student's own answer

B
1C 2F 3D 4A 5E

Vocabulary

A
1. killing
2. holds
3. shape
4. predict
5. hunch
6. pockets
7. infinite

B
1. likely
2. anticipated
3. looming
4. critical
5. intended
6. preserve

C
1c 2a 3f 4d 5b 6e

D
Student's own answer

E
1. can only speculate
2. only make an educated guess
3. felt like an eternity
4. a bad omen
5. he planted an arboretum for posterity

Grammar

A
1c 2e 3h 4b 5g 6a 7f 8d

B
1b 2a 3c 4b 5c 6a 7b 8b

C
1. worked very hard/because she wanted to go to law school
2. is so much competition/find/are finding it very difficult
3. to budget cuts/won't renovate/be renovating
4. so many decisions to make very quickly/surprising that Camilla is feeling
5. to price rises/unlikely to be able
6. that/as you handed in/you can't expect

D
1. Either
2. either of
3. Neither
4. nor
5. either
6. Neither of

E
1d 2g 3c 4h 5f 6a 7e 8b

Listening

A
Student's own answer

C
1. crust
2. hot springs
3. heat and cool
4. transfer
5. melt
6. wells
7. the United States
8. export

Writing

A
1F 2T 3T 4F 5T

B
1b 2d 3c 4a

C
Student's own answer

Review 6

Vocabulary

A
1b 2a 3d 4c 5c 6a 7b 8d 9c
10b 11a 12d 13b 14c 15c 16a
17d 18b 19a 20c

Grammar

B
1d 2c 3c 4d 5b 6b 7a 8c 9a 10d
11a 12b 13c 14d 15c 16a 17b
18c 19c 20a

Use of English

C
1. fanatics
2. burning
3. observers
4. overpower
5. maniacs
6. disqualified
7. commentator
8. referee
9. sharpen
10. captivating

D
1. holds
2. the
3. next
4. seeing
5. as
6. in
7. of
8. off
9. for
10. since/as/because
11. to
12. even
13. so
14. spite
15. being

E
1. shape
2. secret
3. dropped
4. lap
5. hold

F
1. Neither George nor Paul
2. fell at the first hurdle
3. apologised for not making it to
4. if he had practised that
5. congratulated Karen on her
6. made a killing signing with
7. Next to travelling in space, nothing
8. should watch the launch the following